AF652979

The Selected Works of MAULANA ABUL KALAM AZAD

Volume I
(1936 - 42)

Chief Editor
DR. RAVINDRA KUMAR

ATLANTIC
PUBLISHERS & DISTRIBUTORS (P) LTD

Published by
ATLANTIC
PUBLISHERS & DISTRIBUTORS (P) LTD
7/22, Ansari Road, Darya Ganj,
New Delhi-110002
Phones : +91-11-40775252, 23273880, 23275880, 23280451
Fax : +91-11-23285873
Web : www.atlanticbooks.com
E-mail : orders@atlanticbooks.com

Branch Office
5, Nallathambi Street, Wallajah Road,
Chennai-600002
Phones : +91-44-64611085, 32413319
E-mail : chennai@atlanticbooks.com

Copyright © The Author, 1991, 2012

All rights reserved. No part of this publication may be reproduced, stored in a retrieval system, transmitted or utilized in any form or by any means, electronic, mechanical, photocopying, recording or otherwise, without the prior permission of the copyright owner. Application for such permission should be addressed to the publisher.

Printed in India at Glorious Printers, A-13, D.S.I.D.C., Jhilmil Industrial Area, Delhi-110095

TO

MOTHER INDIA

V. N. GADGIL
Member of Parliament
(Lok Sabha)

95, Shahajan Road,
New Delhi-110011
Phone : 387272

संदेश

मुझे यह जानकार अति प्रसन्नता हुई है कि युवा और अति उत्साही विद्वान डा0 रवीन्द्र कुमार द्वारा तैयार किया गया मौलाना अबुल कलाम आजाद पर पहला चयनित कार्य (1936-1942) प्रकाशित हो रहा है ।

मौलाना आजाद हमारे देश की स्वाधीनता के एक महान अगली पंक्ति के सेनानी थे और वे सदैव भारत की एकता के प्रतीक थे । भारत की एकता वे भौगोलिक तथा धार्मिक दोनों रूपों में चाहते थे जो उनकी महानता का प्रतीक था ।

आज जब हमारा देश विभिन्न समस्याओं के दौर से गुजर रहा है और साम्प्रदायिक टकराव की स्थिति गम्भीर रूप से धारण कर रही है ऐसे में मौलाना आजाद के धार्मिक सहिष्णुता और सहनशीलता के विचार वास्तव में लाभकारी और प्रेरक हैं ।

हमारा देश प्राचीन सभ्यता और संस्कृति वाला देश है और इस सभ्यता व संस्कृति ने सदा प्रेम, भाईचारे तथा उच्च विचार का संदेश दिया है । यह ठीक भी था क्योंकि इसके बिना तो देश की ऐकता व अखण्डता पर खतरा ही रहता । इतिहास साक्षी है कि जब-जब भी हम इन सांस्कृतिक मूल्यों से हटे तब-तब हमारी अखण्डता भी सुरिक्षत नहीं रही । हमें इस पर आज पुनः गम्भीरता से विचार करने की आवश्यकता है । डा0 रवीन्द्र कुमार का यह प्रयास इस दिशा में बहुत सराहनीय है ।

(वी0 एन0 गाडगिल)

श्री राज्यपाल
उत्तर प्रदेश

सं॰ 5193/पोल्‍रस-एम्प05इ-गी

राज भवन
लखनऊ

सितम्बर 10, 1990

प्रिय डा० रवीन्द्र कुमार,

आपका पत्र दिनांक 28-8-1990 मिला, धन्यवाद।

मुझे यह जानकर प्रसन्नता हुई है कि आप किसी से बिना आर्थिक सहायता प्राप्त किये, महान स्वतंत्रता सेनानी एवं शिक्षाविद मौलाना अबुल कलाम आजाद द्वारा सन् 1936 से 1942 तक किये गये प्रमुख-प्रमुख कार्यों पर पुस्तकें लिख रहे हैं, जो प्रशंसनीय है और आप इसके लिए बधाई के पात्र हैं। मैं आपकी सफलता के लिए कामना करता हूँ।

भवदीय,

(बी० सत्यनारायण रेड्डी)

डा० रवीन्द्र कुमार,
311, अब लेन,
मेरठ कैन्ट- 250 001

GOVERNOR OF TAMILNADU
TRUTH ALONE TRIUMPHS

RAJ BHAVAN
MADRAS-600 022

MESSAGE

I am glad to know that Dr.Ravindra Kumar who is a reputed scholar is working for the compilation of selected works of Moulana Abulkalam Azad who was a great freedom fighter, educationist and a statesman. He was an embodiment of sentiments of millions of Indians who were struggling to free this great country from the shakles of British empire. He was also a true representative of Indian culture and heritage. I wish this project all success as it will throw light on a very important era in the Indian history.

Surjit Singh Barnala

(SURJIT SINGH BARNALA)

अखिल भारतीय किसान मजदूर

महा पंचायत

गांव-दमदमा, जिला-गुड़गांव, हरियाणा

मुख्य कार्यालय : 25, तुगलक रोड,
नई दिल्ली-1

दूरभाष : 3016800, 3016870

क्रमांक ......

दिनांक 28th Dec.1990

MESSAGE

It gives me a great pleasure to write few lines on the first vloume of the SELECTED WORKS OF MAULANA ABUL KALAM AZAD (1936-42), a great freedom fighter and thinker by Dr. RAVINDRA KUMAR.

In fact, Maulana Azad was ready to give any sacrifice to achieve independence from the subjection of alien rulers but Hindu-Muslim unity and integrity of the country was still so dearer to him. In a sub-continent like India, which had unique cultural heritage of unity in diversity, he rightly believed in the philosaphy that the believer in different religions should go together. This is still the need of hour and from this point of view the volume will be welcomed by the scholors concerned and the general people.

I wish the editor all success.

(RAJESH PILOT)
President.

MAULANA AZAD MEMORIAL ACADEMY

(Regd. Under Societies Regn. Act, 1860)

PATRON :

Maulana S. Abul Hasan Ali Nadwi
RECTOR,
Nadwatul Ulama
Lucknow.

PRESIDENT :

Z. R. Ansari
Union Minister for Environment
and Forest, Govt. of India
New Delhi.

VICE-PRESIDENTS :

Amin Ansari
M. P. (Rajya Sabha)

Professor Usman M. Adhami
Director
Academic Staff College, A.M.U.
Aligarh.

GEN. SECRETARY :

A. J. Jalali

Editor, Azad Journal & Treasurer :

S. G. Mohiuddin
Ex Secy. U. P. Minorities Commission

No · 483 - 90

November 28, 1990.

MESSAGE

Maulana Abul Kalam Azad occupied a place of pre-eminence for over three decades in the struggle for Indian Independence and the evolution of a secular and egalitarian culture for the country At a time like this, when fissiparous forces are attempting to disrupt the unity of the country, it is felt that the propagation of the ideals of patriotism, secularism and intellectual integrity which inspired the life of Maulana Azad would be a positive contribution towards strengthening the fabric of Indian Society.

It is matter of great pleasure and satisfaction that a well known research scholar Dr. Ravindra Kumar is working on the project for the compilation of selected works of Maulana Azad from 1936 to 1942. I wish this project all success.

Yours faithfully,

(A.J. JALALI)

Regd. Office : 7, Bisheshwar Nath Road, Lucknow-226001 — Telephone : 34135, 77929, 74216

Academy Office : 422/1, Birbal Sahni Marg, New Hyderabad, Lucknow.

Phone : Office : 230805
Resi : 35776

Abul Kalam Azad Oriental Research Institute

PUBLIC GARDENS
HYDERABAD-500 004. A. P.
[INDIA]

President :
Dr. Mir AKBAR ALI KHAN
Ex-Governor of U. P. & Orissa
Tel. 36086

Vice-President :
Mir AHMAD ALI KHAN
Ex-Minister, A. P.
Tel. 238753

Vice-President :
VICE-CHANCELLOR,
Osmania University-Ex-officio
Tel. 868048

Secretary & Director :
KHWAJA MUHAMMAD AHMAD
Tel. 35776

Jt. Secretary & Jt. Director :
HASHIM ALI KHAN
I.A.S. [Retd.]
Tel 235184

Jt. Secretary, Jt Director & Treasurer :
S. G. AFZAL BIYABANI
H.C.S. [Retd.]
Tel. ~~237588~~ 237538

Date October 20, 1990.

M E S S A G E

I have had the priviledge of meeting the great leader Moulana Azad. When I was in Parliament he was the Education Minister. I had several opportunities of meeting him and discussing several problems of our Country as well Islamic Countries and the rest of the World. I think he had great qualities of head and heart and India benefitted by his great service to the Country as well as his advice to other countries. I consider it a privilege to offer my respect to the great personality who will be remembered for his services in difficult times before and after Independence. His intimate association with Gandhiji and Jawaharlal Nehru helped the progress of this country in many directions. I offer my respectful homage to Moulana Saheb who is one of the few great Indian leaders who worked for the Communal harmony and progress of the country. May our young generation take lesson from his rich and dignified activities.

I very much appreciate that Dr. Ravindra Kumar is Editing a six Volume Series of the Selected Works of Moulana Azad (1936-1958), I wish him and his Project all success and hope that the young generation will draw inspiration from the books.

(MIR AKBAR ALI KHAN)

Foreword

I am glad to accept the invitation of the Editor, Dr. Ravindra Kumar, to write a Foreword to his First Volume (1936-1942) of the Selected Works of Maulana Abul Kalam Azad who was a great freedom fighter, educationist, thinker, journalist and statesman.

His life and personality manifests the eternal spirit, all that was good and great in the Indian culture, propounded by saints and savants like Kabirdas, Nanakdev, Ravindra Nath Tagore, Arvindo and Mahatma Gandhi. He was a unique synthesis and an outstanding monument of one who lived and died for the cause of revival and rehabilitation of the National glory. He had the privilege of being loved and admired by millions of Indians.

In this volume all speeches, correspondence, writings, circulars, extracts from the talks etc. of Maulana Azad have been included. All these documents will be a source of great inspiration to the present generation of Indians in terms of their devotion to duty, sincerity and love for the country and for forging communal harmony and National amity in a spirit of understanding and co-existence.

Dr. Ravindra Kumar deserves all appreciation in this regard because he has rendered a great national service by having completed this gigantic task.

I wish success to Dr. Ravindra Kumar's efforts.

K. Mahmood Ali Khan

Preface

Dr. Shri Ravindra Kumar is an admirer of Maulana Abul Kalam Azad. This is nothing unusual. Maulana Azad had numerous admirers in the course of India's struggle for freedom. The number increased appreciably after India attained freedom. Partition of India was the heavy price India paid for this freedom. Maulana Azad had throughout his whole political life opposed forces which encouraged separatist trends in our national life. It was in the partitioned India that people realised more vividly the soundness of the views Maulana had expressed on the communal problem.

Maulana Azad was among the major figures in our unique struggle for freedom waged under the leadership of Gandhiji. The selected works which Dr. Ravindra Kumar has edited bring out the greatness of Maulana Azad in several fields of life. He was most assuredly an outstanding scholar, a great journalist, a matchless orator but with equal ease he was also a great statesman who played a significant role in every crisis which India and, in particular, the Indian National Congress faced from time to time in its struggle to make our country free and independent.

He had also his due share in shaping India's destiny in her first decade of Independence. He was an outstanding member of the union cabinet but what was more important was the mature advice he made available to his comrade and fellow warrior Pandit Jawaharlal Nehru as the latter sought to grapple with India's difficult and daunting problems in the first crucial phase of her independence.

Dr. Ravindra Kumar may not yet be a mature scholar but the enthusiasm he has shown in portraying the intellectual and political life of Maulana Azad deserves commendation. The country is still faced with problems which greatly exercised the Maulana's mind. What he thought and said on these problems would still be a source of inspiration and enlightenment to his countrymen in the difficult days through which we are all passing.

Sadiq Ali

Preface

Contents

Messages	v
Foreword	xi
Preface	xiii
Introduction	1
Abbreviations	9
List of Documents	11
Documents	18
Who's Who	294
Glossary	301
Chronology of Events	304
Index	306

Introduction

Maulana Abul Kalam Azad was the Paragon celebrity of the universe of Twentieth Century Chronicle and was esteemed for his splendorous fabrication of the newfangled India, as one of the organiser, party leader and above all an embodiment of cultural heritage. In the history of thirty-two year's (1915-1947) national liberation movement and eleven years (1947-1958) after the dawn of the Independence, Maulana Azad remained as the best organizer and as a statesman in the front line, under the unique leadership of Mahatma Gandhi.

His multidimensional personality assimilated the intensified instinct of freedom from the subjection of alien rulers. He was ready to give any sacrifice for achieving independence. Hindu-Muslim Unity and nationalism were the most important aspects of his deepbrooding. He believed that the problems of the country could not be solved without this unity. Total Independence of the country was certainly his cherished aim, but Hindu-Muslim Unity was still dearer to him. Happily during the Non-Co-operation and Khilafat Movement the spirit of complete unity and communal harmony was in evidence everywhere. But the bonds began to loosen soon. Addressing a conference of Majlis-e-khilafat, he said, "for India, for the freedom of India, and? performing the acts of truth and, dutifulness, Hindu-Muslim Unity and harmony is essential." Unfortunately, however, soon the voice of sanity and passionate humanism was lost in the gathering storm of communal bickerings and bitterness, which shocked every sensible Indian particularly leaders like Mahatma Gandhi and Maulana Azad.

In 1923 Maulana Abul Kalam Azad vehemently stressed the need of unity and addressing the Special Delhi Session of the Congress, he reaffirmed "If an angel were to decent from the high heavens and proclaim from the heights of the Qutub-Minar 'Discord Hindu-Muslim Unity and within 24 hours *Swaraj* is your' I will refuse *Swaraj* but will not budge an inch from my stand. If *Swaraj* is delayed it will effect only India, while the end of our unity will be a loss to the entire human World."

In a sub-continent like India, which had Unique cultural heritage of unity in diversity, he believed in the Philosophy that the believer in different religions should go together and he synchronised this by 'we feeling' so that communal harmony of India can be maintained.

He possessed a multifaced personality. Due to this asset, he was capable of solving any type of problem whether it be a political or organisational. Mahatma Gandhi was also influenced by this competency of Maulana Saheb. His mannerism of writing and oration, and his art of speaking were the main factors in recognising and bringing into limelight his personality. Specially his mode of representing letters displays his whole personality before us. His frankness, supremacy of national interest, faith and feeling of fraternity are fully visualised by his letters, statements and talks. He had the instinct, in his personality of inspiring everybody and this is also depicted by his correspondence.

These characteristics are less seen in today's political leaders and statesmen, keeping in view the advantage of present and future generations, who can know these inspirative characteristics and could follow and lead to the idealistic path showed by Maulana Saheb, I have determined to prepare a six volumes series of his unpublished correspondence, statements and speeches, *etc.,* under the title — The Selected Works of Maulana Abul Kalam Azad. I hope that this project of 6 volumes will cover the period between 1936 and 1958. Volume I: 1936-42; Volume II: 1943-46 : Volume III : 1947-48; Volume IV : 1949-50 Volume V: 1951-54 and Volume VI : 1955-58.

I am very glad to say that in this context, I have compiled and edited the first volume. In this volume all the important correspondence, statements, extracts of speeches and talks, *etc.,* of Maulana Azad, have been included. The important part of this volume is his correspondence with all contemporary national and international personalities but very interesting portion of it contains the correspondence in between Azad and Nehru. The relations in between Azad and Nehru was dependent on reliance and deep friendship. The both had mutual understanding in midst of them. This was the reason Nehru accepted Azad as a true representative of Indian people in whose hand the general people's interest was safe. Nehru met Nahas Pasha in 1938 at the time when he was travelling to Europe. In this very meeting, on 24 November, 1938 they both decided for the representation of Indian people in Wafdist Congress. In this connection Nehru wrote to Azad from London that he should participate in the Congress as an excellent representative (Document 11). The important line of this letter is 'I can not think of a better representative than you.'

In 1939 a Special Session of the A.I.C.C. was decided to take place in Calcutta. For this, Maulana was requested to take the charge of Congress presidentship, which he denied. Pandit Nehru did not like this decision of Maulana. For this, the reason was this that Nehruji knew it very well, that nobody else was capable of handling with this turmoiled situation which had fell on Congress, than that of Maulana. This was the reason that Pandit Nehru, on 22 January, 1939 (Document 21), wrote to Maulana from Almora : 'I have just learnt that Radio has announced your withdrawal from the contest for the Congress presidentship. I am sorry. But I may not criticise your action because you are the best person to judge.'

Maulana's attitude towards Babu Subhash Chandra Bose was absolutely firm. In this connection his ideas were similar of Mahatma Gandhi and Sardar Vallabhbhai Patel. He attributed (Document 26), 'I consider the affair of Subhash Babu to be neither a struggle between the right and the left nor the question of composite and homogeneous working committee. It is only a matter of Subhash and some of his supporters.' On 17th April, 1939 he wrote to Pandit Nehru stressing in this regard also. Nehruji's views were not so firm about Subhash Babu. He (Pt. Nehru) has a long discussion with Subhash Bose in the mid of April and on 20.4.1939 giving details to Maulana he stressed (Document 27), "He (Subhash Bose) has been too much surrounded by one-sided accounts of rumours.... I think it will be a very good thing if you write to him and express the desire to meet him." But, after this also when Subhash Babu neglected the decision of majority of Congress Working Committee and continued to behave inappropriately, then Maulana Azad objected to this. He clearly wrote to Pandit Nehru on 17th August, 1939 when he was requested to express his views in this connection – 'In my opinion the attitude of Subhash Babu was wrong.' (Document 33).

In exchanging views, both Azad and Nehru – fell a feeling of self contentment. The period from 1936 to 1942 was very crucial and in these circumstances a continuous discussion between the two was very much necessary. At that time the feeling of belief was the prime factor. It is clear in a number of letters, included in this volume.

In fact, they both have the deep sense of affection for each other and at the same time sincerity was also there. But Pandit Nehru was a sentimental and sometimes even he crossed the limits also. Maulana never thought of crossing the limits of discipline. It is necessary to give an account of an important event of Second World War of the year 1940. Mahatma Gandhi was on one side and Maulana Azad,

Sardar Patel and Pandit Nehru were on the other, for whether in the War with English people, the Indians and Congress should give their support or not, Gandhiji was not ready at any cost to assist Britishers, whether they (Britishers) declared the independence for India. On the other hand, except Mahatmaji, remaining were of the idea of giving their full support to Englishmen. Even then the Congress Working Committee could not reach to any unanimous decision. In this context, Nehru wanted to issue a statement about his personal views but Maulana was not in favour of this. On 17th July, 1940 Nehru asked Maulana's consent for issuing a statement. In giving reply on 19.7.1940 (Document 73) Maulana stated clearly "Because any resolution has not been passed unanimously by the working committee, I shall be obliged if you do not issue any statement about it just at present."

Maulana Azad had interests in international and economic matters too which is clearly stated by Document No. 69. His view was clear on the position of sugar factories in the year 1940, which is stated by Document No. 76. By part of this letter 'Both groups of sugar factories syndicate are to be consulted, after which some solution may be evolved on behalf of the Congress.'

Azad and Nehru both were tied in the knot of deep affection of Gandhiji. Mahatma Gandhi was the leader of the both. We can take an example from the Document 65.

In his letter of 9th May, 1942, Azad at the time of preparing grounds for Quit India Movement, wrote to Nehru 'I have received a letter from Bapu through Prafulla Babu. He wants me to see. The papers say that he is leaving for Bombay for a week. I am, therefore intending to leave for Bombay on Monday or Tuesday.' The talk seems to be very simple but the deep sense of meeting definitely shows ample affection.

Azad and Nehru were like two members of the same family. Their behaviour was of real brothers. This was the reason, they intervened in the private matters of each other. They were the companions of each other, in the moment of sorrows and happiness. The accurate example of this is in Documents 39, 40, 49, 60, 61, 62, 66 and 67. In February, 1942, at Ahmedabad, Maulana Azad as an elder brother firmly stated Nehru to take care of his health. Even then Nehru was not so careful and when his health became deteriorated then he accepted his fault by asking forgiveness through a letter written to Maulana. In connection to this letter's reply on 13th May, 1942 (Document 36) Azad wrote – 'Now you should admit that you are going to leave the wrong side. You should be little more careful about your health." This is an example of affection between each other.

Under the leadership of Mahatma Gandhi for liberating the country, the front-line team which worked in that, apart from Nehru and Maulana, there are two other top ranking leaders, Sardar Vallabhbhai Patel and Dr. Rajendra Prasad. Azad's relations with both were always of higher quality. Though the views were never alike but for the cause of national interest and unity they worked team-heartedly remaining above all from all differences. From 1936 to 1942 a number of letters were written to each other. These letters are, of the time of Second World War, Gandhiji's indifferent attitude from Congress and the Party crisis *etc.* are the symbol of clarity and maturity in between the two – Maulana Azad and Sardar Patel.

The relations between Dr. Rajendra Prasad and Maulana Azad were developed on maturity since 1923 to 1936. And the mature relations in between the two can be seen in Documents 7, 10, 12, 13, 31, 42, 44, 45, 48 and 86. In 1939, both of them played a crucial role, as the members of the Congress Parliamentary Board, in the organisational matters of Punjab, Bihar and Utkal *etc.* The role played by Azad and Rajendra Babu during the conflict of peasants and the Landlords of Bihar was very important.

It was highly appreciated at that time and in this connection Mahadeobhai Wrote an article in 'Harijan' on 25 December, 1937 (Document 7).

Maulana gave a clear consent in replying to the letter written to him on 23rd July 1939 on Punjab issue by Rajendra Babu. According to the reply, "The Punjab affairs have our immediate attention, but you are right in saying that they cannot be settled unless a strong man goes there." Like this, in connection with the Utkal and Bengal, he stated clear views in giving his sound advice to the then Congress President, Dr. Rajendra Prasad. He wrote on 3 January, 1940 (Doc. 44) 'The Working Committee should be called for this earlier.' His views on Party Organisation were absolutely firm and clear from 1937 to 1942 and this was the main reason which pressed Rajendra Babu to declare Maulana Azad as a perfect party organiser (Document 72).

Acharya J.B. Kripalani, with Maulana Azad was the General Secretary of the Congress. In this period from 1940 to 1942, in which Azad was the Congress president, the country's political situation was very grave. That's why the communication of letters, of this period between Maulana and Kripalani is inspirative. Documents 53, 64, 135, and 141 are the sources of instructive directions of Azad, on the other hand, Maulana's sympathy towards the national language Hindi (Document 135 and 141), inspiring for doing the relief work swiftly (Doc.140...) and his being an eminent organiser. An example from Document 140, "send without delay all the donation received directly in the office about the Congress Medical Mission...I do not understand the cause."

A difficult problem arose before the Indian National Congress in 1940. Mahatma was not prepared to support the British in World War. A group of the Congress leaders including Azad himself, Nehru and Patel were in favour of giving support to the Britishers if they declared a complete freedom to India. Consequently, Gandhiji remained alone in the party and he wrote to Maulana on 30th December 1941 (Document 98) to relieve him from the responsibilities of Congress. Apart from the personal relations, in between Mahatma and Maulana, there was something more cordial. These were in connection with the country's independence and for the security of humanity. This was why, Azad didn't give reply individually but inspired the Congress Working Committee, held at Bardoli, for the unanimous consent issuing public statement. According to this, 'Congressman will render full assistance to Gandhiji in prosecution of his mission, including offering the civil disobedience.'

This was the example of the faith in between the two. It is evident by Documents 56 and 58. The letter of 4.4.1940 of Mahatma Gandhi, written to Lord Linlithgow, the then viceroy (Doc. 58), can be seen by us as Gandhiji's sincerity towards Azad. According to a part, ' I shall be painfully surprised if you confirm the report received by Maulana Saheb.'

Maulana Abul Kalam Azad was not only close to his companions and contemporaries but side by side he was sincere in maintaining relations also. Discipline, organisational unity, respect for the decision of majority and national interest were dear to him and he was not ready to compromise on the cost of these ideals. This is also clarified by this compilation. Firm advice and quick decision-making were the main characteristics of Azad. On 7th of July, 1939, B.C. Misra complained the deficiency of contract between the Congress organisation of 'Surma Valley' and the Assam Government. Maulana clearly mentioned, in his letter of reply of 16th July, 1939 (Document 32), "Creating of a satisfactory machinery through which closer contact between the 'Surma Valley Congress and the Assam Cabinet may be established for Parliamentary Work.'

Documents No. 107 and 129 are the examples of instructions to party leaders and Documents No. 130 and 140 are the criticism of the steps taken by Rajaji, in which he had accepted to pass the resolution of Cripps Plan by Madras Congress Legislative Party in 1942. Maulana Azad was always serious about communal harmony and national unity and this is evident from his historical speech (Doc. 51) of March 19, 1940 at Ramgarh as the president of Indian National Congress. This speech was highly appreciated by M.D. Desai (Document 55) by writing an article in Harijan on 30.3.1940.

In the political arena of India, two most important events took place in March 1940. First was the proposal of the demand of Muslim League for a separate nation for Muslims and the second, was the Session of Congress at Ramgarh, in which there was a proposal for non-co-operation against British Government. Maulana Azad, as stated above, was elected the president in this session and he worked continuously on this post till 1946. The period between 1940 and 1942 was very important and critical in country's history as well as for Congress. The question of supporting British Government in the War arose in 1940. After this the other important event was the 'Cripps Plan' and for which Maulana Azad had to discuss, as Congress president. In this connection he discussed as well as communicated with British officials like Sir Stafford Cripps, British Commander-in-Chief and Lord Linlithgow. In this Maulana's responsibility for national welfare as well as a Congress Leaders, efficient statesmanship, and apart from these, his crystal clear ideas are shown. An example of his statesmanship can be seen in reply to the letter written on the question of India's participation in War, on 8.8.1940 to the viceroy. Maulana wrote (Doc. 78) I would readily avail of pleasure of meeting your excellency but when His Majesty's government have already thought fit to announce a definite line of action may I ask how far there still remains a chance of usefulness of future discussion. An example of his frankness can be seen from his reply (Doc. 142) to Sir Cripps on 4.4.1942. Azad stated, "We are interested, as you know, in the political aspect of the problem, the complete control of defence as well as all other departments of administration. We consider such control essential before responsibility can be taken."

Maulana Azad was a nationalist to the core and being in Congress he always opposed Muslim League. That's why, he has been given the post of Congress president very often. This was knowingly spread by British newspapers as well as by others also. But the fact is that Maulana Azad was a born Satyagrahi and in honour of the post, he held, is clear by a comment (Doc. 50) of the *Hindustan Times* of

28.2.1940 and by an article, of Abdullah Butt of Lahore, written on 24.6.1942.

Several important documents relating to the main events of the period (1936-42) have been included in appendix.

The life and Works of Maulana Abul Kalam Azad are so illustrative and it is not easy to pen down the whole at one place. In this volume I have tried to give an account of his life and works and it is my belief that the coming generations especially historians, politicians and the general people of the country can lay a peep into his towering personality. I hope that the research scholars will also be benefited by this volume.

Azad's life and works are the source of inspiration and teachings of clean and fair deal politics, being up from all the difference for country's welfare and live to be open-eyed for the interest of national cause, unity and integrity. By this point of view, the readers will be benefited.

For the compilations of this volume I am grateful and thankful to the staff of National Archives of India, New Delhi, National Gandhi Museum and Library, New Delhi, the officials of Nehru Memorial Museum and Library, New Delhi, Staff and Officials of Sardar Vallabhbhai Patel National Memorial, Ahmedabad, Navjeevan Trust, Ahmedabad and the Director of Provincial Archives of Lucknow, Calcutta, Bombay and Patna.

I am greatly indebted to His Holiness, Maulana Syed Abul Hasan Ali Nadvi, Rector Nadwatul Ulama, Lucknow, Shri Babubhai J. Patel, Shri Sadiq Ali, Dr. Hari Dev Sharma, Shri A.J. Jalali, Shri S. Mohiuddin, Nawab Akbar Ali Khan and Shri Z.R. Ansari for their kind guidance and encouragement in preparation of this volume.

My thanks are to Mrs. Kamlesh Ravindra Kumar, Dr. Hari Singh, Dr. Malti Malik and Shri A.K. Awasthi for their kind cooperation.

I will be failling in my duty morally if I do not acknowledge the debt of gratitude, I owe to Dr. K.R. Gupta of Atlantic Publishers and Distributors, New Delhi for undertaking the publication of the Selected Works of Maulana Abul Kalam Azad courageously.

Ravindra Kumar

Abbreviations

A.I.C.C.	All India Congress Committee.
A.I.C.P.B.	All India Congress Parliamentary Board.
A.I.M.L.	All India Muslim League.
A.I.S.A.	All India Spinner's Association.
B.H.U.	Banaras Hindu University.
B.P.C.C.	Bombay Provincial Congress Committee.
B.P.C.C.	Bihar Provincial Congress Committee.
B.W.C.	British War Cabinet.
C.D.	Civil Disobedience.
C.D.M.	Civil Disobedience Movement.
C.F.	Cripps' Formula.
C.G.M.A.B.	Committee of Grain Merchants Association of Bombay.
C.L.P.	Congress Legislative Party.
C.O.	Congress Organisation.
C.P.	Central Provinces.
C.P.S.C.	Congress Parliamentary Sub-Committee.
C.S.P.	Congress Socialist Party.
C.W.C.	Congress Working Committee.
D.T.	Delhi Talk.
G.B.	Government of Bengal.
H.C.R.E.B.	Hindu Charitable and Religious Endorsement Bill.
H.M.G.	His Majesty's Government.
I.C.D.M.	Individual Civil Disobedience Movement.
I.N.C.	Indian National Congress.
I.N.T.U.C.	Indian National Trade Union Congress.
K.P.	Khadi Programme.
L.R.M.L.	Lahore Resolution of Muslim League.

M.C.L.P.	Madras Congress Legislative Party.
M.L.A.	Member of Legislative Assembly.
M.L.C.	Member of Legislative Council.
N.P.C.	National Planning Committee.
N.V.	Non-Violence
N.W.F.P.	North-West Frontier Province.
P.C.C.	Provincial Congress Committee.
P.G.	Provincial Government.
P.S.V.	Private Secretary to the Viceroy.
S.D.P.S.P.	Sanatan Dharam Pratinidhi Sabha of Punjab
S.G.P.C.	Shiromini Gurudwara Prabandhak Committee.
T.H.C.P.	The Hindustani Committee of Patna.
U.P.P.C.C.	United Provinces Provincial Congress Committee.

List of Documents

Sl. No.	Document	Date
1	2	3
1.	Brief History of Abul Kalam Azad prepared by the Govt. of India, Home Deptt. Political in 1936	1936
2.	To Vallabhbhai Patel	13-10-1936
3.	To Rajendra Prasad	13-10-1936
4.	To Rajendra Prasad	17-07-1937
5.	From Vallabhbhai Patel	17-07-1937
6.	To Vallabhbhai Patel	18-07-1937
7.	Maulana Azad, Dr. Rajendra Prasad and the situation of Bihar: a report by Mahadeo Desai	25-12-1937
8.	Statement of Abul Kalam Azad and Vallabhbhai Patel in connection with the Central Provinces Ministry	25-05-1938
9.	Abul Kalam Azad's report on the political situation of Bihar	17-07-1938
10.	To Rajendra Prasad	14-09-1938
11.	From Jawahar Lal Nehru	01-10-1938
12.	To Rajendra Prasad	29-10-1938
13.	From Rajendra Prasad to Sardar Patel and Maulana Azad	14-12-1938
14.	From Vallabhbhai Patel	20-12-1938
15.	From B.N. Das	22-12-1938

Contd.

Sl. No.	Document	Date
1	2	3
16.	From N. Kanungo	27-12-1938
17.	To Nilakantha Das	27-12-1938
18.	To N. Kanungo	28-12-1938
19.	From Nilakanth Das	30-12-1938
20.	From G. Misra	31-12-1938
21.	From Jawahar Lal Nehru	22-09-1939
22.	To Rajendra Prasad from Azad and Nehru	18-02-1939
23.	Resolution, passed by the open session of I.N.C., held at Tripuri with Maulana Azad as Acting President	27-02-1939
24.	Text of the three resolutions, moved by Azad as president, in the Tripuri Congress	10-03-1939
25.	From Jawaharlal Nehru	17-04-1939
26.	To Jawaharlal Nehru	17-04-1939
27.	From Jawahar Lal Nehru	20-04-1939
28.	To Jawahar Lal Nehru	03-07-1939
29.	From Jawahar Lal Nehru	08-07-1939
30.	To Rajendra Prasad	10-07-1939
31.	From Rajendra Prasad to Abul Kalam Azad and others	11-07-1939
32.	To B.C. Misra	16-07-1939
33.	To Jawahar Lal Nehru	17-08-1939
34.	From A.N. Sinha	25-08-1939
35.	To Rajendra Prasad	27-08-1939
36.	From Rajendra Prasad	29-08-1939
37.	To Rajendra Prasad	03-09-1939
38.	Joint Statement of Abul Kalam Azad, Jawahar Lal Nehru and Vallabhbhai Patel, in connection with the unity and discipline in Congress Party	16-09-1939

Contd.

Sl. No.	Document	Date
1	2	3
39.	From Jawahar Lal Nehru	13-10-1939
40.	To Jawahar Lal Nehru	11-11-1939
41.	From Gopinath Bardloi	15-11-1939
42.	To Rajendra Prasad	28-11-1939
43.	Statement against the deliverence day of Muslim League	21-12-1939
44.	To Jawahar Lal Nehru	03-01-1940
45.	To Rajendra Prasad	05-01-1940
46.	To Vallabhbhai Patel	25-01-1940
47.	To Vallabhbhai Patel	29-01-1940
48.	From Rajendra Prasad	21-02-1940
49.	From Jawahar Lal Nehru	22-02-1940
50.	Editorial on Maulana Azad	28-02-1940
51.	Maulana Abul Kalam Azad's Presidential address in the Congress Session at Wardha	19-03-1940
52.	Resolutions adopted by the I.N.C. at Wardha with Maulana Azad as President	20-02-1940
53.	To J.B. Kripalani	27-03-1940
54.	To Jawahar Lal Nehru	27-03-1940
55.	Mahadeo Desai's remark on the Congress Session at Ramgarh, held under the Presidentship of Maulana Azad and his analysis of the President's speech	30-03-1940
56.	To Mahatma Gandhi	30-03-1940
57.	Extract of the statement of Abul Kalam Azad, issued against the Lahore Resolution	1940
58.	From Mahatma Gandhi	04-04-1940
59.	From Gopichand Bhargava	10-04-1940
60.	From Jawahar Lal Nehru	20-04-1940

Contd.

Sl. No.	Document	Date
1	2	3
61.	From Jawahar Lal Nehru	21-04-1940
62.	To Jawahar Lal Nehru	24-04-1940
63.	From Master Tara Singh	26-04-1940
64.	To J.B. Kripalani	07-05-1940
65.	To Jawahar Lal Nehru	09-05-1940
66.	From Jawahar Lal Nehru	11-05-1940
67.	From Jawahar Lal Nehru	16-05-1940
68.	To Jawahar Lal Nehru	25-05-1940
69.	From Jawahar Lal Nehru	01-07-1940
70.	To M.A. Jinnah	10-07-1940
71.	From M.A. Jinnah	10-07-1940
72.	From Jawahar Lal Nehru	16-07-1940
73.	To Jawahar Lal Nehru	19-07-1940
74.	From Jawahar Lal Nehru	04-08-1940
75.	From Linlithgow	04-08-1940
76.	To Jawahar Lal Nehru	05-08-1940
77.	From Jawahar Lal Nehru	07-08-1940
78.	To Linlithgow	08-08-1940
79.	From the Assistant Secretary to the Governor of Bengal	10-08-1940
80.	To the Viceroy	10-08-1940
81.	To the Viceroy	11-08-1940
82.	To the Viceroy	19-08-1940
83.	To C. Rajagopalacharier	23-08-1940
84.	To Ex-Prime Ministers	23-08-1940
85.	To Ex-Prime Ministers and Members of Assemblies	27-08-1940
86.	From Rajendra Prasad	13-10-1940

Contd.

Sl. No.	Document	Date
1	2	3
87.	A.I.C.C. Statement with Maulana Azad as President	13-10-1940
88.	A.I.C.C. Resolution with Maulana Azad as President	16-10-1940
89.	From Jawahar Lal Nehru	18-10-1940
90.	From Jawahar Lal Nehru	24-10-1940
91.	From Jawahar Lal Nehru	24-10-1940
92.	From Jawahar Lal Nehru	25-10-1940
93.	From the President of the C.G.M.A. Bombay	06-11-1940
94.	From J.B. Kripalani	18-12-1940
95.	To Rajendra Prasad	25-12-1940
96.	From Parshuram Sharma	13-12-1941
97.	C.W.C. Resolutions, passed at Bardoli with Maulana Azad as President	23-12-1941
98.	From Mahatma Gandhi	30-12-1941
99.	From Parshuram Sharma	01-01-1942
100.	A statement in support of Mahatma Gandhi	03-01-1942
101.	C.W.C. decision with Azad as President	14-01-1942
102.	To Jawahar Lal Nehru	22-01-1942
103.	From Jawahar Lal Nehru	24-01-1942
104.	Congress Working Committee's instructions with Abul Kalam Azad as President	25-01-1942
105.	All India Congress Working Committee's Resolution with Azad as President	01-02-1942
106.	To Jawahar Lal Nehru	27-02-1942
107.	Appeal to the Members of C.W.C.	03-03-1942
108.	From Jawahar Lal Nehru	04-03-1942
109.	From Jawahar Lal Nehru	05-03-1942
110.	To Jawahar Lal Nehru	08-03-1942

Contd.

Sl. No.	Document	Date
1	2	3
111.	From P.S.V.	18-03-1942
112.	To P.S.V.	19-03-1942
113.	To Jawahar Lal Nehru	23-03-1942
114.	Working Committee's Resolution with Maulana Azad as President	27-03-1942
115.	To Four different addresses	27-03-1942
116.	From Stafford Cripps	30-03-1942
117.	From Stafford Cripps	01-04-1942
118.	To Stafford Cripps	01-04-1942
119.	From Stafford Cripps	01-04-1942
120.	From Stafford Cripps	02-04-1942
121.	From Stafford Cripps	03-04-1942
122.	To Stafford Cripps	04-04-1942
123.	From Stafford Cripps	07-04-1942
124.	To Stafford Cripps	10-04-1942
125.	Explanation of the Congress Position on Delhi Talks.	10-04-1942
126.	From Stafford Cripps	10-04-1942
127.	Congress Committee's Resolution on Delhi talks with Maulana Azad as President	11-04-1942 11-04-1942
128.	To Stafford Cripps	11 04-1942
129.	Instructions to the all leaders of P.C.C.	25-04-1942
130.	Reaction through an open letter on the resolution, passed by the M.C.L.P.	25-04-1942
131.	Abdullah Buṭt's analysis of the personality of Maulana Azad	
132.	From C. Rajagopalacharier	30-04-1942
133.	From Jawahar Lal Nehru	08-05-1942
134.	To Jawahar Lal Nehru	09-05-1942

Contd.

Sl. No.	Document	Date
1	2	3
135.	From J.B. Kripalani	13-05-1942
136.	To Jawahar Lal Nehru	13-05-1942
137.	From Sucheta	14-05-1942
138.	To M.S. Anney	18-05-1942
139.	To Jawahar Lal Nehru	18-05-1942
140.	To J.B. Kripalani	20-05-1942
141.	To J.B. Kripalani	23-05-1942
142.	From J.B. Kripalani	25-05-1942
143.	From Jawahar Lal Nehru	30-05-1942
144.	To Jawahar Lal Nehru	31-05-1942
145.	To Jawahar Lal Nehru	June, 1942
146.	From Jawahar Lal Nehru	05-06-1942
147.	All India Congress Working Committee's Resolution with Maulana Azad as President	14-07-1942
148.	From C. Rajagopalacharier	04-08-1942
149.	All India Congress Committee's Resolution with Maulana Azad as President	07-08-1942
150.	Working Committee's Resolution Regarding the Congress Ministries	02-01-1938
151.	Statement of Sardar Patel on C.P. affair	01-06-1938
152.	Text of Judgement delivered by the City Magistrate of Allahabad in the case against Abul Kalam Azad	10-01-1940
153.	Cripps' Draft Declaration	1942
154.	Gandhiji's Appeal to Muslims	20-07-1942

Documents

Document 1

BRIEF HISTORY OF MAULANA AZAD PREPARED BY THE GOVERNMENT OF INDIA, HOME DEPARTMENT POLITICAL, IN 1936

"Maulana Abul Kalam Azad son of the late Maulana Khairuddin of Calcutta. An Arabic scholar who has visited Egypt, was editor of the Al-Hilal an Urdu weekly which had to be proscribed on account of its seditious writings, was one of the organisers of the 'Khuddam-e-Kaba Movement in 1913 and the founder of the 'Dar-ul-Irshad College' at Calcutta. A great Pan-Islamist and rabidly anti-British and extremely fanatical, was an active member of the 'Deoband Jehad Conspirancy' and was believed to have assisted the Hindustan fanatics and certain trans-border tribesmen in the then fighting with money *etc.* Took a leading part in the Khilafat, non-co-operation and Swaraj Movement in Bengal in 1920. Was convicted and sentenced to one year's R.I. in February, 1922. Was president of the special session of the All India Congress held in Delhi in September 1923. A strong supporter of the Congress and follower of Pandit Motilal Nehru. In 1925 he was granted a passport to enable him to proceed to Europe for medical treatment but he failed to use it. He did not come prominently to notice from 1926-29. In August, 1930, he was nominated as acting president of the Indian National Congress. On 28-8-30 he was arrested under the I.-ordinence in connection with a speech, delivered by him at Meerut and was convicted and sentenced six months' S.I. In February 1932 he was served, consequent upon his nomination as Congress President by Sardar Sardul Singh Cavesheer after his arrest, with a notice by the Bengal Government under the Emergency Powers Ordinance restraining him from participation in the Civil Disobedience Movement for a month. On 12-3-32 he was arrested under Section 30 of the said ordinance and sent to Jail. Was released on 11-5-32. Was elected a member of the Working Committee

of the All India Congress Committee after the Bombay Session in 1934; was also elected a member of Congress Parliamentary Board from which he now seems to have resigned.

Document 2

LETTER FROM MAULANA AZAD TO SARDAR PATEL

13-10-1936

My dear Vallabhabhai,

Thank you for your letter of 9th instt. sending therewith a copy of joint appeal[1] to the all Provincial Congress Committees. I am expecting to see you in Bombay on 20th.

Yours Sincerely,

A.K. Azad

Sardar Vallabhbhai Patel,
Bombay

1. See enclosure.

Enclosure:

ALL INDIA CONGRESS PARLIAMENTARY COMMITTEE

Congress House, Bombay
Dated, 8th October 1936

The following appeal has been issued by Pandit Jawaharlal Nehru, President, Indian National Congress, and Sardar Vallabhbhai Patel, President, All India Congress Parliamentary Committee:

> "In the Election Manifesto the Congress has stated its general policy and programme and appealed to the nation to support it in the coming elections. The appeal has been confidently addressed to all classes of our people who stand for the complete freedom of our country. On that fundamental basis, the Congress offers a national platform to our countrymen, and a united front against the forces that work for the continued domination

and exploitation of India. In this national campaign the Congress expects the willing cooperation and help of all; each giving that help according to his capacity. Ours is a mass organisation and it derives its strength from the mass of the people and it relies on them for support. It is also on this broad popular basis that we desire to fight the elections. The preliminary work of setting up the machinery for organising these elections and for setting up proper candidates on behalf of the Congress has been completed. But we have to approach over three million voters and contest about 1,500 seats in constituencies spread over the vast country from one end to the other. It is a huge task and for this purpose our organisations will require money. For the general propaganda of the Congress alone, we will require large sums of money. Besides, it will be necessary to give financial help to some candidates who cannot bear their expenses, particularly those of the Scheduled and Backward Classes and to areas suffering from starvation and scarcity due to natural calamities or other causes. Those who are in a position to meet their expenses are expected to do so.

To our people, therefore, we appeal to subscribe to the election funds of the Congress, so that the message of the Congress may reach each voter and the remotest corner of our vast country, and the success of the Congress at the elections be otherwise assured.

We suggest for this purpose that a special fortnight be devoted to this work all over India, to the collection of funds for the elections and to the broadcasting of the Congress message. We fix the fortnight beginning from November First 1936 for this purpose. All Provincial Committees should make arrangements through their subordinate Committees and otherwise, for these collections to be made on the widest scale during the first half of November. With these collections must always go the message of the Congress, of Indian freedom, of the ending of our exploitation. Thus we shall build up our campaign on the solid and enduring basis of popular support."

Jawaharlal Nehru
Vallabhbhai Patel

Document 3

TELEGRAM FROM MAULANA AZAD TO DR. RAJENDRA PRASAD

CALCUTTA
13-10-1936

RAJENDRA PRASAD
CONGRESS
PATNA

CORRECT PUBLISHED TEXT[1] OF APPEAL HAS REACHED STOP FOUND PROPER STOP.

ABUL KALAM AZAD

1. See Enclosure to Document 2.

Document 4

TELEGRAM FROM MAULANA AZAD TO DR. RAJENDRA PRASAD

July 17, 1937

RAJENDRA PRASAD,
CONGRESS COMMITTEE,
CHANDNI CHOWK,
CUTTACK

SUGGEST YOUR CONSIDERATION INCLUDING MUSLIM IF IN YOUR OPINION SUITABLE PERSON TAKING CONGRESS PLEDGE AVAILABLE STOP AM GOING BOMBAY.

ABUL KALAM AZAD

Document 5

TELEGRAM FROM SARDAR PATEL TO MAULANA AZAD

17-07-1937

MAULANA ABUL KALAM AZAD,
CALCUTTA

ON BOMBAY B 17 37

RAM NARAYAN WIRES QUOTE IGNORING CONGRESS ABILITIES MINISTERS SELECTED COMMUNAL LINES PLEASE ASK BIHAR LEADER STAY ANNOUNCE TILL ENQUIRY BY YOU AND RAJENDRA BABU SERIOUS DEVELOPMENT MAY FOLLOW DELAY UNQUOTE CALL HIM AND SATISFY WIRED RAJENDRA BABU.

VALLABHBHAI PATEL

Document 6

LETTER FROM MAULANA AZAD TO SARDAR PATEL

Calcutta

18-07-1937

My dear Vallabhbhai,

Received your telegram.[1] I am in touch with Rajendra Babu[2] you have need not to be worried about it.

Yours Sincerely,

A.K. Azad

Sardar Vallabhbhai Patel
Bombay

---

1. See Document No. 5, Telegram of 17.7.1937.
2. Dr. Rajendra Prasad.

Document 7

MAULANA AZAD, DR. RAJENDRA PRASAD AND THE SITUATION OF BIHAR: A REPORT BY MAHADEO DESAI DATED 25-12-1937

There is widespread satisfaction over the news that thanks to the efforts of Maulana Abul Kalam Azad and Babu Rajendra Prasad and other Bihar leaders, the Bihar Tenancy Amendment Bill will soon be passed into law. The easy passage of the Bill in the Assembly was the result of friendly and conciliatory talks between the Zamindars and the representatives of the Kisans. This good result represents in one word both the parties will to a voluntary peace. For a forced peace in which one party's interests are sacrificed is no peace, it has the seeds of discontent and conflict. A peace based on understanding and the desire of one party to do justice to the other is the fruit of active goodwill, and Bihar has taken a real step forward in that direction.

The understanding also means the realization on the part of the Zamindars and the Kisans that the Congress represents them both and can safeguard the legitimate interests of both. It should do nothing less and nothing else. The legitimate interests of the Kisans demand the enjoyment by them of the full fruits of their labour nothing less. The legitimate interests of the Zamindars means the enjoyment of the fruits of their trusteeship, which means a commission for the use of their intelligence in wisely directing the energies of their tenants so that the latter can make the best use of the land in their possession and in securing the products of their labour. The Bihar legislation does not achieve all this, but it is a step in that direction.

But there is a growing body of opinion which evidently considers the two interests as wholly conflicting and has no place for the Zamindar. That section claims to speak for the Kisans and evidently proceeds on the belief that the Congress does not, or has failed to, represent them. For years after the organisation of the Congress in 1920 the claim of the Congress to represent the Kisans was never challenged. During the past two or three years it is being challenged by people for whom evidently the Congress creed has no appeal. They are reported to have gone about misrepresenting the Congress and actually fomenting trouble between the Zamindars and the Kisans, so much so that the Working Committee of the Bihar Provincial Congress Committee was compelled to adopt the following resolution:

> "In the opinion of this Committee the kind of propaganda that is being carried on in this province has been responsible for producing a poisonous atmosphere and attacks are being made on the principle of which is the principle of the Congress. An atmosphere is developing in certain parts of the provinces which it is apprehended is likely to do much harm to the country and put obstacles in the way of the country's march towards freedom. The Committee, therefore, considers it necessary and proper to enjoin all Congress workers and those sympathizing with it to keep themselves aloof from such activities and in accordance with the Congress policy, to fight those who may be found indulging in them. In view of the fact that the Committee has before it enough material to prove that many a worker of the Kisan Sabha in each activities and in public meeting organized under the auspices of the Kisan Sabha statements are being made as a result of which the situation is growing from bad to worse, and there is a likelihood of the Congress being hampered, this Committee impresses on such Congress members as are working in the Kisan Sabha that not only their activities but also their passive association with them is improper, and directs the District Congress Committees to keep an eye on these activities of its workers and report them to the Provincial Congress Office."

This in our opinion, is a mild resolution and as Babu Rajendra Prasad explained it does not mean a ban on the Kisan Sabha. But it is warning to the Sabha and its members that if they use the Congress name to promote internal feuds they will invite a ban on themselves. For any Congressman to serve the Kisan and to educate them to know their true interest and the way of securing it is a laudable ambition. A separate organization is hardly necessary for the purpose. The Congress represents many activities. But it is easy to conceive the possibility of the Congress breaking to pieces if every group representing a particular activity were to form a separate organization. It is open to the Congress to form branch organization, but it is hardly open to any Congressman to form an organization and exploit the name of the Congress. The Congress has many activities, but one and only one ideal, *viz.*, the attainment of Complete Independence. Every activity has to subserve that end. Any activity which does not do so cannot be permitted to use the Congress name. If a Kisan Sabha sets up internal feud as between Kisan and Zamindars, it harms the Congress cause. The Congress known best how to deal with the different elements composing the nation. There are undoubtedly conflicting elements in it. But it is for the Congress to lay down policies, not for individuals or for groups to dictate them by a threat or show of force.

Document 8

THE C.P. MINISTRY

Maulana Abul Kalam Azad and Sardar Vallabhbhai Patel issued the following statement to the press on 29th May,1938 :

Shri Rajendra Prasad and we were deputed with working committee to go into and compose the difference that had arisen among the C.P. Ministers and to investigate certain charges that had been brought to the notice of the Working Committee and otherwise to supervise the formation if it became necessary, of a new Cabinet. Minister Shariff's case had already been dealth with by the Working Committee. Shri Rajendra Prasad was taken ill and unfortunately could not accompany us. We reached Pachmarhi on the 24th instant. We had invited the Presidents of the three Provincial Congress Committees to be present and assist us. They had kindly responded to our request. There were members of the Central Assembly Party of the province also present. We had long conferences with the Ministers singly and together. Though difficulties encountered us, we are happy to be able to say that the differences were composed and the Ministers announced to us that they had decided to bury their differences and work together as a team. They will make changes themselves so as to ensure administrative efficiency and to prevent a recurrence of causes for complaints.

We also investigated the graver charges. We are glad to be able to say that the gravest charges of bribery and corruption were not proved. We found that many had been recklessly and even spitefully brought without an iota of proof to support them.

At the same time certain complaints were not without justification. Thus there was undoubtedly administrative inefficiency. We have been assured that these will not be allowed to recur. It was admitted also that in the Debt Conciliation Act, that was intended purely to help the toiling cultivators, the amount of debt limit brought under the law was raged from 50,000 to 1,000,000. This was admitted to be indefensible and the Ministers have promised to reduce the sum to the original level. The charge of undeserving persons being appointed to professorships by the University and to some other positions by the Ministry was sustained. Promise has been made to remedy the wrong in every case. Minor charges have been referred to Shri Jamuna Lalji[1] for disposal.

We are glad to be able to say that wherever errors of judgement had been committed there was a readiness to admit and make amends. We entertain the hope that now that the gravest charges have been found to be groundless and errors of judgement are under promise of prompt rectification all public criticism will cease and the Ministers will be given a chance of proving themselves capable of upholding the Congress tradition of rectitude in public life and affairs.

1. Seth Jamuna Lal Bajaj.

Document 9

SITUATION OF BIHAR [1]

Confidential

When I went to Bihar I had hoped to see a harassed Ministry with its innumerable problems sympathised by at least a substantial section of the population. But I was disillusioned. I heard no word of sympathy but only curses and expression of disgust, officials, non-officials, landlords, Kisans, Muslims, Hindus, and the general and they will all say, "The Ministers are doing a fine job of it, namely, giving jobs to their friends and relatives. As for other things they are just sleeping and sending the province to dogs. The best thing they can do is to resign and get out."

The Ministry is faced not with one but innumerable problems, each acute and urgent in itself. There is the agrarian trouble, then there are the strikes, there are the annual and devastating foods, there is the problem of co-operation which in Bihar is in the most parlous straits, then there is the question of education in which Bihar is in most backward and so on and so forth. Thus, the resources at the disposal of the Ministry are limited but given efficiency and whole-hearted and public-spirited work, the Ministry could have achieved a lot. But lethargic Bihar seems incapable or producing an efficient Ministry for, curiously enough, the present ministers are perhaps the best available.

Let me take the ministry's sins of commission and omission one by one.

Jobbery easily takes the first place in the catalogue. The way the Ministry has been circumventing the authority of the Public Service Commission is most scandalous. In fact the Commission had made a representation to the Governor and also to the Ministers but the latter are unmoved. There are three ways by which the Ministry hoodwinks and defeats the real purpose for which the Commission has been set up. First of all appointments of their favourites are made on a temporary basis for six months and then job is advertised with the result that with the experience gained during six months' service the Ministry's nominee easily comes out best among the candidates. Another way of doing things is to frame the advertisement in such a way that the Ministry's favourite alone can answer the required qualifications. Thirdly, only one candidate is sent up and the Commission asked to say whether he is fit for the job or not. Many are the jobs which have gone to the Ministers' nominees like this.

Casteism among the Ministers is rampant. It assumed the most acute proportions at the time of making appointment to the post of manager of Bettiah court of wards estate. This had become a disgraceful scandal and had caused widespread discontent. When it was once decided to appoint a non-official Indian in that post, all sections, especially from Champaran in which district lies Bettiah, pleaded that Mr. Bipin Bihari Verma (who was at last appointed to the post after a period of nearly one year of suspense at the instance of Gandhiji) should be made the manager. But he is a Kayastha and the Premier is a Bhumihar. The Premier did not like to give that position to Mr. Verma. The Finance Minister threatened to resign. When Mr. Verma came to know of this he decided not to go near it. But unfortunately for the Premier there was no other competent candidate among Bhumihars available. Dr. Rajendra Prasad shifted his burden on to Gandhiji who was asked to finally instruct Mr. Verma whether to take the job or leave it. Gandhiji favoured that Mr. Verma should resign his seat in the Assembly and take the appointment. And so it was that Mr. Verma is now the manager.

This is a case of casteism *par excellence* but other cases are not wanting. Only recently a Bhumihar with only eleven years' service in the provincial cadre has been appointed to be rent officer, a post reserved for the I.C.S. within two years he will be appointed district magistrate. The objection is not that he is from the provincial service but that he is so junior and that he has superseded so many others. His only qualification is that he is a Bhumihar and was for some time private secretary to the Premier.

A relative of one of the Ministers has recently been appointed deputy superintendent of the Government Printing Press. The gentleman has no knowledge of printing and he has been sent to England at Government's expense to get training.

Unlike other ministries the Bihar Ministry has not abolished nominations to local bodies. Even in the municipal amendment bill nominations are only nominally abolished for they have been substituted by cooperation. The main object of this is to give seats in local bodies to relatives and friends.

With so much interest and time devoted to jobbery, it is no wonder that the ministry is most inefficient. It often happens that no Minister at all is present in the Assembly and the work is left to be carried out by the Parliamentary Secretaries and most of all by the advocate-general. We do not even know the names of advocate-generals in some of the other provinces but in Bihar a visitor is struck by the presence of the advocate-general in all the sittings of the Assembly and the Council and by his continuous spokesmanship of the Government. In fact, he can be easily mistaken for the Premier by one now to this province, so much does he dominate the daily proceedings. And he has to do it per force because the job is too much for the Ministers. Each goes his own way and each abuses the other of course in private. One Minister is reported to go even to the length of saying that so long as another minister is surrounded by Bengali officer, he will have nothing to do with other's department.

Hardly if ever do the ministers attend the secretariat. They are supposed to do their work at home and at home, only Durbars are held. The result is that files accumulate for months together and business is unduly delayed. Appointments are given only to be broken. Officers are called to the headquarters from their stations and sent back saying that matters would be talked over later. For hours together officers have to sit at ministers' houses before they can get audience not for personal purposes but for official business.

After this the tale of the manner in which the ministry has handled its problems and kept its promises is easily told.

The ravages of the annual floods in Bihar beggar description. The problem is raised in the legislature times out of number. The ministry's only reply is that they knew the gravity of the problem, that they have ordered surveys and they are paying attention to it. Nothing, however, has been done, not even a bit. Saran is perhaps the worst-affected district. Its contiguity to United Provinces gave at first an excuse to the Ministry in that before anything can be done, consent and cooperation of the neighbouring province must be secured at the problem in that district is common to both. The people, however, clamoured for some immediate relief by reconstructing the bandhs, *etc.*, they could not wait helplessly any more till the preliminaries were over and some measure of permanent relief was decided upon. The people promised to give free labour and even to bear the cost later by paying taxes. The ministry was overwhelmed, a special officer was appointed, conferences were held, schemes draws up but nothing has been done so far. And the rains are already on. The result: immense discontent, another handle to Kisan leader who are now openly preaching lawlessness and it can be taken as a certainty that clashes and riots would soon become a daily occurrence in that district. Meanwhile the ministers are busy attending marriage functions, visiting small villages presiding over unimportant conferences.

It may be added here that while under the pretext of ill-health, the Premier did not go to Bombay to attend the Premiers Conference, he came down to Patna from Ranchi to attend the marriage of the daughter of Police S.P. who is a Bhumihar.

In the very first session after assuming of Office Mr. K.B. Sahay, Parliamentary Secretary, declared that he was proud to announce on behalf of the Congress that the Bihar Ministry would carry out the long demanded reform of separation of judiciary from the executive. A Committee set up by the previous government had already prepared a scheme. All that they had to do was to scrutinise it and prepare a final scheme to be put into operation. A Committee was set up to do the job. It sat and submitted an interim report. The report has been shelved in the pigeon-hole and nothing more is heard of it. And in all likelihood it will lie there for ever.

In the latter part of 1937 the ministry announced that they would launch a rural development scheme. About six months later, chief organisers were appointed. Six months they took to draw up scheme, then came the selection of village organisers. Some months passed. Then started the organisers' training which is still going on. None knows when the scheme will actually start working.

Contrast this as well as the question of separation of functions with the expediency with which the United Provinces Ministry put both the schemes into operation.

A retrenchment committee was set up. It submitted an interim report nearly a year ago. No more sitting has been held. No more perhaps will be held at all. It is only necessary to add that in that committee there is one minister and some parliamentary secretaries.

It is more than a year now that the Governor gave assent to the prohibition Act. The rules are still being prepared.

Provision was made in this year's budget for starting an intermediate college for girls. The college was to be started this year. Nothing of it has been heard yet. Other collages have already opened.

Same with the proposed military training college. People in Bihar are now wondering whether these two institutions will at all start working.

Same with the electrification scheme. The initial mistake was made and this by the way is another instance of nepotism was to employ a civil engineer as special officer for the scheme. After month's of work and expert examination at the hands of renowned engineers, all that has been decided is that the 'scheme is feasible'. Advertisements have been made to appoint a chief electrical engineer who will work out the details of the scheme. The appointment is yet to be made. When and if it is made, it can be safely assumed from the way things are being handled that it will take years before the details are worked out. Only the next generation, if at all, will see the scheme put into operation.

To make a beginning it was decided to electrify a small area with the help of current from a private factory and sink tubewells.

It was over a year ago that the Assembly voted the demand for the scheme. Nothing has been done yet. Meanwhile the special officer who has outlived his job continues to draw his salary of Rs. 800 p.m. all-right.

Prohibition has been a fiasco, an utter fiasco if some reports are to be believed. It really amuses one to hear the derisive manner in which it is spoken of in Bihar. It is reported that today tapping and drinking goes on openly and freely, many times with the connivance of the excise officers. There are reports that preparations for drinking bouts are made with the connivance of the officers who leave the place on the day the event is to come off. People living in villages will tell you that drinking is now perhaps on a larger scale than before the prohibition. Regarding allowance for all exaggeration it cannot be denied that prohibition in Bihar has not been a success at all.

And for this nothing but the ineptitude of the Ministry is responsible. First of all the Pasis (toddy tappers to whose community the Excise Minister belongs) are most infuriated at being deprived of their traditional profession. Not that they mind giving up their ancestral calling but they demand that efforts be made to give them alternative employment. And this the Government have entirely failed to do. Imagine the Excise Minister saying that those among the Pasis (who are illiterate) who are qualified will be given employment in Government service. Imagine again an official note describing that they are being taught bee-keeping and motor-driving. Under the circumstances it is no wonder if the Pasis snap their fingers at prohibition. In fact the Pasis were preparing for an open revolt but when they found that there was no control and no check, they thought it better to go on doing the thing covertly instead of giving it the appearance of a Satyagraha and drawing unnecessary attention towards themselves..

Secondly Government have made no effort to provide alternative attractions to the addicts. No propaganda is made and no effort bestowed on weaning the addicts away.

Thirdly, the administration and control is left entirely to officials. No voluntary organisations have been mobilised into the cause of prohibition. Neither has the staff been increased, with the result that they find it extremely difficult to cope with the work of prevention.

It appears that the Ministry is not at all serious about making prohibition a success; they seem to have no heart in it.

A first class scandal cropped recently. As a measure of mitigation Government allowed four shops for selling sweet toddy to be opened. And it is reported that licences for all the four shops went to the Minister's relatives. Other Pasis kicked up a row and there was big agitation and Government had ultimately to close down the shops.

The Ministry has also bungled in its own inimitable way the agrarian problem. All said and done it now appears that the Congress-Zamindar agreement willingly augured. And the legislation based upon it has been still worse. It is said to be full of drafting mistakes; the administrative difficulties have not been taken into consideration and while doing so good to the Kisans it has helped to hasten the ruin of the petty landlords. It was an initial mistake that neither the Kisans nor the petty landlords were taken into confidence when the pact was made. And now except for the bigger landlords the Ministry has friends neither among the Kisans nor among the smaller landlords.

The bakest problem has assumed now the most serious proportions. But the Ministry seems to be unaffected by it. It is a problem which cries for immediate solution but a solution at the hands of the present ministers seems to be as far as ever. Even the Ministerial organ has been clamouring for tackling the problem immediately but nothing is being done.

And it also cannot be denied that repression in all its forms has not been spared. Some of the incidents such as the lathi charges on peaceful women strikers in Patna, the handcuffing of Rahul Sankrityayna, *etc.*, have been scandalous and they have harmed the reputation of the ministry.

The services have, however, been thoroughly loyal to the ministry but their difficulty is the vascillating and uncertain policy of the Government. I have heard of a story of a district magistrate being rung up at night and asked what policy he was adopting regarding the agrarian situation in his district. The officer replied that he was, of course, following the Ministry's policy but added that his difficulty was that he did not know what their policy was. The Minister quietly put down the receiver. And yet attempts are being made to shelter the ministry by holding the accusing finger at the services, especially the European element which is assumed to be the villain of the peace.

Abul Kalam Azad

July 17, 1938

1. Report of Maulána Azad on the Political Situation of Bihar Province.

Document 10

TELEGRAM FROM MAUALANA AZAD TO DR. RAJENDRA PRASAD

CALCUTTA
SEPTEMBER 14, 1938

RAJENDRA PRASAD
HARIJAN COLONY
DELHI

BARDOLOI[1] TELEPHONED ME AFTER GIVING UNDERTAKING FOR COALITION MINISTRY STARTING SHILLONG TODAY SHALL INFORM YOU LATER

ABUL KALAM AZAD

1. M. Gopi Nath Bardoloi.

Document 11

LETTER FROM PANDIT JAWAHAR LAL NEHRU TO MAULANA AZAD

London
October 1, 1938

My dear Maulana,

I have not written to you since I came here, but I have sent several letters and reports to the Working Committee, which no doubt you must have seen. I have been following, as far as I could, developments in India. You have had a lot of trouble and the burden on you must have been great.

As you know I have been meeting Nahas Pasha and trying to develop contacts with the Wafdist movement. Nahas Pasha is very keen on this and I hope that good will result from our efforts.

I conveyed his invitation to the Congress to send representatives to the Wafdist Congress on November 23rd. I think it is highly important that we should send some representatives – at least two, a Hindu and a Muslim. I cannot think of a better representative than you. I might mention that Nahas Pasha specially suggested to me that one of our representatives should be a Muslim. I do hope that the Working Committee will decide soon about it and will communicate its decision directly to Nahas Pasha.

Perhaps you would write to him direct, not only about this Congress but about other affairs also. I am sure he would be delighted to receive a letter in Arabic from you.

You will notice the reference to the Arab Congress to be held on November 7th. I do not know what the position is in regard to this in India and whether the Muslim League or the Jamiat are sending delegates. What I have said in my letter to Nahas is based on information received in London. It would be worthwhile your finding out how matters stand in India and writing to Nahas Pasha about it.

Perhaps also you might inform Mufti Kifayatullah and other of the Jamiat as to the true character of this congress, which is probably being run to some extent under British influence, although in regard to Palestine it will no doubt criticise British policy. Anyway it is anti-Wafdist.

I am eager to get back to India, but for some time I am rather tied up because of my sister's and daughter's ill-health. I hope to decide in the course of the next week or ten days.

I hope you are keeping well.

Yours Sincerely,
Jawahar Lal Nehru

Document 12

TELEGRAM FROM MAULANA AZAD TO DR. RAJENDRA PRASAD

CALCUTTA
29 OCTOBER 1938

RAJENDRA PRASADJI
PATNA

OWING INDISPOSITION JOURNEY POSTPONED PLEASE DECIDE BHAGALPORE GAYA AFFAIRS REMOVING MUSLIM COMPLAINTS WHICH HAVE PERTURBED MUSLIM NATIONALISTS IMMEDIATE REMEDY NECESSARY PLEASE TELEPHONE ME TO NIGHT

ABUL KALAM AZAD

Document 13

LETTER FROM DR. RAJENDRA PRASAD TO SARDAR PATEL AND MAULANA AZAD

P.O. Ziradei (Saran)
14th December 1938

My dear Vallabhbhai and Maulana Saheb,

Raja Bahadur of Tiloi has been recently elected President of the British Indian Association of Oudh (Taluqdars Association) and Babu Kamakhyadutt Ram the Secretary of the Association, with some other friends have seen me in connection with the proposal for a settlement of the question of tenancy legislation. I understand that the meeting of some Taluqdars which was held on the 27th October last and which decided against arbitration or decision by the Parliamentary Sub-committee was unauthorised and invalid inasmuch as it was not a meeting of the Executive Committee or of the General Body of the Association but only of some Taluqdars. As against this there is a previous resolution of the General Body authorising the Raja Bahadur of Tiloi to take necessary steps in regard to the tenancy question. In any case I am told there is considerable change in the situation and the recently elected President thinks that a majority of the Taluqdars would like to have a settlement. The position of the Zamindars of Agra province is the same as before that is, (the) Nawab of Chhatari and his Association favour a settlement. They are now anxious to have our intervention. I have explained to Raja Bahadur that the resolution of 27th October, valid or invalid still stands and unless something is done to indicate clearly that the Taluqdars and Zamindars desire our intervention it will not be possible for us to move in the matter. On the other side the Assembly engaged in considering the clauses of the Bill. But it is not likely to finish this consideration before the Christmas recess. It is therefore suggested that if the Parliamentary Committee indicates its willingness to intervene, Raja Bahadur will take steps to obtain authority from the Taluqdars for making his formal request to the Parliamentary Sub-committee. The Government in that case have to be asked to stay its hands while the negotiations are completed. I have explained that the Parliamentary Sub-committee can agree to move in the matter only if the Ministry indicates its opinion in favour of such step and in any case postponement of further consideration of the Bill will be very difficult. I have suggested that as two of the members of the Sub-committee and other members of the Working Committee are at Wardha it would be best to see them there. From the talk I have had with them I gather that these friends are taken on a settlement and have always been so. Now that the Rajabahadur has become the President of the Association after a keen contest he may carry his brother Taluqdars with him and it may be worthwhile giving him a chance. I need hardly say that I personally favour an agreed settlement.

Yours sincerely,
Rajendra Prasad

Document 14

LETTER FROM SARDAR PATEL TO MAULANA AZAD

All India Congress Parliamentary Sub-committee

Purushottam Mansion,
Opp. Opera House,
Bombay-4,

20th December 1938

My dear Maulana Saheb,

I have received your letter of the 17th instant and accordingly I am sending you the papers concerning the Orissa controversy over some allegations made against the Prime Minister and his administration by Mr. Chintamani Misra.

Yours sincerely,

Vallabhbhai Patel

Enclosure 1 :

(From Vallabhbhai Patel to Chintamani Misra, Editor, Lokamata)

ALL INDIA CONGRESS PARLIAMENTARY SUB-COMMITTEE

Camp Bardoh,
August 21, 1938

My dear Friend,

I have received your letter of the 11th August, 1938 in which you make serious charges against the Premier of Orissa and his administration. It is impossible for me to give you any answer without making any inquiry in this matter. I do not see how you can blame the Prime Minister for a legislation which has been unanimously approved by the Congress Party in the Assembly. This is the first time that I hear your voice against it. The Tenancy Legislation may or may not get sanction from the Government of India, it is another matter altogether. It is not easy to get the assent of the Zamindars whose interest is affected by. It is not denied that the present rate of rents requires to be reduced. Admitting that as an accepted fact, it is for those who claim the present Bill as an expropriatory measure on the ground that the reduction of rent is unduly high to suggest what amount of reduction would be called legitimate and would not be regarded as expropriatory. I do not think that your criticism about it is justified. The other charges you have preferred against him are more serious and I cannot answer them without investigation.

Yours sincerely,
Vallabhbhai Patel,
Chairman

Document 15

LETTER FROM B.N. DAS TO MAULANA AZAD

Cuttack,
22 December 1938

My dear Azadji,

I have received your letter of 17th December 1938. You will please remember my conversation with you on phone while you were at Patna. It is not good that I should write to Pandit Nilakantha Das to come with all complaints against the Ministry to Calcutta. There is no use also in calling only Pandit Nilakantha Das alone. His lieutenant, Mr. Chintamani Misra, has to come. He is the person who has addressed the letter to Sardarji.[1] If Pandit Nilakantha Das comes alone he may disown the whole thing. Added to this, Pandit Godavarish, Joint Editor of 'Lokamata' with Mr. Chintamani Misra, has also to be called, I would therefore, request you to call these three gentlemen to Calcutta on the first as fixed by you.

I was ill for a few days and hence going to my village, keeping my stenographer here to receive any communication from you and direct them at once to my place. In the absence of any communication I will start for Calcutta on the 31st night by Puri Express.

Hope you have fully recovered your strength.

With Pranams,

Yours sincerely,
Biswanath Das

---

1. Sardar Vallabhbhai Patel.

Document 16

LETTER FROM N. KANUNGO TO MAULANA AZAD

Cuttack,
27th December 1938

Respected Maulana Saheb,

Our Premier Sjt. Biswanath Das[1] has gone to his village home and he would me to know if the arrangement which was made by you in course of the telephone conversation with him, stands good or not, that is Sjt. Biswanath Das has to go to meet you in Calcutta on the Ist January and that in the meantime you would have written to the following gentlemen to be present there on that date also. On receipt of your reply I will have to send a special messenger to Sjt. Biswanath Das so that he can come in time to be present in Calcutta on the 1st January 1939. If any alterations are to be made, you will kindly let me know of the same for communication to him. He has engagements fixed for him on the 4th, 5th, 6th and 7th January, which cannot be altered.

With regards,

Yours sincerely,
N. Kanungo

Addresses of the gentlemen who are to be asked for by you:

1. Pandit Nilakanth Das, Village Sri Ramehandrapur, Post Office Sakhigopal, District Puri.
2. Babu Godavarish Misra, M.I.A. P.O. Banpur, Distt. Puri.
3. Babu Chintamani Misra, Naba Bharat Press, Cuttack.

---

1. The then, Premier of Orissa.

Document 17

LETTER FROM MAULANA AZAD TO NILAKANTHA DAS

December 27, 1938

Dear Nilakantha Das,

Babu Rajendra Prasad was to go to Cuttack in connection with the Orissa Tenancy Amendment Bill. It was decided that he will also go through the complaints against the Hon'ble B.N. Das, Premier, Orissa. It is a pity that he is not keeping good health and is still unable to undertake the journey. As this is a matter which can no more be delayed, I wish to expedite it. But as it is difficult for me also to go to Cuttack at present, I think it would be better if you take the trouble of coming to Calcutta on the 1st January 1939. The Premier will also come, and the needful will be done here. Kindly let me know by wire that you are coming here on the 1st January so that I may inform the Premier also or you may inform him directly so that he may start on 31st instant for Calcutta.

Yours sincerely,
Abul Kalam Azad

Document 18

LETTER FROM MAULANA AZAD TO N. KANUNGO

December 28, 1938

Dear Kanungo,

I am in receipt of your letter of 27th December 1938. I have sent letters to the three gentlemen, according to the proposal of Mr. Biswanath Das, and am waiting for their replies. On receipt of replies about their arrival here on the first January, I shall inform you by wire, so that Mr. Das may also come here. In case I do not get any reply (and) they (cannot) come here on the first, I shall inform you about it even then.

Yours sincerely,

Abul Kalam Azad

Document 19

LETTER FROM NILAKANTHA DAS TO MAULANA AZAD

P.O. Sakhigopal
Naba Bharat Office
P.O. Chandni Chowk
Cuttack,

30 December 1938

Dear Maulana Saheb,

I received your letter today and have acknowledged receipt of it by wire. I returned from Delhi on the 20th when I arranged a week's tour programme from the 27th December to the 4th January in various places in the district. A part of it has been covered. It is not possible to cancel the remaining part of the programme all at once. Orissa University Committee, of which I am the Chairman, meets from the 5th January. It may go on up to the 10th. As soon as I am free I shall be glad to meet you, if you consider it necessary.

I am very sorry that Rajendra Babu is not yet well. He is ailing for a long time. May he get well soon. I have absolutely no definite knowledge of any proposal of his coming to Orissa to go through the allegations against the Hon'ble B.N. Das or in connection with any Orissa Tenancy Amendment Bill. I remember only to have read some such thing in the papers long ago. Even then as far as I recollect, there was no reference to any Orissa Tenancy Amendment Bill. As far as I know no Orissa Tenancy Amendment Bill is on the anvil now. May be the Government are considering another amendment of the Act. Many such amendments, however, are immediately necessary.

If the consideration of the enquiry can be postponed, I shall be highly obliged If you kindly arrange to send me copies of the allegations, or points for consideration, and any other necessary connected matter. Please do so.

Yours sincerely,

Nilakantha Das

Document 20

LETTER FROM G. MISRA TO MAULANA AZAD

P.O. Banpur,
Distt. Puri,

December 31, 1938

Dear Maulana Saheb,

I was away on tour and returning therefrom received your letter No. 566 dated the 27th instant yesterday. I am in the midst of various worries caused by a criminal case and other enquiries started on the initiative of a person who of late has been in the good books of the Hon'ble the Chief Minister. The criminal case is proceeding from yesterday at this place, which is far away from the headquarters of the Court even during the holidays. Besides, there is not time enough now for me to start this evening for Calcutta in order to be able to see you there tomorrow. There is no telegraph office here and I could not therefore intimate to you my inability in the matter earlier than this. There are allegations against the Hon'ble Mr. Biswanath Das. It will take time to prepare to substantiate them properly. Moreover, there may be other, and I know there are some who can be of use in this matter. It will be necessary to meet them all or as many of them as possible. If you think it proper, you may kindly fix some other time and I think that Cuttack will be the suitable place for this purpose.

I am sorry that I am not able to meet you as desired and hope to be excused.

Yours sincerely,
G. Misra

Document 21

LETTER FROM JAWAHAR LAL NEHRU TO MAULANA AZAD

Snow-View
Almora, January 22, 1939

My dear Maulana,

I have just learnt that the Radio has announced your withdrawal from the contest for the Congress Presidentship. I am sorry. But I may not criticise your action as you are the best person to judge of it.

I am glad to find from the newspapers that the Jaunpur by-election matter has been satisfactorily settled. I was very worried over this and I must confess that I disliked the idea of the Muslim League getting their man in unopposed. I felt that this would have been a very bad precedent. As it happens, the Congress position in Jaunpur was so strong that the first Muslim candidate withdrew and a second had to be put in. Even then the League feared failure. I am very glad that the Congress agreed to Ali Zaheer's name and thus avoided the bitterness of conflict, and yet got a decent man in.

I am going down to Lucknow on the 27th

Yours affectionately,

J.L. Nehru

Maulana Abul Kalam Azad,
19-A, Ballygunj Circular Road,
Calcutta

Document 22

TELEGRAM FROM JAWAHAR LAL NEHRU AND MAULANA AZAD TO DR. RAJENDRA PRASAD

LUCKNOW,
18-02-1939

RAJENDRA PRASAD,
PATNA

AGREE MEETING WARDHA EARLIEST POSSIBLE DATE

ABUL KALAM,
JAWAHAR LAL

Document 23

RESOLUTION PASSED BY THE OPEN SESSION OF I.N.C. HELD AT TRIPURI ON 27-02-1939 WITH MAULANA AZAD AS ACTING PRESIDENT

In view of various misunderstanding that have arisen in the Congress and the country on account of the controversies in connection with the Presidential election and after, it is desirable that the All-India Congress Committee should clarify the position and declare its general Policy.

The Committee declares its firm adherence to the fundamental policies of the Congress which have governed its programme in the past years under the guidance of Mahatma Gandhi and is definitely of the opinion that there should be no break in these policies and that they should continue to govern the Congress programme in future. The Committee expresses its confidence in the work of the Working Committee which functioned during the last year, and deplores that any aspersions should have been cast against any of its members.

"In view of the critical situation that may develop during the coming year and in view of the fact that Mahatma Gandhi alone can lead the Congress and the country to victory during such crisis, the Committee regards it as imperative that the Congress Executive should command his implicit confidence and requests the President to nominate the Working Committee in accordance with the wishes of Gandhiji."

Document 24

TEXT OF THE THREE RESOLUTIONS, MOVED BY MAULANA AZAD AS PRESIDENT IN THE TRIPURI CONGRESS ON 10-3-1939

This Congress expresses its sense of sorrow and loss at the deaths of Maulana Shaukat Ali, Sir Mohammad Iqbal, Begam Ansari and Messrs K. Raman Menon, G.S. Khaparde, B. Raju Rau, Nathuji Jagtap, Thakur Gulzar Singh, Raja Ram Shukla, Deviprasad Shukla, K.H. Bhatt, Dhundi Raj Mahadeo Naik, Abdul Wahid, Balwantrai P. Thakore, Maheshprasad Nigam, Pandit Mahabir Prasad Dwivedi, Upendranath Mukerji, Jwala Singh, K. Nageswar Rau, Rajab Ali Patel, Ghaltu Venkat, Chaturanan Das, Bạnchchanidhi Mahanty, Girija Bhusan Dutt, Shrinath Das and Pratap Singh.

Welcome to Egyptian Delegation

The Congress extends its cordial welcome to the fraternal delegation from the Wafd Party of Egypt and considers this visit as symbolising the solidarity of the movements for freedom in Egypt and India. The Congress sends its greetings to the people of Egypt and its earnest wishes for their complete success in achieving full freedom. It trusts that the association of the peoples of Egypt and India will ever grow closer and more fruitful in the furtherance of world peace and freedom.

China

The Congress sends its greetings to the people of China and its deepest sympathy in their trial and privations in their struggle against a ruthless and inhuman imperialism. It congratulates them on their heroic resistance.

The Congress expresses its approval of the sending of a medical mission on its behalf to the people of China, and trusts this mission will continue to receive full support so that it may carry on its work of succour effectively and be a worthy symbol of India's solidaritv with China.

Document 25

LETTER FROM JAWAHAR LAL NEHRU TO MAULANA AZAD

Anand Bhawan
Allahabad

April 17, 1939

My dear Maulana,

I received your letter yesterday afternoon. I felt that it was perhaps too late for me to go to Lucknow to meet Sir Sultan Ahmed. If, however, my presence there is required or he asks me to go, I shall certainly do so.

I sent your letter in original last night by messenger to Rafi Ahmed[1] and asked him to show it to the other ministers. I fear there has been much bungling about this issue. Hafiz Ibrahim was particularly incharge of it and considerable pressure was brought to bear upon him by Maulana Hussain Ahmad. The Deputy Commissioner also was very excited and pressed for an early decision by the government. Pantji[2] unfortunately, was and has been a very sick man, thoroughly tired out and with no freshness left about him. Rafi also had been unwell and had gone away for a few days rest. The matter was thus decided in a hurry without full consideration of the consequences. Of course, they should have referred to you. The fact is that the ministry is weary with work and responsibility and tends to become stale.

Pantji was so unwell that he had to leave Lucknow immediately after and I am not sure that he has come back yet.

I understand that Maulana Hussain Ahmad is very displeased with Moulvi Abdul Shukur as the latter did not play fair with him. Zaffar-ul-Mulk is probably still in prison (though I am not sure of this) because he refused to agree to the settlement.

If I can be of any use whatever, I shall gladly offer myself.

Yours affectionately,
Jawahar Lal Nehru

---

1. Mr. Rafi Ahmed Kidwai.

2. Pandit Gobind Ballabh Pant.

Document 26

LETTER FROM MAULANA AZAD TO JAWAHAR LAL NEHRU

19A, Ballygunge Circular Road,
Calcutta,

April 17, 1939

My dear Jawahar,

When I think of my accident at Allahabad I find that nothing more could have been done for my comfort and treatment by my own people here had it happened in Calcutta. Indeed the nearest and dearest of my relatives could not have felt more than you did for me there. I do not know how to express my feeling of gratitude to you for these. Believe me my heart is extremely grateful for your love and kindness.

There are numerous ordinary things which tend to create deep feelings of heart. While coming from Allahabad you looked into the very minor details about my comforts for a journey which had to last for only a night. I did not know how many things have been sent with me. Here I found that even I do not know whether you have seen the letters of Subhas[1] to Gandhiji.[2] It is a pity that Subhas Babu is exactly in the position where he was before Tripuri, and there is no hope that he will improve the situation by acting on the Tripuri resolution. On the one hand he calls the Pant resolution against the constitution and *ultra vires*, on the other he wants Gandhiji to accept certain conditions. Along with this he does not hesitate in making the extravagant assertion that the Pant[3] resolution would have been lost, had the Socialist group not become neutral.

However there is no hope of the Congress moving along Subhas Babu. The whole thing will come to dead stop. We have therefore, to chalk out the future line of action.

I consider the affairs of Subhash Babu to be neither a struggle between the right and the left, nor the question of composite and homogeneous Working Committee. It is only a matter of Subhas and some of his supporters. It matters little in what form the tangle comes to an end, we have to consider these questions independently and specifically, in order to reach a solution.

I hope you have received my last letter, and you have phoned to Lucknow about Sultan Ahmad.

Yours sincerely,
A.K. Azad

---

1. Netaji Subhas Chandra Bose.
2. Mahatma Gandhi.
3. Pt. Govinda Ballabh Pant's Resolution moved before the open Session of I.N.C. at Tripuri on February 27, 1939.

Document 27

LETTER FROM JAWAHAR LAL NEHRU TO MAULANA AZAD

Anand Bhawan
Allahabad,

April 20, 1939

My dear Maulana,

Your letter of the 17th. Surely you ought to know me better than to thank me for my efforts to look after your comforts here. What else could you expect anyone to do?

I went to see Subhas[1] yesterday at his request and I had a long talk with him. I have looked through the correspondence between him and Gandhiji. This is, as you say, very distressing correspondence, and it creates fresh difficulties. There was some talk of publishing this correspondence but I have dissuaded Subhas from doing So, I have also requested Gandhiji not to issue any statement which might commit him.

I am quite sure that the only thing to be done now is for Subhas to leave the formation of the Working Committee entirely to Gandhiji and to promise his loyal support to whatever is done. There are sure to be difficulties because of the way Subhash thinks as well as other matters. But we have to face these difficulties. Any other course means far greater trouble and difficulty. I think that in practice many of these difficulties will be controlled and Subhas also will not add to them. The main thing is that we should not meet the A.I.C.C. before some solution is found. Subhas was agreeable to what suggested but, of course, I do not know what reservations he might have in his mind. Anyway, I think we shall not trouble ourselves with possible future difficulties. It is something to get over the present difficulty. In view of the national and international situation, it is urgently necessary that we should start functioning here as a Working Committee.

My talk with Subhas was quite friendly and frank. Unfortunately he has been too much surrounded by one-sided accounts and rumours.

I think it will be a very good thing if you write to him and express the desire to meet him. He will be in Calcutta tomorrow night.

I have had a long letter from Rafi Ahmed in which he tells me all the developments in the Shia-Sunni affair. He met Sir Sultan Ahmed. It appears that Sir Sultan Ahmed is going to Lucknow again to see the ministers. Hafiz Ibrahim has gone to Delhi to see the Ulemas there. Rafi[2] suggested to him that the government would accept any recommendation of a committee consisting of you and him. Rafi Ahmed felt that in your letter you had been unfair to Pantji and written in somewhat harsh language about his part in these affairs.

If Gandhiji goes to Calcutta sometimes before the A.I.C.C. I shall also try to get there them.

Yours affectionately,
Jawaharlal

Maulana Abul Kalam Azad
New Delhi

1. Babu Subhash Chandra Bose.
2. Rafi Ahmed Kidwai.

Document 28

LETTER FROM MAULANA AZAD TO JAWAHAR LAL NEHRU

19 A, Ballygunge Circular Road,
Calcutta,

July 3, 1939

My dear Jawaharlal,

I excepted to meet you in Bombay, but owing to the slow progress of recovery I could not undertake the journey. Dr. Roy[1] thinks that it will take at least one month more to become normal.

I am writing this letter for a special matter. Chamanlal, who was some time a reporter of the *Hindustan Times*, will meet you. Why do you not take him on the staff of the *National Herald*. He has acquired sufficient experience in Journalism, and I think the National Herald stands much in need of such men.

He is known to me for the last fifteen years. There are a few defects in him, but I do not think that they will hinder the work.

Much had to be discussed with you about the present and the future, but after your return from Ceylon we may get a chance of meeting each other.

Please convey my message of love to Indira when you write to her next.

Yours sincerely,
A.K. Azad

Pt. Jawahar Lal Nehru
Anand Bhawan,
Allahabad

---

1. Dr. Bidhan Chandra Roy.

Document 29

LETTER FROM JAWAHARLAL NEHRU TO MAULANA AZAD

6, Couper Road, Lucknow,
July 8, 1939

My dear Maulana,

Thank you for your letter of the 5th. Just before receiving it I sent you a copy of a letter I addressed to Rajendra Babu.

I am glad that you are progressing. I hope that you will be completely fit by the end of this month. In case, however, some emergency arises owing to war or otherwise, Rajendra Babu written to me that there will be on immediate meeting of the Working Committee, probably in Delhi. Gandhiji has promised to come down from the Frontier for it. In case such a meeting takes place I hope you will make a point of attending it.

I know Chamanlal very well and realise that he has some very good qualities. I had wanted to help him in the past but he did not take advantage of my suggestions. I shall see what can be done about him.

I am going to Allahabad tonight and staying there three days. Then I go to Bombay where I remain for the 13th and 14th. Then Ceylon. I hope to be back by the end of the month.

Yours affectionately,

J.L. Nehru

Maulana Abul Kalam Azad,
19-A, Ballyganj Circular Road,
Calcutta

Document 30

LETTER FROM MAULANA AZAD TO DR. RAJENDRA PRASAD

19 A, Ballygunge Circular Road,
Calcutta

July 10, 1939

My dear Rajendra Babu,

Your letter of the 3rd instant to hand. The Punjab affairs have our immediate attention, but you are right in saying that they cannot be settled unless a strong man goes there. So far as I am concerned, I am yet unable to use my leg. In the opinion of Bidhan Roy, it still requires one month's treatment, which means that I shall be able to walk about by the middle of August. If someone has to go there immediately, I think either you yourself, Sardar Patel or Pandit Jawaharlal should go. Jawaharlal is going to Ceylon, and he will not be able to return before August. Now the matter devolves on you or Patel.[1] No one else can be of any use.

The malady of the Punjab is chronic and deep-seated. It will not be sufficient to glean at the surface only. The real causes of the disease are to be diagnosed, and firm steps are to be taken to root out the disease absolutely.

If none of you or Mr. Patel can give time for it, then nothing can be done but to wait for my recovery.

The attitude of Subhash Babu[2] as well as of the P.C.C. Bengal have created an important problem. It is necessary that the Working Committee should give its verdict unhesitatingly and without any weakness.

Yours sincerely,
A.K. Azad

Dr. Rajendra Prasad,
President, A.I.C.C.
Ranchi

---

1. Sardar Vallabhbhai Patel.
2. Netaji Subhash Chandra Bose.

Document 31

FROM DR. RAJENDRA PRASAD TO MAULANA AZAD AND OTHERS

Birla House, Ranchi,

11th July 1939

Dear Friend,

You might have seen in the Press the statement issued by me regarding the observance of 9th of July as a day of protest against the resolution of the A.I.C.C. as announced by the left Consolidation Group and Sjt. Subhash Bose. I have seen reports in the papers of meetings having been held in Calcutta, Cawnpore, Nagpur and Jubbulpore. It is possible that similar meetings has been held in some other places. I have seen full reports of the proceedings of the meeting of the Executive Council of the Bengal Provincial Committee and also of the public meeting held in Calcutta which was attended by a large number of prominent members of the Congress Committee. I have received a suggestion from a member of our Working Committee that we should meet at an early date to consider the situation arising out of these demonstrations. As you are aware Pandit Jawahar Lal has gone to Ceylon and will not return before the end of this month. I should very much like to have him present at the meeting of the Working Committee to discuss this question. Mahatmaji has also gone to the Frontier and will not be returning before the end of this month. I should like to have your views about the matter and as to whether I should convene a meeting immediately or wait till we are in a position to get the benefit of the advice of both these gentlemen. I shall be staying here and a reply to this may be sent here.

Rajendra Prasad

Document 32

LETTER FROM MAULANA AZAD TO B.C. MISRA

16th July 1939

Dear friend,

I have received your letter of the 7th July, regarding creating of a satisfactory machinery through which closer contact between the Surma Valley Congress and the Assam Cabinet may be established for parliamentary work. This matter will come up before the Working Committee through the A.I.C.C. office as soon as the opinion of the parties concerned have been received. As you have sent the copy of this representation to the General Secretary of the A.I.C.C.. I have no doubt he will obtain the opinion of the organisations concerned and place the matter before the Working Committee.

Yours sincerely,
A.K. Azad

Sjt Biresh Chandra Misra,
Secretary,
Sylhet, District Congress Committee,
Sylhet

Document 33

LETTER FROM MAULANA AZAD TO JAWAHAR LAL NEHRU

19-A, Ballygunge Circular Road,
Calcutta

August 17, 1939

My Dear Jawaharlal,

Thanks for your letter. I have already sent to you two letters one after the other on your Allahabad address. I hope they have reached you.

I do not know whether Rajendra Babu had presented my letter before the Committee or not. He himself and Vallabhbhai[1] had insisted to send my opinion – in case I could not attend – and therefore, I had written my opinion in detail. In my opinion the attitude of Subhas Babu[2] was wrong, and it was necessary for the Working Committee to express its opinion. But I had suggested not to show too much strictness at this occasion. I proposed that the Working Committee should pass a resolution on the lines of the one passed by you in U.P., and leave the rest to the President. The President may then correspond with them, and if they agree with the resolution of the Committee, then he may drop further action. But if they are not ready even to this extent, then they may simply be removed from their present office. But there should be no bar to their next year's Election.

I had given you the trouble to talk over the phone, as I thought that you would take part in the consideration of this matter. But now it transpires that you remained practically aloof, and the decision was made in the absence of your agreement.

Yours sincerely,
A.K. Azad

Pandit Jawaharlal Nehru,
Allahabad

---

1. Sardar Vallabhbhai.
2. Netaji Subhash Chandra Bose.

Document 34

LETTER FROM A.N. SINHA TO MAULANA AZAD

Camp Poona
7, Yerrowada House,

25 August 1939

My dear Maulana Sahib,

I apologise for not writing to you so long in reply to your letter relating to the nomination to District Boards in Bihar. I was long pondering over the problem and could not make up my mind until I was forced to do when the election reports began to reach me. In making nominations, I am to be guided by three principles laid down in the Local Self-Government Act. I may mention here that the policy to be followed in future is to abolish the system of nomination altogether and with this end in view, a Municipal (Amendment) Bill is pending in the Assembly and has been referred to Select Committee. This Bill provided for representation of Muslim minority on population ratio with freedom to contest general seats. The representation of depressed classes is also to be based on this very principle. System of nomination has been abandoned in this Bill. Since it is not possible to do away with nomination unless the Act has been amended. I am adopting the following formula consistent with the requirements of the Act in dealing with appointment of additional members.

The Act lays down that nomination of additional members should be based upon three principles, *viz.* (1) to make up for unrepresented interests such as trade zamindary, labour, *etc.*, as (2) to give adequate representation to minorities such as Muslims, depressed classes, backward communities, *etc.* and (3) to secure the association of persons of experience and of experts.

After a good deal of thought and consultation, I evolved the following formula to Muslims. As their population varies from district to district, I thought it would be fair to secure their representation on population basis plus 50% of this ratio in each district and if in any district they have not been returned in adequate number by election to make up the district by nomination. In relation to depressed classes, it was not possible to follow the principle on account of limitation of seats. I was advised to guarantee at least two seats on each Board, including the number secured by them. Representation of unrepresented interests like landlords, trade, *etc.*, has to be provided for and it should be noted that in this year's election, landlord who used to dominate before have hardly been able to capture any seat in most districts. Under the third category, *viz.*, experienced (persons) and experts the usual practice was to take in all the S.D.O.s and such other persons who have been in the Board for some years or who have any special qualifications to be there.

Bearing these factors in mind, I proceeded to appoint additional meet, whose number varies from 6 to 10 according to total strength of each Board. If were to follow any other principle, I could hardly comply with the directions in the Act. So far I have announced the results of one Board in each division of Chhotanagpur, Bhagalpur and two in Patna. I have stayed further nominations to observe the reaction to these principles.

In regard to selection of Muslim names, I have kept in view the recommendations of Maulana Sajjad and President of the Jamait-ul-Momin. Muslim Mass Contact has been generally represented by election and in some districts their number has been quite adequate. For example in Bhagalpur and Patna districts as many as five and four have been respectively returned by election and all of them are Muslim Mass Contact has been generally represented by election and in some districts their number has been quite adequate. For example in Bhagalpur and Patna districts as many as five and four have been respectively returned by election and all of them are Muslim Mass Contact Workers. In Chhapra, three have been elected, and three have been nominated. In Gaya, two were elected and four have been nominated. One represents Momins, one an ex-Muslim League and the remaining Mass Contact representatives. In Purnea, two have been elected and two nominated – one representing an independent party and the other Momin. In Manbhum, two have been nominated and both prominent Muslim gentlemen of Dhanbad and Sadar respectively, only one having been elected. One Muslim official was appointed. In Arrah, the quota according to the above formula came to 4 – one having been elected, three were nominated – one representing Momins, one Muslim Mass Contact and one an independent influential gentleman. This is in short the result of nominations made on principles enunciated above. I have now stayed making further nominations and if any other principle is suggested to me consistently with the direction in the Act, I am prepared to follow it. I shall, therefore, await further instructions if you intend to send any.

I shall just take a district and illustrate the points of view which I discussed above. Take the case of Gaya. I have to nominate 10 persons. I have nominated as follows: 4 Muslims, 2 S.D.O.s., one depressed class, 2 landlords and one Socialist = 10.

In this district, there has been no trouble as both election and nomination have been done in pursuance of an agreement between two contesting parties.

As regards particular names, it is impossible to accept any one out of hundreds of names suggested without displeasing the remaining ones. I have, therefore, in acting upon the above principles, I ignored the recommendations made by so many persons and interests and have accepted only one such as, in my opinion, may appear most suitable in the circumstances. I am going to nominate two Muslims at Patna as four have been returned by election and all of them belong to Muslim Mass Contact group. It will be unfair to give all seats to them. I am, therefore, taking one nominee of Maulana Sajjad and another a Momin gentleman.

I have dealt with the subject rather exhaustively. I may make it clear to you that this has been a most unpleasant duty which I have to perform and I do not feel quite happy over it. I have no personal desire in the matter and I have kept no other interest but that of the Congress in view when I have made these appointments. I would be quite happy if the responsibility could have been taken by someone else whom I would have been content to assist.

So many representations, so many deputations and so many communications have been received by me that I have often felt bewildered what to do and had not ignored most of them it would have been impossible for me to make nominations at all. I have done so with a clear conscience and if some interests have not been satisfied or if some dissatisfaction exists, I consider those inevitable in the circumstances.

I am conscious that I am giving you some trouble by inflicting this long note but I think it was not possible to explain my position otherwise. Although I have taken consent of my colleagues in these nominations. I take the entire responsibility upon myself for so doing.

With respectful regards

I am
Yours Sincerely,
Anugrah Narayan Sinha

Maulana Abul Kalam Azad
Calcutta

Document 35

TELEGRAM FROM MAULANA AZAD TO DR. RAJENDRA PRASAD

LUCKNOW,

27-08-1939

DOCTOR RAJENDRA PRASAD,
RAMGARH

STAYING HERE AT PRESENT STOP PATNA SUITABLE WIRE.

ABUL KALAM AZAD

Document 36

TELEGRAM FROM DR. RAJENDRA PRASAD TO MAULANA AZAD

29TH AUGUST 1939

MAULANA ABUL KALAM AZAD,
CARE HONOURABLE IBRAHIM,
LUCKNOW

RECEIVED STILL UNABLE MOVE PROPOSE MEETING RANCHI SECOND OR THIRD WIRING AGAIN WHEN FINALLY FIXED.

RAJENDRA PRASAD

Document 37

TELEGRAM FROM MAULANA AZAD TO DR. RAJENDRA PRASAD

LUCKNOW,

03-09-1939

BABU RAJENDRA PRASAD,
RAMGARH

REACHING CALCUTTA TOMORROW MORNING MEETING SHOULD BE CALLED WITHOUT DELAY WIRE CALCUTTA.

ABUL KALAM AZAD

Document 38

UNITY AND DISCIPLINE HAVE TO BE EMPHASISED[1]

Wardha, 16-09-39

Dear Comrade,

For many years past all of us have lived on the verge of a world crisis and preoccupied as we were with our vital national problems, the Congress had often given thought to the approaching crisis and laid down our broad policy in regard to it. Now that crisis has come and may rages in Europe, in addition to the far eastern war, which has now been going on for two and half years. Every Congressman has been deeply moved by this turn of events and has given earnest consideration to our duty at this juncture. Not only the directions of the Congress and its reason for existence compel us to play a worthy and effective part in the development of events. We have not been onlookers of events in India passively adapting ourselves to what happened. The Congress has essentially been a body of action and struggle in the cause of India's freedom and has shaped India's destiny for many years. That grave responsibility has to be shouldered afresh by the Congress in this crisis which affects India as well as the rest of the world.

As you are aware the working committee have given the most earnest consideration to these developments and have issued a statement in which they have clearly laid down India's attitude. We invite your attention to this statement so that your provincial and local committees and all Congressmen should appreciate the position fully and act in accordance with the advice given. That statement is a dispassionately worded document, clarifying the issues as they affect India, in simple language and indicating the road that India has to travel in these troubled times. The implications of that statement and the possible developments must be clear to you.

The committee has viewed the crisis in the widest perspective and has considered the cause of Indian freedom in relation to world freedom. We who claim to labour for great ends in India cannot lose sight of these perspectives. This crisis will not pass, as the working committee say, leaving the essential structure of the present day world intact. The world is going to be refashioned and India is going to play her part in this refashioning.

Many questions arise as to our day-to-day activities more especially during this period when our final decision has not been taken. We shall endeavour to answer them as they arise and as they are put to us. As you are aware a special sub-committee consisting of us three has been appointed to deal with the war emergency and we shall always be at your disposal for reference or advice. Our sub-committee will of course be guided by Mahatma Gandhi and the Congress President, Sri Rajendra Prasad.

To matters, however, have to be borne in mind for they are of essential importance. Whatever the developments might be, we can only face them with dignity and strength if our organisation is well prepared and has put an end to internal controversy and conflict. No lover of the Congress and of Indian freedom may do anything which impairs our unity and joint will for action. We have all to rise above our petty selves and become, in this crisis of our destiny, true soldiers of India, speaking and acting together with dignity and forbearance and in accordance with the ideals and principles we have cherished.

Our first duty is to tune up our organisation and keep it in fit condition for whatever demands might be made upon it. Secondly, we must not individually or severally act or speak hastily precipitating a development before its proper time. We must function in accordance with the spirit of the working committee's statement and not overreach it or believe it in our words or deeds. That would be a disservice to the larger cause we seek to serve as well as to this unity which is essential in our ranks.

Your provincial and local committees should give the widest publicity to the working committee's statement and explain its implications, more particularly the essential need for tightening up our organisation and preparing it for all the difficulties and trials we may have to face. Unity and discipline have to be emphasised, as well as that the final decision has not been taken yet and this will depend on circumstances and developments. Our position has been frankly and clearly stated before India and the world. To that we shall adhere, and seek, above all, to follow paths which lead to world freedom and reorganisation which must be based on our freedom. But any action taken by an individual Congressman which oppose the working committee's statement will not only lead to a loosening of our discipline but to a weakening of our cause and to controversy when we have to present a united front. This has to be avoided. Strength will not come to us by individual action or by brave speeches but by discipline and united effort. The hour of trial has come again upon us. Let us be worthy of it.

Abul Kalam Azad,
Vallabhbhai Patel,
Jawahar Lal Nehru

1. A Joint Statement of Maulana Azad, Pandit Jawahar Lal Nehru and Sardar Patel.

Document 39

LETTER FROM PANDIT JAWAHAR LAL NEHRU TO MAULANA AZAD

Camp Wardha,

13th October 1939

My dear Maulana Saheb,

You have seen the statement of Sir Sikandar Hayat published in the papers which we got this morning. There is a direct suggestion that the Congress should have consultation with the Muslim League regarding the communal question and come to an agreement with it. It is a public invitation. You also know that our suggestion for an enquiry by an impartial judge into the allegations against the Congress ministries has been rejected by Mr. Jinnah[1] who has practically barred the door for the present at any rate. I should like to have your views in the matter. I had a talk with Mahatmaji. He is of opinion that I should write to Sir Sikandar Hayat asking him for definite suggestions and pointing out to him that Mr. Jinnah has practically barred the door at present. But Mahatmaji has said that I should first consult you and get your advice in the matter.

I am leaving this evening and shall be staying at Benares on the 15th, 16th October with Babu Shivaprasad Gupta, Seveupvan, Benares Hindu University, Benares, and reaching Patna on the 17th. I shall be obliged for an early reply.

Yours Sincerely,

Jawahar Lal Nehru

Maulana Azad,
Calcutta

---

1. Mr. Mohammad Ali Jinnah.

Document 40

LETTER FROM MAULANA AZAD TO PANDIT JAWAHAR LAL NEHRU

Calcutta,

11-11-1939

My dear Jawaharlal,

The Hindustani Committee of Patna has been further postponed to December 15, instead of 18th November. Now I can reach Allahabad on the 19th without any hitch. I shall reach there by the Punjab Mail, and probably Bidhan will be also with me.

My fears about Assam have come to be true. There are only two Congressmen out of the eight Ministers. The remaining six are-non-Congressites, and naturally they are averse to leave the Ministry. In the words of Bardoloi: "Congress circles themselves, and some Congress office-holders too, are supporting them."

However, Bardoloi[1] assures me that he would resign till the 12th November. It is hoped that he may be able to do so.

I wish to remind you an important matter. Fazlul Haq had said in reply to your statement, that he would inform you on reaching Calcutta. More than a week has already passed. Please wire to him immediately that you are waiting for his information, so that you may be able to chalk out your programme accordingly. A copy of this telegram should also be given to the Press.

Your reply has absolutely upset Fazlul Haq. All his colleagues are blaming him for his folly. This is the most opportune time to bring him to his senses by persistently forcing the issues at him, so that the absurdity may end for all time to come; and the public should not get a chance of forgetting this episode.

Yours sincerely,
A.K. Azad

Pandit Jawahar Lal Nehru,
Anand Bhavan,
Allahabad

---

1. Mr. Gopinath Bardoloi.

Document 41

LETTER FROM GOPINATH BARDOLOI TO MAULANA AZAD

Shillong,

November 15, 1939

My dear Maulana Saheb,

After we had telephonic conversations with you and after plenty of heated discussions, we managed to adopt unanimously a resolution, copy of which is enclosed herewith for your perusal.

After the resolution was passed, the Congress members of the Party withdraw from the meeting and the non-Congress members proceeded to discuss the possibilities of an alternative Ministry pledged to execute the Congress programme.

I am sure, from the trend of discussion with Rev. Nichols-Roy on the phase you could well understand the mentality of a fair number of the Coalitionists. I am afraid, out of a body of 23 men at least 10 to 12, including the tribal group consisting of six members, are against what they call creating a deadlock. I tried to convincc them that the withdrawal of co-operation from the Ministry was purely a moral issue which every Indian should join but they seemed inexorable. After plenty of discussions they adopted resolution among themselves, copy of which is also sent herewith. They tried to appoint a leader at the same sitting bút it was only today that they succeeded in electing Rev. Nichols-Roy as Leader and Mr. Ali Haïdar Khan as President of the party.

In the meanwhile, Rev. Nichols-Roy saw the Governor who, it seems, encouraged him with the idea of some kind of alternative Government.

At this evening's sitting they decided to write me the letter which I enclose herewith. I told them that if I were to give a reply, it would be possible for me to do so only after consulting the working committee. I further told them that I could give my personal opinion but that could never bè taken as the opinion of either the Congress Party or the Working Committee. I am awaiting your advice on the matter. I have already given my opinion in a previous letter to you. I hope you will kindly discuss the subject at the next meeting of the Working Committee and communicate your opinion to me early.

We submitted our resignation at 3 o'Clock this afternoon. I had about 15 minutes' talk with the Governor, in the course of which I told him that I expected that Assam would be treated like the seven Congress provinces and that since we command a majority in the Assembly, the only honourable course would be to apply Section 93 and suspend the constitution. The Governor said that in view of the special circumstances of the province, he could not do so straightway but must give the leader of the opposition an opportunity to form an alternative Ministry. He did not accept our resignation and asked for 4 or 5 days' time.

The Governor called Sir Md. Saadulla at 6.30 this evening. To the pressmen Sir Saadulla said that he had an informal discussion with the Governor and that if he was formally asked to form a Ministry tomorrow he would take time. As far as I can see, nothing is going to happen during the next 4 or 5 days.

We seem to have today a majority of 58 members including the Speaker. Since there is the hope of an alternative Ministry with the Congress programme, other members (non-Congress) of the coalition also show a definite disposition not to go to Saadulla's side. It seems that if this attitude is real, the Congress constructive programme has at any rate caught their imagination. I feel some degree of selfishness is also there.

With kind regards,

Very sincerely yours,

Gopinath Bardoloi

Maulana Abul Kalam Azad,
19-A, Ballyganj Circular Road,
Calcutta

Document 42

LETTER FROM MAULANA AZAD TO DR. RAJENDRA PRASAD

19-A, Ballygunge Circular Road
Calcutta,

November 28, 1939

My dear Rajendra Babu,

Sarat Babu[1] has sent me yesterday a cheque of Rs. 5,000 and a fixed deposit receipt for Rs. 10075 in connection with the Assembly Party Fund. Now a balance of Rs. 521/13/6 remains in his Current Account; which he has not transferred in order that the Account may remain open in the Bank for future. As nothing was said in the Resolution of the Working Committee for the future, he thinks that he will continue depositing the contributions of the members in the Bank as usual. I did not deem it expedient to say anything to him in this connection at present. We shall think over it in future.

He has sent a lengthy letter to me about this matter, which, he has requested me to present to the next Working Committee. He has taken strong exception to the decision of the Working Committee. I have acknowledged his letter saying, that I will present it before the next Working Committee.

I hope you are doing well, I am still as before, yet I have decided to start for Patna on December 4. There we shall have the occasion to meet and talk in detail.

Yours sincerely,

A.K. Azad

Dr. Rajendra Prasad,
Sadagat Ashram,
Patna

---

1. Mr. Sarat Chandra Bose, Elder Brother of Netaji Subhash Chandra Bose.

Document 43

MAULANA AZAD'S STATEMENT DATED 21-12-39 AGAINST THE DELIVERANCE DAY OF MUSLIM LEAGUE

"Now when the Congress has given up the Government of eight provinces of its own choice and free will, what advice has the League president to offer to the Muslims? If is this that they should march towards the mosques and thank God on their deliverance from the Congress Ministries, which have prefered duty to power, and have resigned not only on the issue of India's freedom but for the rights of all down-trodden peoples of the East. It is difficult to imagine that any group of Muslims, however at longgerheads, with the Indian National Congress, would tolerate to be presented to the world in such colours."

Document 44

LETTER FROM MAULANA AZAD TO DR. RAJENDRA PRASAD

19-A, Ballygunge Circular Road
Calcutta,

January 3, 1940

My dear Rajendra Babu,

I am fuly in agreement with your opinion which you have formed about Utkal.

We have decidedly to take a final step about Bengal, if the Provicial Committee to be held on the 6th allows the decision of the executive to stand as it is. The Working Committee should be called for this, not on the 15th, but earlier. You have written to the Bengal Provincial to send its statement to you till the 10th January. You can call the Working Committee on the 11th by a telegram. I write this simply because I want to get a chance of going sooner to the Punjab.

Yours sincerely,

A.K. Azad

Dr. Rajendra Prasad
President, I.N.C.
Wardha

Document 45

LETTER FROM MAULANA AZAD TO DR. RAJENDRA PRASAD

Calcutta,

January 5, 1940

My dear Rajendra Babu,

Many telegrams have been received from the Punjab saying that the Tribunal there has been formed on party lines by the P.C.C., which is not expected to work in a non-partisan spirit. It is also said that the man selected for the Tribunal have no social standing and ordinary clerk of the *Pratap* office has been made a member.

The tribunal would have been appointed in August last, so complaint was received at that time. The difficulty now is that the complaints are pouring in just at the time of the selection of the delegates which will begin there from the 8th January.

Moreover, the complaints regarding the PCC should go to the office, or direct to you not to me.

However, I am sending the telegram to you, You may please wire them some reply.

There is a complaint from Jammu that the Punjab Congress has ignored their delegation. The telegram[1] is enclosed herewith, for inquiry and necessary action.

Yours sincerely,
A.K. Azad

Dr. Rajendra Prasad

---

1. Not included.

Document 46

LETTER FROM MAULANA AZAD TO SARDAR PATEL

19-A, Ballygunge Circular Road,
Calcutta,

January 25, 1940

Dear Vallabhbhai,

This situation which arose in connection with the Multan by-election seems to have been caused by some in the working of the parliamentary sub-committee. The Punjab Provincial applied for the approval of one and the same from two different places, at the same time. It wanted your approval as Chairman of the Sub-committee, and mine, as a member of the Sub-committee incharge of the province. We both were in the dark about each other. You did not get the application of Shanno Devi, and therefore, you gave your approval. I had received her application, and I, therefore, hesitated in giving approval.

In order to avoid complication, we had divided the work between ourselves in 1937, and had informed the Provinces accordingly. But I do not know, how the Provinces failed to abide by the division. They began to send a matter to you, another to Rajendra Babu and a third to me. We did not take any notice of his irregularity. The result is, that the Punjab created a situation unnecessarily by asking approval from two places, at one and the same time, and you and I had to form two different opinions about one and the same matter.

Recently I read in the papers, that elections of the Upper House in U.P. are about to take place. But I have received no information about it from there. Probably they might have written to you and got your approval.

I think that we would once again make this matter clear between ourselves, in order that a situation like that of the Punjab may not arise again. If the division of work we had made in 1937, according to which we have been working since then, still holds good, then a circular might be sent on behalf of you to the Provincial Congress

Committees and the Assembly Parties of U.P., the Punjab, and the Frontier. They should be reminded therein that they should take directions and approval from me in all matters concerning the by-elections and the parliamentary activities.

Rajendra Babu[1] had to deal with matters relating to Bihar, Assam and Orissa. He could not give much time to it owing to his indifferent health. Nevertheless this should continue in future.

Yours sincerely,

A.K. Azad

Sardar Vallabhbhai Patel,
68, Marine Drive,
Bombay

1. Dr. Rajendra Prasad.

Document 47

LETTER FROM MAULANA AZAD TO SARDAR PATEL

Calcutta,

29-01-1940

My dear Vallabhbhai,

I am receiving numerous letters from Mr. Sethi. He is also sending recommendations from other persons. I think this matter should not be kept in suspension any further. You may give, whatever decision you think fit, in this matter. I shall have no objection.

Yours sincerely,

A.K. Azad

Sardar Vallabhbhai Patel,
68, Marine Drive,
Bombay

Document 48

LETTER FROM DR. RAJENDRA PRASAD TO MAULANA AZAD

Ramgarh,

February 21, 1940

My dear Maulana Sahib,

I am sending you copy of a letter I have received from Bhulabhai[1] today. I have sent copies of it to Vallabhbhai,[2] Jawaharlalji[3], Kripalaniji[4] also and asked them to let me have their opinions. If you think the members of Parliament should be invited then you may call them or if you like I can do so.

Yours sincerely,

Dr. Rajendra Prasad

---

1. Mr. Bhulabhbhai J. Desai.
2. Sardar Vallabhbhai Patel.
3. Pandit Jawahar Lal Nehru.
4. Acharya Jivatràm Bhagwandas Kripalani.

Document 49

LETTER FROM JAWAHAR LAL NEHRU TO MAULANA AZAD

Express Delivery

Anand Bhawan,

Allahabad, February 22, 1940

My dear Maulana,

There are some points which I should like to place before you for your consideration. We had very little time to discuss anything at the station yesterday.

1. The whole policy of the British Government since the War began has gone to show that they are deliberately and consistently following an imperialist line. Before the War the Chamberlain[1] Government was well-known to be utterly reactionary and on many occasions they encouraged the fascist and Nazi Powers and crushed democracy in Europe. This was evident in the case of Abyssinia, Spain, Austria, Czechoslovakia and Albania. Their policy in Manchuria was also of the same kind. Mr. Chamberlain's Government was known to be the most reactionary and imperialist Government that England has had for more than a hundred years.

When, however, their own Empire was threatened, they took refuge under places of democracy and started the war. It was difficult to believe that they had become suddenly democratic. Subsequently events have shown that their old policy has not changed at all and indeed it is being more intensively followed now, with this difference that they want to remove Hitler who has become a danger to their Empire. This old policy was one of encouraging all the reactionary elements in Europe and the Far East and even in America, and trying to weaken Russia which stood as a challenge to all these reactionary elements as well as to imperialism. While on the one hand fear of the growing Nazi power made them sometimes look to Russia for help, their dislike of Russia and of the growth of democracy was so great that they could not cooperate in any way with Russia.

So till the last moment they followed the policy of appeasement towards Hitler and Mussolini and thereby strengthened them greatly. Their object was to get Hitler entangled in a war against Soviet Russia and thus weaken their two chief enemies. On no account did they want Germany or Italy to have progressive regime.

In this way they played about till Russia felt that there was great danger for it in the situation and, full of suspicion against British policy, it tried to upset it by coming to an agreement with Nazi Germany. This upset British plans for the moment.

The fundamental anti-Soviet British policy continued and it is curious to notice that even today, while England is at War with Germany, the British Government is far more anti-Soviet than anti-German. They are aiming at some kind of an internal change in Germany whereby Hitler might give place to the control of the German army leaders and then to make peace with them. This to be followed by joint attack by England, France, Germany and other countries on Russia. Whether this development will take place or not, it is difficult to say. But the point is that British policy before and after the War has been consistently reactionary and pro-imperialist, notwithstanding all their proclamations.

2. Russia has made many mistakes and notably, I think, her invasion of Finland was a avery serious error, both from the point of view of principle and expediency. It is true that Finland was being used by England as a place for intrigue against Russia and as a future jumping platform for an invasion of Russia. Munitions were being accumulated there. Russia was frightened of this development and tried to forestall them by a rapid invasion. This was very foolish and it played into the hands of England and France and at the same time alienated progressive opinion all over the world. It gave the chance which England wanted of posing as the friend of democracy and of making people forget its own sense in the past few years. The League of Nations, which had never even discussed fascist and Nazi aggressions and invasions, suddenly woke up to condemn Russia. Now there is no doubt in my mind that Russian policy recently has been wrong and must be condemned. But at the same time one must remember how this policy took shape because of the consistent attempts on the part of the British Government to encircle Russia. What is more important now is that we should realise that England is trying to exploit the situation in Finland to its own imperialist advantage and to spread the War to Russia. This is full of danger for us, because if there is War between England and Russia, our own frontiers

become involved and it becomes important for us to be clear about our policy. While we must criticise and disapprove of much that Russia has done, it will be dangerous in the extreme if we permit British imperialism to use that to its own advantage.

I think it would be a tragedy if Soviet Russia was crippled and weakened by a War against her, for then the only powerful opponent of imperialism would be removed. But even apart from this, anything that goes to strengthen British imperialism, is dangerous for us. Therefore, it is very important that we should be clear in our minds about the present British policy towards Russia and that we should declare that we are against it and in no event can we support or approve of British action against Russia. I think a clearly expressed policy on our part will make a difference. If Britain thinks that India will accept everything that she does without much objection, then there is every chance of the War spreading and Russia being involved in it with consequences to our own Indian frontier. On the other hand, if England feels that there is strong objection in India to any attack on Russia by England and that any such policy would be resisted in India, then England might well hesitate before she spreads this war to other regions. The British Government is doubtful at present as to what it should do. It wants to attack Russia but is afraid of the consequences. If it is assured that it will have peace in India, it will go ahead with the attack. Otherwise it will hold its hands. Therefore, our attitude in this matter counts, and it is desirable to express it as clearly and as strongly as possible.

3. What is happening in England and France shows how very reactionary these countries are grewing. France today is a military dictatorship with complete suppression of civil liberty. Scores of members of the Parliament, there have been arrested because the Government does not like their views. Several hundred municipalities have been suppressed for the same reason. In England matters have not gone quite so far but the tendency is the same. In effect both England and France are becoming more and more Fascist in their Government, though they talk about democracy. They refuse to say anything about war aims and are clearly aiming as they did in 1914, entrenching their own empires and to weaken their rival imperialisms as well as all progressive forces within or outside their empires. The question that the Congress put to the British Government in September has been answered very clearly by British policy as well as French policy. That answer is that we stand for imperialisms and we fight to maintain it. Now we condemn fascism and Nazism and it would

be bad if Hitler won in the war. We do not want that. On the other hand a victory of British imperialism means a continuation of Chamberlainism, more strengthened than before. That is equally bad and would lead to constant wars. Hence it would be folly for us, from every point of view, national and international, to help in any way such a victory. Quite apart, therefore, from any internal solution of India's problem as between England and India, it should be clear that we are not going to throw our weight in an imperialist war to preserve the British Empire.

4. You will have noticed the rebirth of the idea of Pan-Islamism. This is not merely due to the Muslim League here or to other organisations. This is fundamentally due to the desire of the British Government to encourage it. Pan-Islamism in 1914 and later was an anti-imperialist force. It weakened the British people in their war effort and later it coloured the background of the Khilafat Movement in India. Today this very idea is being used in support of British imperialism. This breaks, to some extent, the national front in India and helps to influence Muslim opinion in the near East in favour of England. The fact that Turkey is a friendly Power in alliance with England also helps British policy in this regard. I do not know what the effects of the British propaganda have been in the Muslim countries. But what I wish to point out is the definitely imperialist character of the new phase of Pan-Islamism.

5. All this shows how all our own internal problems, whether it is the communal problem or the larger problem of independence, are intimately connected with the larger war issues and those of British foreign policy. If we consider India apart, we fall into an error. The main diffuculties of the communal problem are due to the attitude of the British Government today. It becomes very difficult for us to solve it even if the Muslim League or Sikandar Hyat were agreeable. Of course the British Government wants a solution of the Indian problem in order to strengthen itself in the war and entrench its own imperialism. Sikander Hyat, acting entirely on behalf of British policy, wants to do the same. But fundamentally this policy is based on strengthening British imperialism. That is the basic difference which prevents compromise and no amount of talks with the Viceroy or with the Muslim League will get over that, till the British Government itself is prepared to renounce its imperialism. The Working Committee's statement of September 14th demanded this renunciation. Far from that having been done, the British Government has affirmed its imperialism. India's attitude is of great importance because it effects

America and other neutral countries. America at present is very strongly anti-Hitler, and in that sense, pro-British. At the same time it is certainly not in favour of British imperialism and, therefore, it hesitates to join the British. If the British could explain to American that they had come to terms with India, it would be a tremendous help to them.

6. During the last few months there has been so much confusing talk about compromise with the British Government that both our own people and the world at large have been misled and no one knows what is going to happen. It seems to me that we should make it clear once for all that there can be no compromise with us in the structure of imperialism and the sooner all such attempts are given up the better. There must be a finality about this.

7. British policy in India during the last few months has progressively been a reversion to autocratic rule and it is surprising to the people outside India how we have calmly submitted to it. Not only have the popular Provincial Governments been upset but actually the scope or Provincial autonomy has been limited by Amending Acts in Parliament. This kind of thing shouts louder than all the sweet words of the Viceroy. Ordinarily even a suspension of the Constitution, this should have led to a severe conflict. But we have calmly put up with it. We have also put up with the Amending Bills. This amendment of the Constitution is not important so far as we are concerned except insofar as it shows the trend of British policy. All this indicates that there is nothing in common between us and the British Government, and British imperialism is going as strongly as ever.

8. As I mentioned to you last evening, it seems to me very dangerous to agree to a Constituent Assembly consisting of the present provincial legislatures. That is giving up our basic demand of adult franchise which we have made for the last four years. That means also that our Constituent Assembly will be within the framework of British imperialism. This would lead, under present circumstances, to the same communal and other conflicts and thus our own weakness will be shown up and there will be no agreement as regards the Constitution. It would mean, in effect, that we are functioning almost within the framework of the Act of 1935 with some minor changes. If a Constituent Assembly is to succeed, it must be completely outside the framework of this Act as well as of British imperialism. The question of our relations with the British Government can only be considered after the Constituent Assembly has framed our Constitution. The technical difficulty of adult franchise can be got over by having

an intermediate step of indirect election. The point in that this Constituent Assembly must be looked upon as the organ of the Indian people functioning completely outside the orbit of British imperialism and the British Parliament. Otherwise it will just become an offshore of some enactment of the British Parliament.

9. I think it should be made clear also that there can be no going back by our Provincial Governments under existing conditions of services, control *etc.* I am glad that Pantji has laid stress on this. The whole structure of Government must change from top to bottom.

I hope you will forgive me for writing at such length. There are so many other ideas in my head but I must stop now.

Yours

J.L. Nehru

Maulana Abul Kalam Azad,
13-A, Ballygunge, Circular Road,
Calcutta

1. British Government, Headed by Mr. Chamberlain.

Document 50

EDITORIAL ON MAULANA AZAD[1]
28-02-1940

A comment in a British newspaper on the Congress presidential election seems to indicate that Maulana Azad's election was arranged, especially as he was a Muslim, and that in view of the communal situation, this would be to the advantage of the Congress.

Nothing could be further from the truth. The suggestion is unfair to the Maulana and the Congress. Of course, Maulana Azad is eminently qualified to tackle the communal problems, and the Congress and the country should take full advantage of his services in this as in other matters. But Congress Presidents today have to bear a terribly heavy burden, and they are elected because Congress delegates consider them worthy of this. Never before has India had to face a more difficult problem in the national and international sphere than today. Even the communal problem, important as it is, occupies a back place in relation to these vast issues.

It is right that Muslims and members of minority groups should occupy the honourable and responsible position of Congress President, as they are as much concerned with this election and with India's future as any others. We welcome, therefore, the election of a Muslim. But it is wrong to think that Congress Presidents are elected for communal reasons. Certainly not Maulana Abul Kalam Azad.

We welcome the Maulana's election because he represents in an eminent measure the Congress tradition and the Congress viewpoint. I do not speak of his great ability and learning, which he carries so lightly, or his long and proud record of service in the cause of Indian nationalism and freedom, for every child in India knows about them. Though young in years, he is one of the giants of old, still fortunately with us, and he combines in a rare measure the solidarity and strength of the old guard with a flexibility of the mind and understanding of youth and the new currents that are disturbing and yet vitalizing the country.

It is well-known that for some years past the Congress Presidentship has been his, if he would but agree to accept it. Last year, after much persuasion he agreed, but then changed his mind. Probably, he would have been elected unopposed then, if he had not withdrawn. This year he has at last agreed, though not without hesitation, for he is not of the sort who care for honour and office. It is good for the Congress and for India that he placed the interest of the country over his own personal inclination. We welcome him, therefore, as a brave and tried captain of our forces in an hour which will demand from him and from each one of us the best that we can give.

Document 51

MAULANA ABUL KALAM AZAD'S PRESIDENTIAL ADDRESS IN THE CONGRESS SESSION AT WARDHA ON MARCH 19, 1940

Friends,

In 1923 you elected me President of this National Assembly. For the second time, after seventeen years, you have once again conferred upon me the same honour. Seventeen years is not a long period in the history of national struggles. But now the pace of events and world change is so rapid that our old standards no longer apply. During these last seventeen years we have passed through many stages, one after another. We had a long journey before us and it was inevitable that we should pass through several stages. We rested at many a point no doubt, but never stopped. We surveyed and examined every prospect but we were not ensnared by it and passed on. We faced many ups and downs but always our faces were turned towards the goal. The world may have doubted our intentions and determination but we never had a moment's doubt.

Our path was full of difficulties and at every step we were faced with great obstacles. It may be that we did not proceed as rapidly as we desired but we did not flinch from marching forward. If we look back upon the period between 1923 and 1940, nineteen twenty-three will appear to us a faded landmark in the distance. In 1923 we desired to reach our goal but the goal was so distant then that even the milestones were hidden from our eyes. Raise your eyes today and look ahead. Not only do you see the milestones clearly but the goal itself is not distant. But this is evident that the nearer we get to the goal the more intense does our struggle become. Although the rapid march of events has taken us further from our old landmark and brought us nearer our goal, yet it has created new troubles and difficulties for us. Today our caravan is passing a very critical stage. The essential difficulty of this period lies in its conflicting possibilities. It is very probable that a correct step may bring us very near our goal, and on the other hand, a false step may land us in fresh troubles and difficulties.

At such a critical juncture you have elected me President and thus demonstrated the great confidence you have in one of your co-workers. It is a great honour and a great responsibility. I am grateful for the honour and crave your support in shouldering the responsibility. I am confident that the fullness of your confidence in me will be a measure of the fullness of the support that I shall continue to receive.

I think that I should now come straight to the real problem before us without further delay.

The first and the most important question before us is this whither is the step taken by us in consequence of the declaration of War on the 3rd September, 1939, leading us? And where do we stand now?

Probably in the history of the Congress, the 1936 Session at Lucknow marked a new ideological phase, when the Congress passed a long resolution on the international situation and placed its viewpoint clearly and categorically before the public. After this a consideration of the international situation, and a resolution thereon, became an essential and integral part of the annual declarations of the Congress. Thus this decision on this subject was arrived at the placed before the world with full deliberation. These resolutions embodied at one and the same time, two declarations to the world: Firstly, we stated, what I have described as a new ideology in Indian politics, that we could not remain in isolation from the political events of the outside world, even in our present state of helplessness. It was essential that while we forget our way ahead and fashioned our future, we must not confine ourselves merely to our own surroundings but should keep a vigilant watch on the conditions of the outside world. Innumerable changes in the world have brought countries and nations nearer to one another, so that the waves of thought and action, rising in one corner of the world, and produce immediate reactions in other places.

It is therefore, impossible today for India to consider her problems while confining herself within her own four walls. It is inevitable that events in the outside world should have their repercussions in India; it is equally inevitable that our decisions and the conditions prevailing in India should affect the rest of the world. It was this consciousness and belief which brought about our decisions. We declared by these resolutions against reactionary movements like Fascism and Nazism which were directed against democracy and individual and national freedom. These movements were gaining strength day by day and India regarded this as the greatest danger to world progress and peace. India's head and heart were with those peoples who were standing up for democracy and freedom and resisting this wave of reaction.

But while we were considering the dangers arising from Fascism and Nazism, it was possible for us to forget the older danger which has been proved to be infinitely more fatal to the peace and freedom of nations than these new dangers, and which has in fact supplied the basis for this reaction. I refer to British imperialism. We are not distant spectators of this imperialism, as we are of the new reactionary movements. It has taken possession of our house and dominates over us. It was for this reason that we stated in clear terms that if new entanglements in Europe brought about War, India, which has been debarred from exercising her will and making free decisions, will not take any part in it. She could only consider this question when she had acquired the right of coming to decisions according to her own free will and choice.

India cannot endure the prospect of Nazism and Fascism, but she is even more tired of British imperialism. If India remains deprived of her natural right to freedom, this would clearly mean that British imperialism continued to flourish with all its traditional characteristics, and under such conditions, India would on no account be prepared to lend a helping hand for the triumph of British imperialism. This was the second declaration which was constantly emphasized through these resolutions. These resolutions were repeatedly passed from the Lucknow session onwards till August, 1939 and are known by the name of "War Resolutions".

All these declarations of the Congress were before the British Government when suddenly, in the third week of August, 1939, the war clouds gathered and thundered and, at the beginning of September, the war began.

At this stage I will ask you to pause for a moment and look back. What were the conditions prevailing in August last?

The Government of India Act of 1935 was imposed upon India forcibly by the British Government and, as usual, resorting to the old stratagem, it tried to make the world believe that it had conferred a big instalment of India's national right upon her. The world knows the decision of the Congress to reject this Act. Nevertheless the Congress decided to avoid a conflict at that stage and preferred a respite. It resolved to take charge of Provincial Governments on a certain definite condition. After this decision the Congress Ministries were functioning successfully in eight out of the eleven Provinces, and it was in the interest of Great Britain herself to maintain this state of affairs for as long a period as possible. There was yet another factor. So far as the war was concerned, India had clearly condemned Nazi Germany. Her sympathies were with the democratic nations, and this was a point in Britain's favour. Under such circumstances, it was natural to expect that if the British Government had changed its old imperialistic mentality in the slightest degree, it would, even though as a measure of expendiency, change its old methods at this juncture and afford an opportunity to India to feel that she was breathing in a changed atmosphere. But we all know how the British Government behaved in this matter. There was not even a shadow of change discernible in its methods. Its policy was dictated exactly in accordance with the habits of an imperialism a hundred and fifty years old. It decided its course of action and, without India being afforded in any manner and in the slightest degree an opportunity to declare freely her opinion, her participation in the War was announced. It was not even considered necessary to give those representative assemblies, imposed upon us by British diplomacy for purpose of show, an opportunity of expressing their opinion.

The whole world knows, and so do we, how all the Empire countries were given freedom of decision, the representative assemblies of Canada, Australia, New Zealand, South Africa, Ireland, all of them arrived at an independent decision, in regard to their participation in the War, without the least outside interference. Not only this but when Ireland decided to remain neutral, no surprise was shown nor was a single voice raised against it in Great Britain. Mr. De Valera, in the very shadow of England, refused to extend his help to Britain in the war unless the question of Ulster was settled to his satisfaction.

But what place did India occupy in this picture of the British Commonwealth? India is being told today that the generous hand of Britain will confer upon her the precious gift of Dominion Status in the near but unknown future. When the war began, a war which will probably be one of the greatest in the world, India was pushed into it suddenly without her even realising that she was entering it. This fact alone was sufficient to show us which way the wind was blowing. But there was no need for us to hurry. Other opportunities were to come and the time was not distant when we could see the face of British imperialism even more unmasked and at closer quarters.

When in 1914 the first spark was ignited in a corner of the Balkans, England and France raised the cry of the rights of small nations. Later, President Wilson's fourteen points came into view; their fate is well-known to the world. On that occasion the situation was different. After the last war, England and France, intoxicated with victory, adopted a course of action which necessarily resulted in a reaction. This reaction grew. It took the shape of Fascism in Italy and Nazism in Germany, and unrestrained dictatorship, based on brute force, challenged the peace and freedom of the world. When this happened, inevitably the world aligned itself in two rival camps: one supporting democracy and freedom; the other encouraging the forces of reaction. And in this way a new picture of the coming war began to take shape. Mr. Chamberlain's Government, to which the existence of Soviet Russia was much more unbearable than the existence of Fascist Italy and Nazi Germany and which considered Russia to be a living challenge to British imperialism, continued to watch this situation for three years. Not only this, but by its attitude it clearly and repeatedly encouraged Fascist and Nazi ambitions. Abyssinia, Spain, Austria, Czechoslovakia and Albania, disappeared as free countries, one after the other, from the map of the world. And Great Britain, by her vascillating policy, continually assisted in the destruction of their freedom. But when this course of action produced its natural and ultimate result and Nazi Germany marched ahead unchecked, the British Government found itself compelled to enter the arena of war. Had it not done so then, the power of Germany would have become an intolerable menace to British imperialism. Now the new slogans of freedom, world peace, democracy, took the place of the old cry of saving the smaller nations, and the whole world began to ring with these cries. The declaration of war on the 3rd September by Britain and France was made to the accompaniment of the resounding echoes of these slogans. The peoples of the world were bewildered and harassed by the brutal trial of strength and the world wide unrest created by these new reactionary forces, and they lent a willing ear to the siren voice of these slogans.

War was declared on the 3rd of September and on the 7th September the All India Congress Working Committee met at Wardha to deliberate upon the situation. What did the Working Committee do on this occasion? All the declarations of the Congress made since 1936 were before it. It had also to face the action taken by the British Government in declaring India as a belligerent country. Undoubtedly the Congress could not have been blamed had it come to a final decision in accordance with the logic of the situation. But it continued to keep vigilant watch on its mind and heart, it resisted the natural urge of the moment for an acceleration of pace, it deliberated upon every aspect of the matter, unemotionally and dispassionately, and took the step which today entitles India to raise her head and say to the world that this was the only correct step which could have been then taken. The Congress postponed its final decisions and asked the British Government to state its war aims, for on this depended not only peace and justice for India, but for the whole world. If India was being invited to participate in this war, she had a right to know why this war was being fought. What was its object? If the result of this grim tragedy was not to be the same as that of the last war, and if it was really being fought to safeguard freedom, democracy and peace and to bring a new order to the world, then, in all conscience, India had right to know, what would be the effect of these aims on her own destiny.

The Working Committee formulated this demand in a long statement which was published on the 14th September, 1939. If I express the hope that this statement will occupy an outstanding place in recent Indian history, I am sure I am not claiming too much of the future historian. This is a simple but irrefutable document, based on truth and reason, and it can only be set aside by the arrogant pride of armed force. Though this cry was raised in India, in fact it was not of India only, but it was the agonised cry of wronged humanity, whose hopes had so often before been betrayed. Twenty-five years ago the world was plunged into one of the biggest infernos of death and destruction known to history, and yet this was but a preparation for a still bigger catastrophe. The world was bewitched and its hopes were kindled by cries of freedom for small nations, collective security, self-determination, disarmament, League of Nations and international arbitration, and of similar high sounding phrases. But what was the result in the end? Every cry proved false; every vision that seemed so real to us, vanished as a dream. Again nations are being plunged into the blood and fire of war. Should we part with reason and reality so completely as not even to ask why this is being done and how this affects our destiny before plunging into this deluge of death and destruction?

In answer to this demand of the Congress a regular series of statements were made on behalf of the British Government, both in England and in India. The first link of the series was the Delhi declaration of the Viceroy, dated the 17th October. This lengthy statement is perhaps a finished example of that peculiarly involved and tiring style which characterises the official literature of the Government of India. After reading page after page of this statement, the curtain is at last lifted with hesitation. We have a glimpse. We are told then that if we want to know the war aims we must read a speech by the Prime Minister of Britain, and this speech deals only with the peace of Europe and with the adjustment of international relations. Even the words "Freedom" and "Democracy" are not to be found in the Viceroy's statement. So far as India is concerned, it only reaffirms the policy laid down in the preamble of the 1919 Act, which is now embodied in the 1935 Act. Today that policy continues to be the same; there is nothing to add to it or to improve it.

On the 17th of October, 1939, the statement of the Viceroy was published and the Working Committee met to deliberate upon it on the 22nd October at Wardha. Without any discussion it came to the conclusion that this reply could under no circumstances be considered satisfactory, and that it should now unhesitatingly give the decision, which it had postponed till then. The decision of the Working Committee was as follows:

> "In the circumstances, the Committee cannot possibly give any support to Great Britain, for it would amount to an endorsement of the imperialistic policy which the Congress has always sought to end. As a first step in this direction, the Committee call upon the Congress Ministries to tender their resignations."

As a result of this decision the Congress Ministries in eight provinces resigned.

This was but the first step which the Congress took in the series of events. Now we have to see to what these events led. The communique of the Viceroy issued on the 5th February from Delhi giving the resume of the talk between him and Mahatma Gandhi, and Mahatma Gandhi's statement of the 6th February may be regarded as the last of this series. We all know the substance of the Viceroy's statement. The British Government, it is stated, fully desires that India should, in the shortest time possible under the circumstances, attain the status of a British dominion, and that the transition period should be as short as possible. But it is unwilling to concede to India the right of framing her own constitution and deciding her own destiny through her own elected representatives without outside interference. In other words, the British Government does not accept the position that India has got the right of self-determination.

At the first touch of reality the structure of make-belief fell to pieces. For the last four years the world resounded with cries of democracy and freedom. The utterances of the most responsible spokesmen of England and France in this regard are so fresh in our memory as not to need recall. But the moment India raised this question, the reality behind these utterances was unveiled. Now we are told that, without doubt, safeguarding the freedom of nations is the aim of this war but that this is confined within the geographical limits of Europe. The peoples of Asia and Africa should not dare to have any such hopes. Mr. Chamberlain has made this even more clear in his Birmingham speech of the 24th February, though we never had any doubts about the matters. He confirmed the British Government's action by his words. Proclaiming British War aims, he stated that they were fighting to secure that small nations in Europe shall henceforth live in security, free from the constant threat of aggression against their independence.

Though this answer about war aims has been given through a British spokesman, yet in reality it interprets the real mentality of Europe as a whole, which has been known to the world for the last two hundred years. In the eighteenth and nineteenth centuries whatever principles were accepted for individual and collective human freedom, the right to claim them and to benefit from them was limited to European nations. And even amongst them, its application was confined to the Christian nations of Europe. Today, in the middle of the twentieth century, the world has so changed that the thoughts and actions of the last century read like ancient history, and appear to us as faded landmarks in the distance. But we will have to admit that there is at least one distinctive landmark of Europe emphasizing human rights, which has not faded and is still with us. We have not passed it yet, or achieved those rights.

This reality has been brought home to us again by the problem of our own political and national rights in India. When, after the declaration of War, we raised the question of war aims and their effect on India's destiny, we were not forgetful of British policy in 1917 and 1919. We wanted to know how in the year 1939, when the world was covering the track of centuries in the course of days, England looked at India. Had that look changed? We were given a clear reply that it had not; even now there was no change in that imperialist outlook. We are told to believe that the British Government is very desirous that India should attain the status of a dominion, in the shortest possible period. We knew even before that the British Government had expressed this desire. Now we know that they are very anxious indeed.

But it is not a question of the desire or of the measure of the desire of the British Government. The straight and simple question is of India's rights; whether she is entitled to determine her own fate or not. On the answer to this question depend the answers to all other questions of the day. This question forms the foundation stone of the Indian problem; India will not allow it to be removed, for if it is displaced, the whole structure of Indian nationalism will collapse.

So far as the question of war is concerned our position is quite clear. We see the face of British imperialism as clearly now as we did in the last war, and we are not prepared to assist in its triumph by participating in the war. Our case is crystal clear. We do not wish to see British imperialism triumphant and stronger and thus lengthen the period of our own subjection to it. We absolutely refuse to do so. Our way lies patently in the opposite direction

Let us return to our starting point and consider once again whither the step that we took after the declaration of war on the 3rd September is leading us. Where do we stand today? The answer to both these questions is by this time apparent to your minds and is hovering on your lips. It is not even necessary that your lips should tell me for I fell the quivering of your hearts. The step of temporary and partial cooperation which we took in 1937, we withdrew after the declaration of war. Inevitably we inclined towards further step in non-cooperation. As we stand today, we have to decide whether we should march forward in this direction or go backward. When once a step is taken, there is no stopping. To cry halt is to go back, and we refuse to go back. We can only, therefore go forward. I am sure that the voice of every one of you joins mine when I proclaim that we must and will go forward.

In this connection one question naturally faces us. It is the verdict of history that in a struggle between nations, no power forgoes its possessions unless compelled to do so. Principles of reason and morality have affected the conduct of individuals but have not affected the selfish conduct of powers that dominate. Today even in the middle of the twentieth century, we witness how the new reactionary forces in Europe have shattered man's faith in individual and collective human rights. In place of justice and reason, brute force has become the sole argument in the determination of rights. But while the world is presenting this depressing picture, there is another side, the hopeful side, which cannot be ignored. We see countless millions all over the world, without any distinction, awakening to a new consciousness which is spreading everywhere with great rapidity. This new consciousness is tired of the utter hopelessness of the old order, and is impatient for a new order based on reason, justice and peace. This new awakening which arose after the last war and took root in the deepest recesses of the human soul, has now come to dominate men's minds and their utterance. Perhaps there is no parallel in history to the speed of this awakening.

In these circumstances was it beyond the realm of possibility that history should, contrary to its old record, take a new step? Was it impossible that two great peoples of the world, who had been tied together by the course of events as rulers and the ruled, should create a new relationship between them, based on reason, justice and peace? If that had been possible, the sorrows born of World War would have given place to a newborn hope; and the new order of reason and justice would have ushered in a new dawn. If the British people could have proudly said to the world today that they had added such a new example to history, what a vast and unparalleled triumph this would have been for humanity. Certainly this was not an impossibility, but it was an amazingly difficult thing to do.

In the prevailing darkness of the times, it is faith in the bright side of human nature which sustains the great soul of Mahatma Gandhi. He is always prepared to take advantage of every opening which might lead to a mutual settlement without feeling that he is weakening his unassailable position.

Since war began, several members of the British Cabinet have tried to make the world believe that the old order of British imperialism has ended, and that today the British nation has no other aims except those of peace and justice. Which country could have more warmly acclaimed such a declaration than India? But the fact is that in spite of these declarations, British imperialism stands in the way of peace and justice today exactly as it did before the war. The Indian demand was the touch-stone for all such claims. They were so tested and found to be counterfeit and untrue.

I have briefly placed before you the real question of the day. That is the vital question for us, all else are subsidiary to it. It was in relation to that question that the Congress put forward its invitation to the British Government in September last, and made a clear and simple demand, to which no community or group could possibly object. It was not in our remotest thoughts that the communal question could be raised in this connection. We realise that there are some groups in the country which cannot keep step with the Congress in the political struggle or go as far as the Congress is prepared to go; we know that some do not agree with the method of direct action which the great majority of political India has adopted. But so far as the right of the Indian people to independence is concerned and the full admission of India's birthright to freedom, an awakened and impatient India has passed far beyond the early stages, and none dare oppose our demand. Even those classes who cling to their special interest and fear change lest this might affect them adversely, are rendered helpless by the spirit of the times. They have to admit and to agree to the goal we have set before us.

A time of crisis is a testing time for all of us, and so the great problem of the day has tested us and exposed many an aspect of our present day politics. It has laid bare also the reality that lies behind the communal problem. Repeated attempts were made, in England and India, to mix up the communal question with the vital political question of the day, and thus to confuse the real issue. Again and again, it was sought to convince the world that the problem of the minorities barred the way to a proper solution of India's political problem.

For a hundred and fifty years British imperialism has pursued the policy of divide and rule, and by emphasising internal differences, sought to use various groups for the consolidation of its own power. That was the inevitable result of India's political subjection, and it is folly for us to complain and grow bitter. A foreign government can never encourage internal unity in the subject country, for disunity is the surest guarantee for the continuance of its own domination. But when we were told, and the world was asked to believe, that British imperialism had ended, and the long chapter of Indian history dominated by it had closed, was it unreasonable for us to expect that British statesmen would at last give up this evil inheritance and not exploit the communal situation for political ends ? But the time for this is yet distant ; we may not cling to such vain hopes. So the last five months with their succession of events have established. Imperialism, in spite of all assurance to the contrary, still flourishes; it has yet to be ended.

But, whatever, the roots of our problems might be, it is obvious that India, like other countries, has her internal problems. Of these, the communal problem is an important one. We do not and cannot expect the British Government to deny its existence. The communal problem is undoubtedly with us, and if we want to go ahead, we must need take it into account. Every step that we take by ignoring it will be a wrong step. The problem is there; to admit its existence, however, does not mean that it should be used as a weapon against India's national freedom. British Imperialism has always exploited it to this end. If Britain desires to end her imperialistic methods in India and close that dismal chapter of history, then the first signs of this change must naturally appear in her treatment of the communal problem.

What is the Congress position in regard to this problem? It has been the claim of the Congress, from its earliest beginnings, that it considers India as a nation and takes every step in the interest of the nation as a whole. This entitles the world to examine this claim strictly and the Congress must establish the truth of its assertion. I wish to examine afresh this question from this point of view.

There can be only three aspects of the communal problem: its existence, its importance, and the method of its solution.

The entire history of the Congress demonstrates that it has always acknowledged the existence of the problem. It has never tried to minimise its importance. In dealing with this problem, it followed a policy which was the most suitable under the circumstances. It is difficult to conceive of a different or better course of action. If, however, a better course could be suggested, the Congress was always, and is today, eager to welcome it.

We could attach no greater importance to it, than to make it the first condition for the attainment of our national goal. The Congress has always held this belief; no one can challenge this fact. It has always held to two basic principles in this connection, and every step was taken deliberately with these in view.

(i) Whatever constitution is adopted for India, there must be the fullest guarantee in it for the rights and interests of minorities.

(ii) The minorities should judge for themselves what safeguards are necessary for the protection of their rights and interests. The majority should not decide this. Therefore, the decision in this respect must depend upon the consent of the minorities and not on a majority vote.

The question of the minorities is not a special Indian problem. It has existed in other parts of the world. I venture to address the world from this platform, and to enquire whether any juster and more equitable course of action can be adopted in this connection, than the one suggested above? If so, what is it? Is there anything lacking in this approach, which necessitates that the Congress be reminded of its duty? The Congress has always been ready to consider any failure in the discharge of its duty. It is so prepared today. I have been in the Congress for the last nineteen years. During the whole of this period there is not a single important decision of the Congress in the shaping of which I have not had the honour to participate. I assert that during these last nineteen years, not for a single day did the Congress think of solving this problem in any way other than the way I have stated above. This was not a mere assertion of the Congress, but its determined and decided course of action. Many a time during the last fifteen years, this policy was subjected to the severest tests, but it stood firm as a rock.

The manner in which the Congress has dealt with this problem today in connection with the Constituent Assembly, throws a flood of light on these two principles and clarifies them. The recognised minorities have a right, if they so please, to choose their representatives by their votes. Their representatives will not have to rely upon the votes of any other community except their own. So far as the question of the rights and the interests of the minorities is concerned, the decision will not depend upon the majority of the votes in the Constituent Assembly. It will be subject to the consent of the minority. If unanimity is not achieved on any question, then an impartial tribunal, to which the minorities have also consented, will decide the matter. This last proviso is merely in the nature of a provision for a possible contingency, and is most unlikely to be required. If a more practical proposal is made, there can be no objection to it.

When these principles are accepted and acted upon by the Congress, what is it that obliges British statesmen to remind us so often of the problem of the minorities, and to make the world believe that this stands in the way of Indian freedom? If it is really so, why does not the British Government recognise clearly India's freedom and gives us an opportunity to solve this problem for ever by mutual agreement amongst ourselves?

Dissensions were shown and encouraged amongst us, and yet we are taunted because of them. We are told to put an end to our communal conflicts, but opportunity to do so is denied us. Such is the position deliberately created to thwart us; such are the chains that bind. But no difficulties or constraints can deter us from taking the right steps with courage and fortitude. Our path is full of obstacles but we are determined to overcome them.

We have considered the problems of the minorities of India. But are the Muslims such a minority as to have the least doubt or fear about their future? A small minority may legitimately have fears and apprehensions, but can the Muslims allow themselves to be disturbed by them? I do not know how many of you are familiar with my writings, twenty-eight years ago, in the "Al-Hilal". If there are any such here, I would request them to my conviction, and I repeat this today, that in the texture of Indian politics, nothing is further removed from the truth than to say that Indian Muslims occupy the position of a political minority. It is equally absurd for them to be apprehensive about their rights and interests in a democratic India. This fundamental mistake has opened the door to countless misunderstandings. False arguments were built up on wrong premises. This error, on the one hand, brought confusion into the minds of Musalmans about their own true position, and, on the other hand, it involved the world in misunderstandings, so that the picture of India could not be seen in right perspective.

If time had permitted, I would have told you in detail, how, during the last sixty years, this artificial and untrue picture of India was made, and whose hands traced it. In effect, this was the result of the same policy of divide and rule which took particular shape in the minds of British officials in India after the Congress launched the national movement. The object of this was to prepare the Musalmans for use against the new political awakening. In this plan, prominence was given to two points. First: that India was inhabited by two different communities, the Hindus and the Musalmans, and for this reason no demand could be made in the name of a united nation. Second: that numerically the Musalmans were far less than the Hindus, and because of this, the necessary consequence of the establishment of democratic institutions in India would be to establish the rule of the Hindu majority and to jeopardise the existence of the Muslims. I shall not go into any greater detail now. Should you however wish to know the early history of this matter, I would refer you to the time of Lord Dufferin, a former Viceroy of India, and Sir Auckland Colvin, a former Lieutenant Governor of the NWFP, now of the United Provinces.

Thus were sown the seeds of disunity by British Imperialism on Indian soil. The plant grew and was nurtured and spread its nettles, and even though fifty years have passed since then, the roots are still there.

Politically speaking, the word minority does not mean just a group that is numerically smaller and therefore entitled to special protection. It means a group that is so small in number and so lacking in other qualities that give strength, that it has no confidence in its own capacity to protect itself from the much larger group that surrounds it. It is not enough that the group should be relatively the smaller, but that it should be absolutely so small as to be incapable of protecting its interests. Thus this is not merely a question of numbers; other factors count also. If a country has two major groups numbering a million and two millions respectively, it does not necessarily follow that because one is half the other, therefore it must call itself politically a minority and consider itself weak.

If this is the right test, let us apply it to the position of the Muslims in India. You will see at a glance a vast concourse, spreading out all over the country ; they stand erect, and to imagine that they exist helplessly as a "minority' is to delude oneself.

The Muslims in India number between eighty and ninety millions. The same type of social or racial divisions, which affect other communities, do not divide them. The powerful bonds of Islamic brotherhood and equality have protected them to a large extent from the weakness that flows from social divisions. It is true that they number only one-fourth of the total population; but the question is not one of population ratio, but of the large numbers and the strength behind them. Can such a vast mass of humanity have any legitimate reason for apprehension that in a free and democratic India, it might be unable to protect its rights and interests?

These numbers are not confined to any particular area but spread out unevenly over different parts of the country. In four provinces out of eleven in India there is a Muslim majority, the other religious groups being minorities. If British Baluchistan is added, there are five provinces with Muslim majorities. Even if we are compelled at present to consider this question on a basis of religious groupings, the position of the Muslims is not that of a minority only. If they are in a minority in seven provinces, they are in a majority in five. This being so, there is absolutely no reason why they should be oppressed by the feeling of being a minority.

Whatever, may be the details of the future Constitution of India, we know that it will be an all-India federation which is, in the fullest sense, democratic, and every unit of which will have autonomy in regard to internal affairs. The federal centre will be concerned only with all-India matters of common concern, such as, foreign relations, defence, customs, *etc.* Under these circumstances can any one who has any conception of the actual working of a democratic constitution, allow himself to be led astray by this false issue of majority and minority. I cannot believe for an instant that there can be any room whatever for these misgivings in the picture of India's future. These apprehensions are arising because, in the words of a British statesman regarding Ireland, we are yet standing on the banks of the river and, though wishing to swim, are unwilling to enter the water. There is only one remedy; we shall realise that all our apprehensions were without foundation.

It is now nearly thirty years since I first attempted to examine this question as an Indian Musalman. The majority of the Muslims then were keeping completely apart from the political struggle and they were influenced by the same mentality of aloofness and antagonism, which prevailed amongst them previously in 1888. This depressing atmosphere did not prevent me from giving my anxious thought to this matter, and I reached quickly a final conclusion which influenced my belief and action. I saw India, with all her many burdens, marching ahead to her future destiny. We were fellow passengers in this boat and we could not ignore its swift passage through the waters; and so it became necessary for us to come to a clear and final decision about our plan of action. How were we to do so? not merely by skimming the surface of the problem but by going down to its roots, and then to consider our position. I did so and I realised that the solution of the whole problem depended on the answer to one question: Do we, Indian Musalmans, view the free India of the future with suspicion and distrust or with courage and confidence? If we view it with fear and suspicion, then undoubtedly we have to follow a different path. No present declaration, no promise for the future, no constitutional safeguards, can be a remedy for our doubts and fears. We are then forced to tolerate the existence of a third power.

This third power is already entrenched here and has no intention of withdrawing and, if we follow this path of fear, we must need look forward to its continuance. But if we are convinced that for us fear and doubt have no place, and that we must view the future with courage and confidence in ourselves, then our course of action becomes absolutely clear. We find ourselves in a new world, which is free from the dark shadows of doubt, vacillation, inaction and apathy, and where the light of faith and determination, action and enthusiasm never fails. The confusions of the times, the ups and downs that come our way, the difficulties that beset our thorny path, cannot change the direction of our steps. It becomes our bounden duty then to march with assured steps to India's national goal.

I arrived at this definite conclusion without the least hesitation, and every fibre of my being revolted against the former alternative. I could not bear the thought of it. I could not conceive it possible for a Musalman to tolerate this, unless he has rooted out the spirit of Islam from every corner of his being.

I started the "Al Hilal" in 1912 and put this conclusion of mine before the Muslims of India. I need not remind you that my cries were not without effect. The period from 1912 to 1918 marked a new phase in the political awakening of the Muslims. Towards the end of 1920, on my release after four years of internment, I found that the political ideology of the Musalmans had broken through its old mould and was taking another shape. Twenty years have gone by and much has happened since then. The tide of events has ever risen higher, and fresh waves of thoughts have enveloped us. But this fact still remains unchanged, that the general opinion amongst the Muslims is opposed to going back.

That is certain; they are not prepared to retrace their steps. But again they are full of doubts about their future path. I am not going into the reasons for this; I shall only try to understand the effects. I would remind my co-religionists that today I stand exactly where I stood in 1912 when I addressed them on this issue. I have given thoughts to all those innumerable occurrences which have happened since then; my eyes have watched them, my mind was pondered over them. These events did not merely pass me by; I was in the midst of them, a participant, and I examined every circumstance with care. I cannot be false to what I have myself seen and observed; I cannot quarrel with my own convictions; I cannot stifle the voice of my conscience. I repeat today what I have said throughout this entire period, that the ninety millions of Muslims of India have no other right course of action than the one to which I invited them in 1912.

Some of my co-religionists, who paid heed to my call in 1912, are in disagreement with me today. I do not wish to find fault with them, but I would make appeal to their sincerity and sense of responsibility. We are dealing with the destinies of peoples and nations. We cannot come to right conclusions if we are swept away by the passions of the moment. We must base our judgements on the solid realities of life. It is true that the sky is overcast today and the outlook is dark. The Muslims have to come into the light of reality. Let them examine every aspect of the matter again today, and they will find no other course of action open to them.

I am a Musalman and am proud of that fact. Islam's splendid traditions of thirteen hundred years are my inheritance. I am unwilling to lose even the smallest part of this inheritance. The teaching and history of Islam, its arts and letters and civilisation are my wealth and my fortune. It is my duty to protect them.

As a Musalman I have a special interest in Islamic religion and culture and I cannot tolerate any interference with them. But in addition to these sentiments, I have others also which the realities and conditions of my life have forced upon me. The spirit of Islam does not come in the way of these sentiments; it guides and helps me forward. I am proud of being an Indian. I am a part of the indivisible unity that is Indian nationality. I am indispensable to this noble edifice and without me this splendid structure of India is incomplete. I am an essential element which has gone to build India. I can never surrender this claim.

It was India's historic destiny that many human races and cultures and religions should flow to her, finding a home in her hospitable soil, and that many a caravan should find rest here. Even before the dawn of history, these caravans trekked into India and wave after wave of new-comers followed. This vast and fertile land gave welcome to all and took them to her bosom. One of the last of these caravans, following the footsteps of its predecessors, was that of the followers of Islam. This came here and settled here for good. This led to a meeting of the culture-currents of two different races. Like Ganga and Jamuna, they flowed for a while through separate courses, but nature's immutable law brought them together and joined them in a *sangam*. This fusion was a notable event in history. Since then, destiny, in her own hidden way, began to fashion a new India in place of the old. We brought our treasures with us, and India too was full of the riches of her own precious heritage. We gave our wealth to her and she unlocked the doors of her own treasures to us. We gave her, what she needed most, the most precious of gifts from Islam's treasury, the message of democracy and human equality.

Full eleven centuries have passed by since then. Islam has now as great a claim on the soil of India as Hinduism. If Hinduism has been the religion of the people here for several thousands of years, Islam also has been their religion for a thousand years. Just as a Hindu can say with pride that he is an Indian and follows Hinduism, so also we can say with equal pride that we are Indians and follow Islam. I shall enlarge this orbit still further. The Indian Christian is equally entitled to say with pride that he is an Indian and is following a religion of India, namely Christianity.

Eleven hundred years of common history have enriched India with our common achievements. Our languages, our poetry, our literature, our culture, our art, our dress, our manners and customs, the innumerable happenings of our daily life, everything bears the stamp of our joint endeavour. There is indeed no aspect of our life which has escaped this stamp. Our languages were different, but we grew to use a common language; our manners and customs were dissimilar, but they acted and reacted on each other and thus produced a new synthesis. Our old dress may be seen only in ancient pictures of bygone days; no one wears it today. This joint wealth is the heritage of our common nationality and we do not want to leave it and go back to the times when this joint life had not begun. If there are any Hindus amongst us who desire to bring back the Hindu life of a thousand years ago and more, they dream, and such dreams are vain fantasies. So also if there are any Muslims who wish to revive their past civilization and culture, which they brought a thousands years ago from Iran and Central Asia, they dream also and the sooner they wake up the better. These are unnatural fancies which cannot take root in the soil of reality. I am one of those who believe that revival may be a necessity in a religion but in social matters it is a denial of progress.

These thousands years of our joint life has moulded us into a common nationality. This cannot be done artificially. Nature does her fashioning through her hidden processes in the course of centuries. The cast has now been moulded and destiny has set her seal upon it. Whether we like it or not, we have not become an Indian nation, united and indivisible. No fantasy or artificial scheming to separate and divide can break this unity. We must accept the logic of fact and history and engage ourselves in the fashioning of our future destiny.

I shall not take any more of your time. My address must end now. But before I do so, permit me to remind you that our success depends upon three factors: unity, discipline and full confidence in Mahatma Gandhi's leadership. The glorious past record of our movement was due to his great leadership, and it is only under his leadership that we can look forward to a future of successful achievement.

The time of our trial is upon us. We have already focused the world's attention. Let us endeavour to prove ourselves worthy.

Document 52

RESOLUTIONS ADOPTED BY THE INC AT WARDHA ON 20.3.1940 WITH MAULANA AZAD AS PRESIDENT

This Congress, having considered the grave and critical situation resulting from the War in Europe and British policy in regard to it, approves of and endorses the resolutions passed and the action taken on the war situation by the AICC and the Working Committee. The Congress considers the declaration by the British Government of India as a belligerent country, without any reference to the people of India, and the exploitation of India's resources in this War, as an affront to them, which no self-respecting and freedom-loving people can accept or tolerate. The recent pronouncements made on behalf of the British Government in regard to India demonstrate that Great Britain is carrying on the war fundamentally for imperialist ends and for the preservation and strengthening of her Empire, which is based on the exploitation of the people of India, as well as of other Asiatic and African countries. Under these circumstances, it is clear that the Congress cannot in any way, directly or indirectly, be party to the war, which means continuance and perpetuation of this exploitation. The Congress therefore strongly disapproves of Indian troops being made to fight for Great Britain and of the drain from India of men and material for the purpose of the war. Neither the recruiting nor the money raised in India can be considered to be voluntary contributions from India. Congressmen and those under the Congress influence cannot help in the prosecution of the war with men, money or material.

The Congress hereby declares again that nothing short of complete independence can be accepted by the people of India. Indian freedom cannot exist within the orbit of imperialism, and dominion or any other status within the imperial structure is wholly inapplicable to India, is not in keeping with the dignity of a great nation, and would bind India in many ways to British policies and economic structure. The people of India alone can properly shape their own constitution and determine their relations to the other countries of the world, through a Constituent Assembly elected on the basis of adult suffrage.

The Congress is further of opinion that while it will always be ready, as it ever has been, to make every effort to secure communal harmony, no permanent solution is possible except through a Constituent Assembly, where the rights of all recognised minorities will be fully protected by agreement, as far as possible, between the elected representatives of various majority and minority groups, or by arbitration, if agreement is not reached on any point. Any alternative will lack finality. India's Constitution must be based on independence, democracy and national unity, and the Congress repudiates attempts to divide India or to split up her nationhood. The Congress has always aimed at a constitution where the fullest freedom and opportunities of development are guaranteed to the group and the individual, and social injustice yields place to a juster social order.

The Congress cannot admit the right of the Rulers of Indian States, or of foreign vested interests to come in the way of Indian freedom. Sovereignty in India must rest with the people, whether in the states or the provinces, and all other interests must be subordinated to their vital interests. The Congress holds that the difficulty raised in regard to the states is of British creation and it will not be satisfactorily solved unless the declaration of the freedom of India from foreign rule is unequivocally made Foreign interests, if they are not in conflict with the interests of the Indian people will be protected.

The Congress withdrew the ministries from the provinces where the Congress had a majority in order to dissociate India from the war and to enforce the Congress determination to free India from foreign domination. This preliminary step must naturally be followed by Civil Disobedience, to which the Congress will unhesitatingly resort as soon as the Congress organisation is considered fit enough for the purpose, or in case circumstances so shape themselves as to precipitate a crisis. The Congress desires to draw the attention of Congressmen to Gandhiji's declaration that he can only undertake the responsibility of declaring Civil Disobedience when he is satisfied that they are strictly observing discipline and are carrying out the Constructive Programme prescribed in the Independence Pledge.

The Congress seeks to represent and serve all classes and communities without distinction of race or religion, and the struggle for Indian independence is for the freedom of the whole nation. Hence, the Congress cherishes the hope that all classes and communities will take part in it. The purpose of Civil Disobedience is to evoke the spirit of sacrifice in the whole nation.

The Congress hereby authorises the All India Congress Committee and in the event of this being necessary, the Working Committee, to take all steps to implement the foreign resolution, as the Committee concerned may deem necessary.

Document 53

LETTER FROM MAULANA AZAD TO ACHARYA KRIPALANI

Wardha,

March 27, 1940

My dear Kripalani,

Yours of the 15th. I had already seen your circular regarding the Congress Resolution in the Press, and I was happy over it. I think you did well in issuing these circulars.

Fifteenth is a suitable date for the Working Committee. Please do not change it. I want to send additional invitation to the following gentlemen:

1. Pattabhi.[1]
2. Dr. B.C. Roy.
3. Master Tara Singh.
(Inform him that the Working Committee would like to gather from him some informations about the Shromani Akali Dal.)

I am issuing a statement on the National Week.

I hope to reach Allahabad on the 30th.

Yours sincerly,

A.K. Azad

Shri J.B. Kripalani,
Allahabad

---

1. Dr. B. Pattabhi Sitaramaiah.

Document 54

LETTER FROM MAULANA AZAD TO JAWAHAR LAL NEHRU

March 27, 1940

My dear Jawaharlal,

When on the 15th's morning you handed me on the train the English version of my Address, I just skipped over it to form a general impression of the translation. I had no time until now to go through it. Now that I am comparatively free, I have made a close study of the document. The impression it has created on me compels me to shake off my useful reserve for the moment, and offer my sincere tribute to you first-rate intellect and your exception talents. Your mastery over English extends far beyond what I imagined until now. I dare...some of the most accomplished men of our day could hardly undertake to perform a task of such magnitude in so many days, whereas, it took you just a few hours and that too, without any special effort.

Translating, in a way, is much more difficult than composing in original. It is not so easy to maintain the literary contact of the original writing and at the same time convey through translation the literary style of the writer. Only a person with equal command over both the languages could have attempted such a task. What particularly strikes me in your translation is the fact that no feature of the original has suffered through it, and you have conveyed my Urdu literary style so successfully in English that I should not be surprised if it occurs to the reader that the original was English and not Urdu.

An equally impressive feature is your remarkable grasp of the architectonic imagination from which the details flow. You have perfectly visualized my imagination which gave form and shape to my sentences and composition. In fact, you had a full picture of my theme when you started translating. Surely, it was a stupendous task, specially when my own compositions could not directly assist you.

In some places you have slightly changed the Urdu version and expanded or abbreviated it to suit the agencies of the English rendering.

I have carefully taken note of all these variations and I am happy to find that you have improved upon my writing in some cases. In...case, has the spirit or the form of my writing suffered. Commenting on the Viceregal declaration I wrote as follows:

> *Safhay par safhay parjanay kay baad bhi*
> *bamushkil isqadar batanay par musta-ed hota hai...*

Now, *ba-mushkil* is the keyword of my metaphorical expression. While maintaining the background of my metaphor, you have conveyed it as follows:

> *After reading page after page the curtain is at last lifted with hesitation. We have a glimpse...*

What I wanted to convey through *ba-mushkil* your expanded phrase brings out the meaning with greater emphasis, and I must confees that your version is more apt than mine. This is just to mention one among many such embellishments.

I expect to reach Allahabad probably on the 30th.

I hope you will be staying in Allahabad until then.

Yours sincerely,
A.K. Azad

Pandit Jawaharlal Nehru,
Allahabad

Document 55

RAMGARH CONGRESS AND MAULANA AZAD

Mahadeo Desai's Remark of the Congress Session of Ramgarh, held under the Presidentship of Maulana Azad, and His analysis of the President's speech, The Non-cooperation of the Elements

When Rajendra Babu[1] and his colleagues fixed upon Ramgarh as the venue of this year's Congress, they little knew the hardships they would have to bear due to the non-cooperation of the elements. From the point of view of convenience Daranagar would have been a much better and much less expensive place. But Daranagar was ruled out as not being a village-venue. Ramgarh was right in the midst of the unsophisticated villagers, and, though the cheap village-Congress of Gandhiji's conception still remains a dream, we have, since Faizpur, been succeeding in planting a Congress City in the midst of villages to the material benefit of the villagers who for three or four months get full employment, a satisfactory wage, and a custom for village products. In a vague sort of way the message of the Congress does reach these folks. But we have not yet learnt to go to the Congress with village mentality, and therefore, the principal object of having the Congress in the villages, *viz.*, annihilation of the distance between the city-dweller and the villager is still far from being realised.

But Ramgarh proved a handful in a most unexpected way. The exhibition, for which Laxmibabu and others has laboured like Trojans, was to have been opened by Gandhiji on the 10th, but heavy rains ruined their work. They had to toil over again and the Exhibition could be opened only on the 14th. For five days the skies remained clear, the workers heaved a sigh of relief, when suddenly at the exact hour of the opening of the Congress it began to pour and the amphitheatre with its enchanting environment soon became a lake.

How inauspicious, some exclaimed, 'No' was the reply, rain is never inauspicious and certainly never so disastrous as fire. How human nature always tries to derive consolation from all acts of God. And really speaking the non-cooperation of the elements proved not a small blessing in disguise. The Maulana Saheb[2] declared that come what may he was determined to open the Congress. Pandit Jawaharlal stood by him and their determination was innocuous. Nearly a hundred thousand people, men, women and children, the riches with the costly westing apparel and the poorest in their simple Khadi[3] shirt and dhoti, sat smiling and laughing with but making the slightest stin. When the downpour was unbearable they lifted the bambootattis from under themselves and held them up for shelter, and only when there was knee-deep water, and no sign of the fury abating, did they make for their camps. But even then there was no scrimmage to get back, everyone bowed to the inevitable. The orange-clad sisters and the men volunteers gave all the help they could in carrying children and helping people who slipped and fell, and not a soul was hurt. Rajendra Babu, sore at heart, greeted the people in a brief speech, the Maulana[4] followed with a similarly brief address, and Pandit Jawaharlal moved the main resolution which Prof. Kripalani[5] seconded, and the house was adjourned. The inclement elements continued their mad fury, but finding that everyone was undaunted, the tempest ceased and the skies cleared in the morning, and at nine o'clock the Congress met again in the Chowk with fifty thousand people again ready to face the threatening weather with a cheer. The President could have made short work of the amendments which did not deserve the permission to be moved, seeing the utter lack of support they had in the Subjects Committee, but he gave everyone as long a rope as was asked for, and in a little more than three hours brought the proceedings to a close. Nothing could have been more expeditious, more telling, more significant of the temper of the people. The non-cooperation of the elements was thus turned into co-operation and work, and has left a lesson for all time.

The Exhibition

If the rains taught the workers the lesson of selecting for the Congress a rain-proof venue, they taught people like me not to leave until tomorrow the work that you can do today. For I was foolish enough to defer until the last day a careful and examining look of the Exhibition, with the result that I have come away having seen only the Khadi Court to which one day I devoted a couple of hours. And I know that if I gave a couple of hours to the Khadi Court there were courts like the Basic Education Court, planned by Shrimati Ashadevi and the Jamia Milia workers with elaborate care which deserved more than that time. The Khadi Court was arranged this time not by professional people like Shri Jerabhai but by an amateur in the field Shrimati Kuwerbai Vakil who with his husband runs the pupils in her, own school in Vileparle, a Suberb of Bombay. Her amateur had left nothing to be desired in the way of exquisite taste and attractiveness and though I have not beside me the figures of Khadi sales.. I know this must have contributed not a little to push up the sales Bihar has been lucky in the manufacture and sale of Khadi, luckier than other provinces. The Congress Government purchased last year Rs. 80,000 worth of Khadi from the Bihar Branch of the A.I.S.A. This year the new incumbents have placed an order for Rs. 400,000 worth of Khadi-policemen's uniform to be made of cloth costing 17 annas a square yard. No wonder, therefore, that the Bihar workers should be forging ahead every day in the matter of new patterns, new designs and finer texture. Thus they were able to exhibit this year a piece of muslin woven out of yarn of 300 counts – remininscent of the famous gossamer-like Dacca muslin – spun by a sister who was present on the spot to exhibit the beauty of her art. Devasundary of Darbhanga sat in the middle of the court with her wheel, spinning with patient care from her own handmade slivers the 300 count yarn. Though the workers had succeeded in coaxing her to give up purdah, it was difficult to make her answer many questions. (By the by, the Congress in spite of the heavy expenses and trouble it meant for the organisers, has helped to bring about a revolution among women-folk. Nearly 200 Bihar sisters have discarded their purdah and, having worked as volunteers, will now be so many workers in the field of social reform and will help in the abolition of the purdah from the province.) Devasundary told me that she had made her silvers out of Cambodia cotton and that a tola of silvers took her a month to spin. The sari which had been exhibited there weighed 15 tolas. Rs. 5 was her monthly earning. Abdulla the weaver said that it took him three months to weave her yarn with the help of four men.

The other exhibits – coatings and shirtings, saris, dhotis, curtains, bed-spreads – showed the rapid march we have made in producing stuff suited to the most varied taste and varied needs, and left no excuse for people to say that no Khadi to suit their tastes was available. There were the exquisite door curtains from Sambalpur (Orissa) and U.P. the fine Patola from Orissa, not quite so elaborate and exquisite as the one from Patan, but costing ten times less and therefore within the reach of fashionable middle class women, the charming printings from Bombay and Meerut, and the beautiful saris from Andhra and Tirupur, and the Kashmir shawl with all kinds of pashmina products which tantalised but were beyond the reach of the ordinary khadi lover. The reversible pashmina waistcoat and pashmina pull-over were worth their price, and rug clipped wool-work told a tale that is worth recording. The art had died out until one of the A.I.S.A. workers recently tumbled upon an old man working as a stone breaker who casually told him that he could weave designs that would bewitch the eye but had no customer. He was asked to give up stone-breaking and revive the dead art. The rug with the clipped wool giving the appearance of for outside and the silky pashmina inside measuring 3 yards was worth Rs. 172-8-0.

There were other courts worth a visit and a careful study, but as I have said before, I missed them as I deferred seeing them. I had, however, rushed through the Exhibition with Gandhiji on the day he opened it, and therefore knew from a distance the wealth that it contained. The Basic Education Court, in which, as Gandhiji said, one could see Hindu-Muslim-Christian unity at work, was where Dr. Zakir Hussain and his colleagues, Shrimati Ashadevi and Shri Aryanayakem had tried to show the advance and the illimitable scope of basic education.

There was the place where the villagers in Bihar were extracting iron out of sand and making tools out of it; the manufacture of paper by hand and the rapid strides made in that department, the tannery and the leather-goods factory dealing exclusively in dead cattle hide, the stall where sugar and all kinds of sweetmeats were made from the juice of the palm tree which grows wild in most provinces of India, and of which the number in Bihar is enough to produce gur and sugar for the whole of India. The harvest is rich, the reapers are few and far between.

Its Meaning

In a speech which I shall not attempt to reproduce here Gandhiji explained the vast possibilities of the movement for the revival of these village crafts and occupations. 'You can show the villagers,' he said, 'that they have in their possessions crafts that can stand invasion of bombs from aeroplanes.' But they are ignorant of their treasures which have been mostly looted, and are on the brink of extinction. We have to awaken them to a sense of those treasures, and dispel their ignorance and darkness. That is the function of these exhibitions.

A wag had remarked the other day that Gandhiji aimed not at the civilisation of India, but at the Charkha-civilisation of India. Whatever one may say about the meaning and implications of the

Charkha and Gandhiji's conception thereof, is there any doubt that the civilisation which has been the pride and the admiration of all historians was the charkha civilisation? Gandhiji adverted to this aspect and said: 'The true Indian civilisation is in the Indian villages. The modern city civilisation you find in Europe and America, and in a handful of our cities which are copies of the Western cities and which were built for the foreigner, and by him. But they cannot last. It is only the handicraft civilisation that will endure and stand the test of time. But it can do so only if we can correlate the intellect with the hand. The late Madhusudan Das used to say that our peasants and workers had, by reason of working with bullocks, become like bullocks; and he was right. We have to lift them from the estate of the brute to the estate of man, and that we can do only by correlating the intellect with the hand. Not until they learn to work intelligently and make something new everyday, not until they are taught to know the joy of work, can we raise them from their low estate'.

Touching on another aspect of the exhibition he said in another speech in the exhibition after the evening prayer: 'This exhibition is the real Congress for the masses. Our chosen delegates will attend the Congress, and pass resolutions there as to what we have to do during the year. But what are the masses to do? The exhibition serves to provide intellectual pabulum for the masses, and those who visit the exhibition owe it to them to take to them what they learn here. There is no institution where 35 crores of our people can go. The Kumbha Mela is attended by several lakhs of people, but what is that number in a population of 35 crores? But if you who attend the exhibition can take some of the crafts which are being demonstrated here to the villagers, you can reach the millions who inhabit the villages and revolutionise their lives.... There is the talk of civil disobedience in the air. But who is fit to practise civil disobedience? Not those who will not spin, who will not wear Khadi, who do not care for the handicrafts. They will do some other kind of disobedience, but it will be anything but civil. That is not the disobedience. I would like to teach or would care to live for. I want to turn the quiet and living strength that spinning gives you into the channel of civil disobedience. If you will, therefore, see the exhibition with my eyes, you will carry the gospel of Khadi and the spinning wheel to the villages, and lay the foundation of a handicraft civilisation and universalise Khadi and handicrafts. If you do so, I assure you there will be no necessity for civil disobedience. If you will not do so, if you do not spin, do not universalise Khadi, I may go to jail and be there for a number of years, but it will be all in vain. Without Khadi and without handicrafts the Congress boat, far from carrying us to the port, will sink in midstream.

At the Helm

The candidature of Maulana Abul Kalam Azad was the acid test of the Congress delegate's nationalism, their faith in Hindu-Muslim unity, and their courage to entrust the destinies of the nation to a Muslim leader at a time of unprecedented crisis. But by an overhelming majority they declared their faith in him. They would have done so in 1939 too but their having done so in this critical year of our nation's history is especially notable. I had an occasion to ask the Maulana what he meant when he was reported to have said in a Lahore interview that now that the parliamentary programme had been put aside he had no difficulty in consenting to be president.'That' said the Maulana, with a smile, 'is the trouble of having a reporter who cannot understand and express correctly what you say in Urdu, Don't you see the absurdity of the statement? How could I decry the parliamentary programme having been so closely associated with the conduct of it? What I meant to say was this: 'The parliamentary programme is over. I have had my share in the Working Committee resolution asking the ministers to resign, and if I am called upon to preside over the next Congress and if I declined, I should be rightly held guilty of having shirked the natural consequences of that resolution. Sometime or other, unless the Government revise their attitude, we are sure to have civil disobedience, and I did not want anyone to say or feel that because civil disobedience was a certainty. I got funky. And then to have reposed their trust in me in ordinary times would be good enough; but to have done so in a crisis like the present is something that compelled me to respond.' I think this explanation is enough to silence all criticism on the score of that misreported interview. And the Maulana's presidential address and his conduct of the proceeding at Ramgarh have more than justified that nation's choice. The address whose characteristic of the Maulana, a closely reasoned piece, strictly confined to the question of the hour, and studiously refraining from touching any other subject. If the Working Committee at Patna decided to have only one resolution, the Maulana decided to have only one topic for exhaustive treatment in his address. Not a paragraph in it is superfluous and he has wasted no words on adjectives and epithets. 'You might have said something on civil disobedience and the constructive programme.' I said to the Maulana. 'No,' he said, 'having said that everything depended on discipline, unity and full confidence in Mahatma Gandhi's leadership, it would have been an act of supererogation on my part to have said anything on these topics. He has said all that is worth saying. He who accepts his leadership accepts all that he has said on civil disobedience and the intimate connection of the constructive programme with it, and he has no business to add anything of his own. If I did, should set a bad example.'

The Address

The address has been printed in extension by the daily press, but as a number of foreign readers this paper, and as *The Times* and *The Daily Telegraph* have disposed it of in a summary of 39 and 40 words. I shall extract here the cream of the address. India's fight is not against the British people but against British imperialism, and the Maulana has made this abundantly clear.' But while we were considering the dangers arising from Fascism and Nazism, it was impossible for us to forget the older danger which has been proved to be infinitely more fatal to the peace and freedom of nations than these new dangers, and which has in fact supplied the basis, for this reaction. I refer to British imperialism. We are not distant spectators of this imperialism, as we are of the new reactionary movements. It has taken possession of our house and dominates over us. It was for this reason that we stated in clear terms that, if new entanglements in Europe brought about War, India which has been debarred from exercising her will and making free decisions, will not take any part in it. She could only consider this question when she had acquired the right of coming to decision according to her own free will and choice.

India cannot endure the prospect of Nazism and Fascism, but she is even more tired of British imperialism. If India remains deprived of her natural right to freedom, this would clearly mean that British imperialism continued to flourish with all its traditional characteristics, and under such conditions India would on no account be prepared to lend a helping hand for the triumph of British imperialism. This was the second declaration which was constantly emphasized through these resolutions. These resolutions were repeatedly passed from the Lucknow session onwards till August, 1939 and are known by the name of 'War Resolutions'.

Also:

'But it is not a question of the desire or of the measure of the desire of the British Government. The straight and simple question is of India's right; whether she is entitled to determine her own fate or not. On the answer to this question depend the answers to all other questions of the day. This question forms the foundation stone of the Indian problem; India will not allow it to be removed for if it is displaced, the whole structure of Indian nationalism will collapse.

So far as the question of war is concerned our position is quite clear. We see the face of British imperialism as clearly now as we did in the last war, and we are not prepared to assist in the triumph by participating in the War. Our case is crystal clear. We do not wish to see British imperialism triumphant and stronger and thus lengthen the period of our own subjection to it. We absolutely refuse to do so, our way lies patently in the opposite direction.'

Lastly:

> 'Since war began, several numbers of the British Cabinet have tried to make the world believe that the old order of British imperialism has ended, and that today the British nation has no other aims except those of peace and justice. Which country could have more warmly acclaimed such a declaration than India? But the fact is that, in spite of these declarations, British imperialism stands in the way of peace and justice today exactly as it did before the war. The Indian demand was the touchstone for all such claims. They were so tested and found to be counterfeit and untrue.'

The portion of his address on Hindu-Muslim Unity and the Minority Problem is likely to endure in history. Ever since he started his weekly, Al-Hilal in 1912, he has waged unrelenting war against the policy and efforts to divide Hindus and Muslims, and he declares in his address:

> 'I would remind my co-religionists that today I stand exactly where I stood in 1912 when I addressed them on this issue. I have given thought to all those innumerable occurrences which have happened since then; my eyes have watched them, my mind has pondered over them. These events did not merely pass me by; I was in the midst of them, a participant, and I examined every circumstances with care, I cannot be false to what I have myself seen and observed; I cannot quarrel with my own convictions, I cannot stifle the voice of my conscience. I repeat today what I have said throughout this entire period that the ninety millions of Muslims of India have no

> other right course of action than the one to which I invited them in 1912.'

He scouts the idea that the Muslims are in a minority and that the democratic institutions in India would therefore jeopardise their interests and existence:

> 'Politically speaking, the word minority does not mean just a group that is numerically smaller and therefore entitled to special protection. It means a group that is so small in number and so lacking in other qualities that give strength, that it has no confidence in its own capacity to protect itself from the much larger group that surrounds it. It is not enough that the group should be relatively the smaller, but that it should be absolutely so small as to be incapable of protecting its interests. Thus this is not merely a question of numbers; other factors count also. If a country has two major groups numbering a million and two millions respectively, it does not necessarily follow that, because one is half the other, therefore, it must call itself politically a minority and consider itself weak.'

Also:

> 'Full eleven centuries have passed by since then, Islam has now as great a claim on the soil of India as Hinduism. If Hinduism has been the religion of the people here for several thousands of years, Islam also has been their religion for a thousand years. Just as a Hindu can say with pride that he is an Indian and follows Hinduism, so also we can say with equal pride that we are Indians and follow Islam. I shall enlarge this orbit still further. The Indian Christian is equally entitled to say with pride that he is an Indian and is following a religion of India, namely Christianity.'

Lastly:

> 'Do we, Indian Musalmans, view the free India of the future with suspicion and distract or with courage and confidence? If we view it with fear and suspicion, then undoubtedly we have to follow a different path. No present declaration, no promise for the future, no constitutional safeguards, can be a remedy for our doubts and fears. We are then forced to tolerate the existence of a third

> power. This third power is already entrenched here and has no intention of withdrawing and, if we follow this path of fear, we must needs look forward to its continuance. But if we are convinced that for us fear and doubt have no place, and that we must view the future with courage and confidence in ourselves, then our course of action becomes absolutely clear. We find ourselves in a new world, which is free from the dark shadows of doubt, vacillation, inaction and apathy, and where the light of faith and determination, action and enthusiasm never fails. The confusions of the times, the ups and downs that come our way, the difficulties that beset our thorny path, cannot change the direction of our steps. It becomes our bounden duty then to march with assured steps to India's national goal.
>
> I arrived at this definite conclusion without the least hesitation, and every fibre of my being revolted against the former alternative. I could not bear the thought of it. I could not conceive it possible for a Musalman to tolerate this, unless he has rooted out the spirit of Islam from every corner of his being.'

So much for the Musalmans. As for the British who are not tired of repeating the obstacle of the communal question as an insuperable one, he declares:

> 'We could attach no greater importance to it, than to make it the first condition for the attainment of our national goal. The Congress has always held this belief; no one can challenge this fact. It has always held to two basic principles in this connection, and every step was taken deliberately with these in view :
>
> (1) Whatever constitution is adopted for India, there must be the fullest guarantees in it for the rights and interests of minorities.
>
> (2) The minorities should judge for themselves what safeguards are necessary for the protection of their rights and interests. The majority should not decide this. Therefore the decision in this respect must depend upon the consent of the minorities and not on a majority vote... ....

> The manner in which the Congress has dealt with this problem today in connection with the Constituent Assembly, throws a flood of light on these two principles and clarifies them. The recognised minorities have a right, if they so please, to choose their representatives by their votes. Their representatives will not have to rely upon the votes of any other community except their own. So far as the question of the rights and the interests of the minorities is concerned, the decision will not depend upon the majority of votes in the Constituent Assembly. It will be subject to thc consent of the minority. If unanimity is not achieved on any question, then an impartial tribunal, to which the minorities have also consented, will decide the matter. This last provision merely in the nature of a provision for a possible contingency, and is most unlikely to be required. If a more practical proposal is made, there can be no objection to it.'

The Background

Many people have described the Ramgarh Congress and the passing of the single resolution as a unique triumph for Gandhiji. But I wish I had the words to give even a faint picture of the awesome travail the Gandhiji was going through during the last three days of the Congress. There was no question before him of triumph or failure. There was before him the sole question of whether he would be able to shoulder the terrible responsibility that was being placed upon him, to bear the weight of the unthinking trust that was being responded in him. He had pleaded with the members of the Working Committee to relieve him of the burden. It would free them from what might be acting upon them as an incubus, and it would at the same time leave him free to pursue his experiment of Ahimsa more intensively and without thought of the millions who looked to him for direction. I may be a broken reed and my well land you into unexpected troubles. I might not begin the movement for an indefinite length of time, and I might stop it abruptly. However much you may agree with me, your Ahimsa does not go as far as mine. And if after twenty years of practice of it I have not been able to win the affection and trust of the Musalmans, my Ahimsa must be of a very poor quality indeed. Why not then let me further examine myself, and make further researches? To the Maulana he said: 'I have not the slightest doubt that the Congress and the nation can have nothing to lose and everything to gain by the step. There is no question of my distracting you or other members of the Working Committee or the nation. It is a question of my distrust in myself. I am sure that, if you release me, I shall be able to give even civil disobedience a purer and a nobler shape.' But the Maulana demurred. He somehow could not reconcile himself to the step.

'You must not forget,' he said with visible emotion' that it was at your command that I accepted to serve this year, and you cannot now forsake me.' There was not nothing for it but to bear the burden. The speeches at the subjects committee and the open Congress made after the passing of the resolution, translated fairly fully in this issue, should be read with this background in view.

---

1. Dr. Rajendra Prasad.
2. Maulana Abul Kalam Azad.
3. Indian Loin-Cloth.
4. Maulana Azad.
5. Acharya J.B. Kripalani.

Document 56

LETTER FROM MAULANA AZAD TO MAHATMA GANDHI

19-A, Ballygunj, Circular Road,
Calcutta,

Dated: 30-03-1940

My Dear Mahatmaji,

A friend from Delhi who very often meets the Viceroy,[1] has sent a letter to me. He says that the impression left by your last interview on Linlithgow was that at first you wanted to lead him up to a certain point, and when he tried to reach it, then you lift him altogether. He further writes that if you had cleared the position from the very beginning that the Dominion Status of the Westminster variety would not be acceptable to you, the Viceroy would have comprehended the situation. But it was not done. You insisted on the reply of the question whether the status conferred on India would be of the Westminster variety or not. Linlithgow draw the conclusion that if he would get this point cleared, a way for further negotiations would be opened. He drew the attention of the Home Government to this fact with all emphasis, and assured her that his position would be strengthened if he gets a chance of making such a statement. He also insisted that so far as that declaration was concerned, it should not be mixed up with the communal problems. The League may be opposed to it to any extent but the political destiny of India could not be now changed. But when the basis of negotiations was clarified, and he (Viceroy) made an announcement with the surest hope of your approval, then all of a sudden changed your attitude and declared quite unequivocally that India could not accept it. This weakened the position of Linlithgow, and the Home Government considered him to be incapable of understanding and dealing with Indian situation. In short Linlithgow had a deep grievance against your attitude.

Here ends the letter when I was in Delhi last time, I had come to know of similar things through other sources.

So for as the real question is concerned, I do not think that the Viceroy has a reasonable cause of the grievance. Your question about the Westminster status clearly meant that when it continues the right of cessation, the British Government should not hesitate to allow India to decide it through her own free will. You did not mean that India would give up the right of self-determination and recede to a position where she would accept whatever the British Government condescends to give her in a patronising way. But leaving aside the real problem, perhaps it would have been better to remove the misunderstanding if Linlithgow so feels that he has reason to be aggrieved. The reaction of the Delhi letter on me is that Linlithgow feels that he has been met with the tactics of a politician, rather than in a way which is solely yours. However, the reactions of Linlithgow have no foundation in reality, and there would be no harm if only this aspect of the affair is clarified through a letter.

You may take up whatever line of action you deem fit in this respect. I have only laid the full information I got from the letter before you. The writer of the letter is a responsible and respectful man.

Yours faithfully,

A.K. Azad

Mahatma Gandhi
Sewagram, Wardha

Document 57

EXTRACT OF THE STATEMENT OF MAULANA AZAD ISSUED AGAINST THE LAHORE RESOLUTION, PASSED BY THE ALL INDIA MUSLIM LEAGUE IN 1940

"Harmful not only for India as a whole but for Muslims in Particular. I must confess that the very term Pakistan goes against my grain. It suggests that some portions of the world are pure while others are impure. Such a division of territories on a pure and impure is un-Islamic and a repudiation of the very spirit of Islam."

Document 58

LETTER FROM MAHATMA GANDHI TO MAULANA AZAD

Sevagrame, Wardha,

April 4, 1940

Dear Maulana Saheb,

You shall address me as you like, I do not know that you address me differently.

I have written to Lord Linlithgow as suggested by you. Copy is enclosed herewith.

I quite agree with you about the Pattabhi[1] episode.

I am inclined to think that there should be a considered reply from you to the Labour resolution.

Yours Sincerely,
M.K. Gandhi

Encl. 1

Maulana Abul Kalam Azad
Calcutta

Enclosure:

(Mahatma Gandhi's letter to the Viceroy Lord Linlithgow, dated 04-04-1940)

Dear Lord Linlithgow,

Maulana Abul Kalam Azad writes a long letter from which I enclose herewith the relevant portion.

I shall be painfully surprised if you can confirm the report received by the Maulana Saheb. Mine was a simple inquiry. We had come so near each other that there was no mental reservation between us. And if anything was left obscure there was no difficultly about going straight to the point and clearing obscurities. That dominion status may not be acceptable to the Congress had been cleared at the interview which led to my inquiry. The object was to know where each party exactly stood. I should be very sorry indeed to discover that I left on your mind the impression that if Dominion Status of the Statute of Westminster variety was meant, the Congress would accept it.

I must refuse to give any credence to the suggestion that you had lost caste with the Cabinet because you had allowed yourself to be over-reached by me as the report implies. I have not known British statescraft to be so easily moved from its dispositions as suggested by Maulana Saheb's correspondent. And I shall hope that you could never consider me quite of wanting to overreach you.

Whilst I am writing to you I want to have another thing also of my mind. I have already told you that in my son Devdas you have a warm-hearted champion. He has been writing long letter to me trying to convince me that I did you a gross injustice in abruptly terminating our last conversation. He discounts my assurance that the conversation ended because both you and I saw that the gulf between us was found to be too unbridgeable to be handled at that moment by prolonging conversations. Indeed it was your expression that it would be more manly for as to end the conversations the very day we began them and make the confession to the public. I at once accepted the accuracy of your characterisation. Devdas says that was said out of courtesy, if not British pride, and that you were eager to prolong the conversations. He is thus most disconsolate and thinks that my interpretation of your attitude is wrong. You alone can help me to settle domestic dispute.

M.K. Gandhi

1. Dr. B. Pattbhi Sitaramaiah.

Documents 59

LETTER FROM GOPICHAND BHARGAVA TO MAULANA AZAD

Lajpatrai Bhawan,
Lahore, 10-4-1940

Respected Maulana Sahib,

As desired by you I phoned you last night. I told you that as far as the question of nomination by the Congress was concerned, it was not the party consideration that actuated me to express an opinion that Pandit Thakurdatt be nominated in preference to Shrimati Shanno Devi. I had also submitted that whatever she represented was not correct. The recommendation of the W.C. was unanimous. Shannodeviji had canvassed individually almost all the members of the W.C. and members of Assembly party. But in spite of all this, you thought it proper to believe her and nominate her.

I had formerly received a telegram from Sardar Patel approving nomination of Pandit Thakurdatt. After the receipt of the telegram I had worked for Vaid Ji. Now I am told that Vaid Ji's name is not approved by you and Sardar Sahib has also cancelled his approval. I feel that it humiliates me in the eyes of my friends and those whom I addressed only on Sunday.

I feel very strongly that nomination of Srimati Shannodevi is not in best interests of Congress. Now it is said it is due to party politics that we did not nominate her but where was party politics when Mrs. Dunichand was nominated by her party friends from the very seat she had contested against a Congress candidate. It is not a personal humiliation that I feel but I think it is humiliation of the big institution that such a person has been nominated.

I do fully realise that it is the Central Parliamentary Board whose will is to prevail and we have only to recommend. And it is, therefore, that their commands are being obeyed.

But I feel that it is not possible for me now to work as a member of the Assembly. Therefore, I am submitting my resignation to you.

In all humility, I would request you to forward it to the Governor. I would also like to add that it is not out of anger or in haste that, I am taking this step. But I feel that there is no other alternative left for me.

I must thank you and other members of the Central Parliamentary Board for the consideration they have shown me during these last 3 years.

With best regards,

Yours very sincerely,
Gopichand Bhargawa

To, Maulana Abul Kalam Sahib Azad,
19/A, Ballygunj, Circular Road,
Calcutta

Copy forwarded to Sardar Vallabhbhai Patel for information.

Document 60

LETTER FROM PANDIT JAWAHAR LAL NEHRU TO MAULANA AZAD

Bombay,

April 20, 1940

Dear Mr. President,

I have to report to you about the activities of the National Planning Committee. It was our hope and intention to finish the preliminary work of this Committee within a year from its inception, but the magnitude of the task has prevented us from completing it within that period. I addressed last year's Congress President, Shri Rajendra Prasad, on this subject and he was good enough to extend the period for our report. The National Planning Committee at their last sessions appointed 29 sub-committees on various subjects. Each of these sub-committees in effect has to deal with an important sphere of economic and other activity and there has been great in the delay in the sub-committees' presenting their reports. This has reacted on the National Planning Committee which cannot do its work till it has received the reports of its sub-committees. Because of this reason, we have repeatedly had to postpone our meetings.

The full Committee is now meeting on the 1st May and will probably continue in session for two weeks. We have received full reports from 5 sub-committees, namely:

1. Heavy Engineering 2. River Training and Irrigation

3. Labour 4. Population 5. Horticulture.

Interim reports have been received from the following sub-committees:

1. Chemicals 2. Public Finance 3. Transport.

Final or interim reports are expected within the next few days from the following sub-committees:

1. Rural Marketing 2. Industrial Finance 3. Housing 4. Animal Husbandry 5. Communications 6. Currency and Banking 7. Insurance 8. Manufacturing Industries.

Apart from the above mentioned sub-committees, there still remain 13 sub-committees to report. The next meeting of the National Planning Committee will consider such reports and interim reports as are placed before it and may also discuss some general issues of policy. After that we shall have to give some more time to the remaining sub-committees for their reports. When all the reports have come in, they will have to be considered together and the final report of the planning committee itself drafted and considered. All this is likely to take at least 4 to 5 months more, and may be 6 months. In view of the critical political situation, it is possible that our work may suffer or be delayed. It is our desire, however, to complete as rapidly as possible the work of the sub-committees so that all the material may be ready for any future use.

We have tried to carry on our activities within the limits of our finances. This has often resulted in delay. Owing to the expansion of our work and the heavy burden that this has cast on us, our expenses have been considerable. And yet I would venture to say that work has been carried on far more economically than is usually possible under such circumstances. We have carried on our work for a year and five months with funds which were intended for half period. Our present resources will probably be exhausted about the end of June. It is necessary for us, therefore, to arrange for further contributions for another four or five months, in particular, for the printing of our own report and the reports of the 29 sub-committees. This printing is likely to be a heavy item in our budget.

I am giving you this information of our financial position so that you may be in touch with developments in the National Planning Committee. I am not making a request for a grant from the Congress funds. It is our desire not to burden the Congress with this expenditure insofar as we can help it. We have avoided of course accepting any money from any private or non-official agencies so far, as this was not considered proper by us. We have depended solely on contributions from provincial governments and some state governments (Hyderabad, Mysore, Baroda and Bhopal). It may be that these governments might help us a little still further. I am addressing them on the subject.

Our office is sending to the A.I.C.C. office the audited statement of our accounts up to the 31st December 1939 and another statement till the end of March 1940.

We are also sending to the A.I.C.C. office copies of the reports of the sub-committees received by us so far.

In view of the Circumstances mentioned, I would beg of you to extend the time for the submission of our report. I cannot suggest any definite time but provisionally it might be fixed at the end of September 1940, or to be on the safer side, till the end of the year.

There is considerable interest from the press and the public for the reports of our sub-committees. We have so far treated them as confidential but it is difficult to keep them so, as unauthorized reports go to the press and sometimes mislead the public. It is our intention, therefore, to issue a brief synopsis of our sub-committee's report to the press after the report has been presented to the N.P.C. I trust you approve of this procedure. The sub-committees' reports or the synopsis will of course in no way bind the National Planning Committee, much less the Congress. It is just a report of certain experts appointed for a particular task. This fact will be made clear.

It is quite likely that in these sub-committees' reports there will be considerable variety of opinions and sometimes even conflict in regard to vital matters of principle. This is inevitable, as the number of people working in the N.P.C. is large and represents a variety of opinions. The N.P.C. will try to coordinate these opinions as far as possible, though this may not always be possible. And finally it will be for the Congress Executive to consider the N.P.C. report and give its own opinion in regard to it.

I am sending a copy of this letter to the General Secretary of the A.I.C.C. at Allahabad. As I have mentioned above, sub-committees' reports are also being sent to him, as I did not wish to burden you with this voluminous material. Should you, however, desire to have these reports or any other information, we shall gladly send them to you.

Yours sincerely,
Jawaharlal Nehru

Maulana Abul Kalam Azad
Calcutta

Document 61

LETTER FROM JAWAHAR LAL NEHRU TO MAULANA AZAD

Bombay

April 21, 1940

My dear Maulana,

You will remember your discussing with me the question of someone going on our behalf to America. No suitable person could be thought of at the time and in view of the developing political situation here, it is even more difficult now to think to sending any prominent person.

At the same time it seems to me very necessary to do something about America, not just a propaganda tour delivering speeches, *etc.*, but someone with sense who could meet our many friends in America and make arrangements for future work on an efficient basis. America is full of goodwill for us and I have many friends there among Americans who write to me repeatedly that something should be done. Unfortunately the Indians in America are a very unsatisfactory lot. They should a lot and do no good work. Often they do injury to our cause, we cannot rely upon any single one.

My own view is that we should not have any formal or official representation in America, but at the same time we might have close unofficial contacts with some group who could work efficiently and responsibly. Something of the kind we have had in London through the Indian League, which does not represent us in any way or commit us and yet which does good work for us. Whether this is possible or not in America, I do not know. But an effort should be made.

As it is not possible to send anyone from here, I have been thinking of some suitable person going from England to America for this purpose. This is much more feasible and would not cost much. The only such person I can think of in England is Krishna Menon who might go for a month or two to America. Even if he went, I should like him to do so not as our formal representative but unofficially, though with our goodwill.

I had not mentioned this at all to Krishna Menon, but he has been thinking on the same lines and he has written to me independently that he was considering the prospect of going to America. His chief difficulty is one of funds and he has asked me whether it would be possible for some private arrangement to be made for a hundred pounds. He realises that it would not be fitting for him to commit the Congress in any way or to have any official authorisation. All he would like is a letter of goodwill from you which would contain briefly a reference to our present Congress position and to our desire to have interaction contacts with men of goodwill.

Personally, I think that it would be a very good thing for Krishna Menon to go to America. The position in England is such that little good work can be done at present. In America many of our people have made themselves thoroughly objectionable and decent Americans, who are our friends, do not want to have anything to do with them. It is essential that any work on our behalf should not get tied up with particular parties or groups abroad. Krishna Menon's[1] visit will be good in itself and will lay the foundation for future work.

I do not know that can be done in this respect by you or whether you approve of my suggestion or not. You will remember that sometime in December or January, the Working Committee sanctioned £200 to be sent to Krishna Menon to cover the cost of cables and other expenditure incurred more or less on our behalf. It was then thought that further financial help might be sent to him two or three months later if necessary. Those three months have expired and in view of the developing political situation, it seems to me essential that we should make some further provision for further work there. We may not have a chance to do this later. I would have liked, therefore, for a further sum of £200 to be sent to him on he same conditions as before. This sum may be utilised at his discretion for work in England or, if he so chooses, for a visit to America or for both. Having regard to the magnitude of the work both in England and America, this sum is a very small one. If, however, the sum is considered too much then we should send less at present. I would suggest that at least £100 be sent to him as soon as possible. Apart from this, I shall personally try to contribute something to this end.

I shall be grateful to you if you could let me have your opinion as early as possible. Events are developing rapidly and it may become too late to take any such action after some time. I would also request you, if you agree, to send a letter to Krishna Menon expressing your goodwill at the prospect of his visiting America and hoping that he will explain the Congress viewpoint to our friends there. You might add that all we desire is that the world should be correctly and truly informed of the facts in India and of what we stand for. It would be good if you would add a note as to the present Congress position in India. You could send this letter and note to Krishna Menon directly or through me. It would be preferable to do both to avoid your letter going astray. Krishna Menon's address: V.K. Krishna Menon, C/o India League, 165, Strand, London, W.C. 2.

As you know, I expect to be here for another two weeks or more.

Yours sincerely,
Jawaharlal Nehru

1. Mr. V.K. Krishna Menon.

Document 62

LETTER FROM MAULANA AZAD TO PANDIT JAWAHAR LAL NEHRU

Calcutta,

24.4.40

My Dear Jawaharlal,

Thanks for your letter of 21st April. I agree with you that if Krishna Menon goes to America on his own accord, it would be useful to the demand of the time to some extent. Had it come before us previous to the meeting of the Working Committee, it would have been decided in it. However I am writing to the General Secretary to send £100 immediately to him, and hope you would make arrangements for at least another £100 from Bombay.

You say that I should write a letter to him also. I think that if I write to him as the President, it would necessarily mean that he is going there on behalf of the Congress; and as you yourself write, it would be against expediency to carry the matter to such an exent. It would be better if you write him a letter saying "I am glad to hear that you are going to America. I hope your presence there would enable them to understand the existing Indian situation. "Your letter will fully help him in giving him a responsible capacity. And along with it this would save the position which might be created in writing it directly on behalf of the President.

There were three houses of friends on Mussoorie which have already been occupied. Can any one amongst your friends arrange a house at Mussoorie? If it be not possible in this way, I am ready to pay rent. The house should however be good and commodious. Please wire for the arrangement, if you have any such person in mind. The weather of Calcutta is straining upon me.

I thought of Nainital and Almora after Mussoorie, I am wiring to Pantji[1] at night.

Yours sincerely,
A.K. Azad

Pt. Jawahar La[illegible]nru,
Sakeena Mansion,
Carmichael Road,
Bombay

1. Pandit Govind Ballabh Pant.

Document 63

LETTER FROM MASTER TARA SINGH TO MAULANA AZAD

Lahore,
26.4.1940

My dear Maulana Saheb,

I read your statement which you issued from Wardha on 19th April. In this statement you say "so far as the Congress is concerned, I have no hesitation in saying that this matter may also be entrusted to the Muslim representatives of the proposed Assembly. The right to take such step can vest only in Musalmans who are selected by the Musalmans themselves." You say this with reference to the proposal of creating Hindu India and Muslim India. I may here remind you that the Indian National Congress passed a resolution in its Session of 1929 held at Lahore assuring the Sikhs and other minorities that the Congress will not agree to any constitution which does not satisfy the Sikhs and other minorities. In the history of Indian National Congress published by the Working Committee of the Congress, the following words are given:

> "But as the Sikhs in particular, and the Muslims and the other Minorities in general, had expressed dissatisfaction over the solution of communal questions proposed in the Nehru Report, this Congress assured the Sikhs, the Muslims and other Minorities, that "no solution thereof in any future Constitution would be acceptable to the Congress that did not give full satisfaction to the parties concerned."

The said resolution of the Congress was a pledge given to the Sikhs who felt at the time that they had been ignored by the Congress in the Nehru Report. After this pledge the Sikhs who were going out of the Congress, rejoined the Congress; and we are in the Congress relying upon the above referred resolution. Now you wish to leave the Pakistan Scheme solely in the hands of the Muslims. This evidently is opposed to the pledge given to the Sikhs by the Congress. A good deal of suspicion is spreading amongst the Sikhs. I, therefore, request you to kindly clear your position and that of the Congress. Does the Congress mean to stick to the pledge given to the Sikhs and thus will not become a party to any communal settlement which does not give full satisfaction to Sikhs or has the Congress changed its policy, and is prepared to give a blank card to the Muslims in the matter of the Muslim Pakistan Scheme?

This is a serious matter. The Sikhs must know where they stand. The statements of the Congress leaders are simply increasing the suspicion created by your statement. I hope you will see our difficulty. The Sikhs joined the Congress upon clear conditions and shall insist that the Congress should stick to their promise.

Yours sincerely,
Master Tara Singh

Document 64

LETTER FROM MAULANA AZAD TO J.B. KRIPALANI

19-A, Ballyganj, Circular Road,
Calcutta,
7 May 1940

My Dear Kripalani,

You might have received my last letter. I do not know whether the office has received any donations in connection with my appeal for the Medical Mission. If it has received any, please arrange it to be sent to me. Moreover please inform Messrs Bachhraj & Co., Bombay to send me the donation received in this connection direct on my Calcutta address soon, for expenses is urgently needed.

Yours sincerely,
A.K. Azad

Acharya J.B. Kripalani
A.I.C.C. Office
Allahabad

Document 65

LETTER FROM MAULANA AZAD TO PANDIT JAWAHAR LAL NEHRU

"The Mahal"
Nainital
Dated, 9th May, 1940

My dear Jawaharlal,

I had received your telegram about Mussorie for which I am obliged. Due to arrangements in Nainital, I gave up the idea of Mussorie.

I reached here on the 6th. Circumstances permitting, I shall stay here up to July. You might stay in Bombay till the end of May, and then leave for Allahabad. Why not come to Nainital, and stay here with me for some time? You can work here on the compilation of the report of the Planning Committee. There would be no difference between Allahabad and Nainital, so far as the Provincial work is concerned. You can remain in touch with the work equally from here as from Allahabad. Moreover your presence here would be useful for prompt consultations about many matters.

I had a talk with Mr. A. Patwardhan at Wardha. He said that he would talk to me at another occasion, but he could not see me. Please inquire of him about the membership of the Working Committee. I give you the trouble, as I do not know his address. Socialist friends have proved to be quite hopeless. They have not courage enough do work. They fear opposition, and dare not stand firmly on their own legs. I expected to get some help from them at this critical juncture, but all my hopes proved to be false.

If Patwardhan[1] is not prepared for it, some other person should be nominated soon. Could you suggest some name?

The Imperial Tobacco Company has sent a note to me, which shows the nature of the strike to be quite different from what it was represented by the workers. However I am trying to find out some means of honourable compromise.

Yours sincerely,
A.K. Azad

---

1. Mr. Achyut Patwardhan.

Document 66

LETTER FROM JAWAHAR LAL NEHRU TO MAULANA AZAD

Bombay,
May 11, 1940

My dear Maulana,

Thank you for your telegram and your letter of the 9th. It was my intention to go to the Frontier Province towards the end of this month as I stated at the time of the Working Committee Meeting. But if you intend holding the Working Committee meeting early in June, I cannot go to the Frontier in this month.

Achyut Patwrdhan's address is Ahmednagar. That I think is enough. I am writing to him that you wish to appoint him a member of the Working Committee and that he should write to you directly. If you consider it necessary, you might write to him directly. I am afraid I can suggest no name for the Committee.

I am thinking of going to Wardha for a day on the 15th on my way back to Allahabad and Lucknow. In view of international developments I should like to have a talk with Gandhiji. After that I shall be busy with our provincial Congress meeting and at Allahabad. I have been away for so long that a great deal of work has accumulated.

I am afraid I cannot come to Nainital as I have too much work to do which I cannot do there. Apart from this, I dislike greatly going to these hill stations like Nainital or Mussoorie. These places do not suit me at all and the crowds of people who are there do not fit in with my temperament. At this time of great world crisis it would specially produce a feeling of tension in my mind if I went to a hill station.

Yours sincerely,
Jawahar Lal Nehru

Document 67

LETTER FROM PANDIT JAWAHAR LAL NEHRU TO MAULANA AZAD

Wardha,
16.5.1940

My dear Maulana,

Thank you for your telegram agreeing to the 15th June for the Working Committee meeting. This date enables me to go to the Frontier Province and the Punjab. I have to be back in Bombay on June 21st.

Of course the Working Committee meeting should not be postponed just to suit individual convenience. If the situation demands it, it should be held regardless of other factor. I feel however, and Mahatmaji agrees, that it is better for us to wait some time so that we might know how the present situation develops. Events are marching ahead rapidly and even a month may make a great deal of difference. Therefore, from this point of view also, it is desirable not to have an early meeting of the Working Committee.

I came here today and had a talk with Mahatmaji. I was very glad to find that his reaction to international developments was more or less the same as mine. I wonder if you saw a statement I made to the press five or six days ago. I enclose a copy. I was sorry to read Rajendra Babu's press interview on that day. And now I learn from the radio that Asaf Ali has issued some kind of appeal for political parties to come together and join in helping Britain and in organising our defence. I think it was very improper of Asaf Ali, as a member of the W.C., to issue such a statement. It must lead people to think that the W.C. is prepared to adopt this line and, so far as I know, this is certainly not going to be done.

Rajendra Babu has written a letter to Gandhiji and sent him a copy of his letter to you dated 14th May. At Gandhiji's suggestion I am sending a reply to him, a copy of which I enclose. This will give you some idea of how my mind is working. I hope that the U.P.P.C.C., which meets on the 18th will pass a resolution on these lines.

I am quite clear in my mind that our policy must remain unchanged and we must go ahead, as before with our organisational and other preparations. Our enrolment and training of Satyagrahis must go on. I do not think that Satyagraha should be started soon, even if we are ready for it. But the possibility of a loosening of central authority demands that we should be ready to meet any situation that might arise.

To talk about our joining hands in the defence of India is ridiculous. Defence against whom? and to help the British Empire? I think this will be wrong and degrading, apart from the fact that we are not in a position to do anything effective on these lines. Even the defence of India can only be undertaken by us on the lines of developing the Satyagraha organisations. I do not myself see any real danger of foreign invasion. I do see a danger of internal trouble. For that also we have no other remedy except on disciplined Satyagrahi lines.

I am quite clear that we must not budge an inch from the position we have taken up, and, what is more, we must not be caught in any trap laid out by the new British Government or the Viceroy. I think they are bound to take some step – invite Gandhiji and others, or make some other vague statement. Our answer to all this must be clear. We are going to cooperate in the preservation of empire. The independence of India must be recognised – not Dominion Status and the like – and the people of India must frame their constitution through a Constituent Assembly. No small group of men for this purpose will be accepted. It is only on this basis that we can talk. If this basis is not present, then there is no good of talking.

The British Empire is doomed. It is almost a thing of yesterday already. And yet, such is human folly and arrogance, that the British Government in India continues to behave in an imperialist manner. There is not the slightest change. The members of the British Parliament still patronise us and advise us and behave generally in a manner which I find to be intolerable. If even catastrophic events cannot open their eyes to realities, I do not see why we should join the company of the blind.

To say that because Nazism is worse than British imperialism, therefore we prefer to be ruled by the British, is to me the height of degradation. If we are so helpless that we cannot look after ourselves, then the sooner we perish the better. We are not going to change masters. We shall fight against all domination.

Gandhiji has shown me your letter about Dr. Gopi Chand and the appointment of Sardar Sampooran Singh as leader of the Punjab

Assembly Party. I entirely agree with you that this was improper but I am not clear as to what should be done now. I am going to Lahore for two days soon to attend the Satyagraha camp. Iftikhar has invited me. If you have any directions to give me, please send them soon.

I enclose a copy of my reply to a correspondent of Gandhiji's. This also deals with the Akalis and the Congress.

My provisional programme is as follows, but the exact dates have not been fixed yet:

In Lucknow for P.C.C. meetings	May 18, 19, 20
In Allahabad	May 21, 22, 23
In Lahore	May 24, 25
In Peshawar	May 26 to 30th
Srinagar, Kashmir	May 31st for a week

Yours sincerely,
Jawahar Lal Nehru

Document 68

LETTER FROM MAULANA AZAD TO JAWAHAR LAL NEHRU

"The Mahal"
Nainital,

May 25, 1940

My dear Jawaharlal,

Thanks for you letter of the 16th instant. I read the statement of Rajendra Babu[1] in the papers with surprise, and in the meanwhile I received his letter which gave me clearly the trend of his thoughts. I am sorry that I cannot send you a copy of the letter which I sent him in reply, as it was in Urdu; and no copy but of official letters is kept in the office. So far as the present attitude of the Congress is concerned, this letter was nearly the same as yours. I am pleased to find that our thoughts are going the same way in this respect; and it is most gratifying to find that Gandhiji is also in full agreement with it.

The statement of Asafali[2] was still more objectionable as compared to that of Rajen Babu. In fact it grieved me. I wrote him two biting letters one after the other. Now he assures me that he will abstain from such statements in future.

Whatever, you write in your letters addressed to me and Rajen Babu, are quite correct; so far as the Congress attitude is concerned. There seems to be no reason why should any question of change should arise at this stage. But along with it, you have written two things to which I do not agree, and I wonder how they can be adjusted in the plan which your mind is forming in relation to the Congress's line of action. You say in the letter of Rajen Babu "The Satyagraha is not immediately indicated even if we were ready for it. I think it would be wrong for us at this particular moment, when Britain is in peril, to take advantage of her distress and rush at her throat. "You have also expressed, this idea in the Lucknow speech, and the *Pioneer* thought it necessary to quote your original words: *Yeh baat Hindostan ki shann kay khilaff hae, Ke woh England kee kamzoree sey faa-e-daa uthaa Kar iss waqt satyagraha shuroo kar dey.*

I absolutely fail to grasp this mode of thinking. In fact this very method is totally wrong that we should first formulate such premises in matters of political struggle, and then draw wrong conclusions about our line of action. I do not know what is the *Shaan* of India. I only want to know what is the considered decision, and where does it lead to? We cannot grope in the dark like blind men. We should adopt a way with open eyes. Nothing can be more absurd than to chalk out a way, then refuse to tread upon it.

We gave Britain fullest opportunity to take us with her, but she stubbornly refused to do so. We were forced to decide not to participate in this Imperialistic War. If our present stand is such that it "embarrasses" her (in the words of Gandhiji); or in your words it is against the *Shaan* of India – there can be no remedy to it. We are not responsible for it, it lies with the imprudent vanity of the British Government.

You say that we should not launch Satyagraha at this moment. But, what do you mean by Satyagraha? Would be a new declaration of war, which the Congress has yet to formulate? The war of the Congress is nothing but to stop any help in the War. This checking process has not yet been carried onward from a certain limit in actual practice. It is inevitable to carry it further on in future. I would automatically take the form of Civil Disobedience, because of the existence of War ordinances, and individual arrests.

If your moral Philosophy be taken to be correct in religion to the dignity of India, it will mean only one thing, *i.e.*, Ramgarh decision was absolutely against the honour and dignity of India.

You tell further on in this letter about our future attitude if some form of agreement is reached with the Government. You say: "Even if all this is agreed to (*i.e.* Independence, Self-determination, and Constituent Assembly with adult franchise) it does not follow that we throw our main power into the War."

"But if it does not follow, why should we hope that British Government would give us all that we ask for? Surely, she can grant all these things reluctantly, if forced to do so. But there is no question of using force at this juncture, when even the use of moral force of Satyagraha seems to be against the "dignity" of India.

I do not understand how this confused and illogical conception could find a way to your mind. You, least of all, are not expected to think in such a way.

I hope your stay in Lahore will be fully helpful to its activities.

I have received a telegram of Sikander Hayat today, a copy of which has probably been sent to you also. I have wired in reply that the responsibility of the present situation lies not on us, but on the British Government.

Yours sincerely,
A.K. Azad

J.L. Nehru
C/O Dr. Khan Saheb,
Ex-Premier,
Peshawar

1. Dr. Rajendra Prasad.
2. Mr. Asaf Ali, then a member of C.W.C.

Document 69

LETTER FROM PANDIT JAWAHAR LAL NEHRU TO MAULANA AZAD

Bombay,
July 1, 1940

Dear Mr. President,

I write to inform you that the fourth sessions of the National Planning Committee concluded yesterday. During these sessions we considered the reports of several additional sub-committees and passed resolutions on them. The position is that we have considered reports, final or iterim, of over twenty sub-committees. Seven sub-committees have still to report to us and some reports which have only partly been considered will have to be more fully considered later. Among the reports that require consideration are those on crop planning, public health, technical education, trade and women's role in planned economy.

Our work has grown more and more intricate and comprehensive as we have proceeded with it. There is much to be done but we are gradually approaching the end of our labours. We have to finish the sub-committees stage before very long and then to proceed to the drafting of the report of the National Planning Committee. This task will be a heavy and difficult one.

Our present programme is to have another session of the Planning Committee in the last week of August next. During the sessions we shall deal with some more sub-committees of the National Planning Committee is likely to be a big document and it will require great care in its drafting. It will have to be preceded by a careful collation of our previous decisions and then an attempt to put forward a picture of planned activity in India. This drafting of the final report is likely to take to three months. This means that it will not be ready for final consideration before the end of November. After that this draft report will have to be circulated among the members and we shall later have to consider it formally and to adopt it. So far as I can see this final consideration cannot take place before the middle of December. At the earliest, therefore, the report cannot be passed before the end of December. It will then require revision to give it its final shape before it is presented to you. If this programme is adhered to, our report should be ready for presentation to you some time in January next, but it is difficult to fix a definite time-table.

I sent you a letter at the end of our third session in May last requesting you to be good enough to extend the time for the presentation of our report. I did not receive any reply to it but I presumed that you were agreeable to the proposal I had made. I would beg of you now to extend the time further to the extent suggested above.

After our report is presented to you considered by the Working Committee, it will have to be printed for public circulation. Should you so desire it, it may be printed at a somewhat earlier stage to facilitate its consideration by the Working Committee. We feel that all our sub-committees' reports should also be printed at some stage or other, as they have been presented to us, together with our resolutions on these reports. This volume of literature will be bulky and may run over several thousand pages. But I have no doubt that it will be of considerable value. The final decisions will have to be taken by the Working Committee. But it will certainly be worthwhile to place all the reports before the public to enable them to profit by the large amount of information that has been gathered together, and by the attempt made by us to coordinate it and bring it into a single picture of planned activity.

As I pointed out to you in my last letter, we have been considerably handicapped by our lack of sufficient funds. We are however carrying on our work in as economical a manner as possible. We are likely to have difficulties in the future and certainly we shall not have enough funds for the publication of the reports. This question does not arise immediately but I am keeping you informed of our position. Not much help is likely to be forthcoming in future from the provincial governments or states cooperating with us. Indeed many of these provincial governments have informed us that they cannot send us any contributions in the future. We realise that the extreme gravity of the international and national situation must fill your mind as well as the minds of the members of the Working Committee. It was even proposed to us by some of our members that we should postpone our work till this crisis was over. But a great majority of our members were strongly of opinion that our work must be carried on, so long as this is possible, and indeed that the international situation made it all the more incumbent on us to proceed with this work and to bring it to a successful conclusion. The problems we are facing in the Planning Committee are vital problems for India and it may well be that we shall have to solve them in the near future.

This present work of the Planning Committee must of necessity help greatly in the future consideration of these problems as well as in their solution. We have, therefore, proceeded with our work and intend to continue to do so.

Yours sincerely,
Jawaharlal Nehru

Document 70

TELEGRAM FROM MAULANA AZAD TO MR. JINNAH AS ON 4-7-1940

"I HAVE READ YOUR STATEMENT OF JULY 9. THE DELHI RESOLUTION OF THE CONGRESS DEFINITELY MEANS BY NATIONAL GOVERNMENT A COMPOSITE CABINET NOT LIMITED TO ANY SINGLE PARTY. BUT IS IT THE POSITION OF THE LEAGUE THAT SHE CANNOT AGREE TO ANY PROVISIONAL ARRANGEMENT NOT BASED ON TWO NATION SCHEME? IF SO PLEASE CLARIFY BY WIRE."

ABUL KALAM AZAD

Document 71

TELEGRAM OF MR. JINNAH TO MAULANA AZAD AS ON 4-7-1940

I HAVE RECEIVED YOUR TELEGRAM. I CANNOT RECIPROCATE CONFIDENCE. I REFUSE TO DISCUSS WITH YOU BY CORRESPONDENCE OR OTHERWISE AS YOU HAVE COMPLETELY FORFEITED THE CONFIDENCE OF MUSLIM INDIA. CANNOT YOU REALISE YOU ARE MADE A MUSLIM SHOW-BOY CONGRESS PRESIDENT TO GIVE IT COLOUR THAT IT IS NATIONAL AND DECEIVE FOREIGN COUNTRIES? YOU REPRESENT NEITHER MUSLIMS NOR HINDUS. THE CONGRESS IS A HINDU BODY. IF YOU HAVE SELF-RESPECT RESIGN AT ONCE. YOU HAVE DONE YOUR WORST AGAINST THE LEAGUE SO FAR. YOU KNOW YOU HAVE HOPELESSLY FAILED. GIVE IT UP!

Document 72

LETTER FROM PANDIT JAWAHAR LAL NEHRU TO MAULANA AZAD

16 July 1940

My dear Maulana,

I read the other day your explanation of the Working Committee resolution in which you stated that the resolution clearly meant full support in the war efforts. Also that every member of the Working Committee was unanimous about this. Rajendra Babu has also said something to this effect. My own recollection is somewhat different and I thought I had made it clear that I was not prepared to go so far. Indeed the words in the original draft were changed from war efforts to the country at my instance. I stated that it was conceivable that we might later have to take part in the rest of the war effort and therefore, I could not rule this out completely. But I was not prepared to commit myself to any such proposition at this stage. I thought this would be contrary to our previous decisions as also wrong tactics. I want to make this clear, as you have stated that every member of the Working Committee was unanimous. This would not represent attitude nor the deliberate change in the wording of the resolution.

Yours Sincerely,
Jawahar Lal

Document 73

LETTER FROM MAULANA AZAD TO PANDIT JAWAHAR LAL NEHRU

"The Mahal"
Nainital,

July 19, 1940

My dear Jawahar Lal,

Thanks for your letter of 15th instant. Please re-read my statement. I did not say that the resolution was unanimously passed, I have only explained the mental aspect of the resolution, saying that all were clear in their "minds" that in case the Indian demand is accepted, she (India) should participate in war. Accordingly the Statesman and others have taken the same meaning of the statement.

I shall be obliged if you do not issue any statement about it just at present, till we meet in Poona. I wish to have a detailed talk with you in this respect. It is a pity that we could not get such a chance in Delhi. I have received the copy of the letter from China.

Yours faithfully
A.K. Azad

Document 74

LETTER FROM PANDIT JAWAHARLAL TO MAULANA AZAD

August 4, 1940

My dear Maulana,

I have just returned from Bombay. I find in today's paper a statement that the Working Committee might meet towards the end of August or early in September. I hope the meeting will take place about the 26th as previously suggested. As I told, we have tried to fit in the Planning Committee's meeting with this date and have fixed it for the 30th August. This session of the Planning Committee is likely to last from the 30th August to the 8th September. I do hope that the Working Committee meeting will not conflict with these dates.

Ranjit Pandit has gone to the Frontier Province this morning in connection with volunteering. The situation in the Frontier, from reports received by me, is a difficult one and has to be handled very carefully. Abdul Ghaffar Khan's resignation from the Working Committee and the A.I.C.C. has naturally created a great deal of consternation in people's minds and confusion prevails as to where everybody is. The average Pathan does not understand the finer points of politics. He sees that Badshah Khan has resigned from various Congress Committees and he thinks there must be something wrong somewhere. This applies to Khudai Khidmatgars especially.

There is likely to be trouble on the border. In fact there has been trouble. It appears that the Faqir of Ipi wants to assume the offensive on a large scale. We have heard about this Faqir of Ipi for a long time But I came across not so much about him. Not even Khan Sahib. He needs a great deal of watching.

Under the circumstances, I think it will be definitely better for you to invite Dr. Khan Sahib to join the Working Committee of course through Abdul Ghaffar Khan. Not to do so may lead to further complications.

According to your advice I have written to Ceylon people welcoming their suggestion. I think this matter might be placed before the Working Committee at their next meeting.

Yours sincerely,
Jawaharlal Nehru

Document 75

LETTER FROM LINLITHGOW TO MAULANA AZAD

Ootacamund,
August 4, 1940

Dear Maulana Sahib,

1. You will be aware that I have in the last few weeks been in contact with various political leaders, including Mr. Gandhi, in regard to the Indian political situation. I have, I need not say, informed His Majesty's Government of the results of my discussions with the various leaders concerned; and I am glad to say that I have in the result been authorised to make the statement of which I now enclose an advance copy. That statement will appear in the morning papers of Thursday, 8th August, and I would ask that until its appearance it should be treated as for your entirely secret and personal information.

2. As you will see, I have been authorised to invite a certain number of representative Indians to Join my Executive Council. I have been authorised further to establish a War Advisory Council which would meet at regular intervals and which would contain representatives of the Indian States and of other interests in the national life of India as a whole. I trust sincerely that the Indian National Congress will feel able to join with me in the Central Government and in the War Advisory Council: and I should welcome it if you could let me have a very early answer on that point, if possible not later than the 21st of August.

3. I readily conceive that it might be convenient for you to discuss this matter further with me before you send me a formal reply on behalf of the Indian National Congress. I shall, as at present arranged, be in Poona from 6th to 11th August, and in Bombay from 11th to 14th August, and I hope to reach Delhi on my way back to Simla on 20th August. I shall be very glad to see you and any friend whom you may care to bring with you at any of these places at any time convenient to you, should you desire to pursue the matter as I have suggested in conservation before sending me a more formal reply to this invitation.

Perhaps you would be good enough to let me know whether you would see advantage in this, and if so what date and time would be convenient to you. I would only add that I am, as you will, I know, understand, anxious that effect should be given with as little delay as possible to the decisions of His Majesty's Government: and that I am concerned, to announce the personnel of the expanded Executive Council by the end of August, and of the War Advisory Council at the latest by about the middle of September, but in any event with as little delay after the announcement of the personnel of the expanded Executive Council as practicable.

Yours sincerely,
Linlithgow

Document 76

LETTER FROM MAULANA AZAD TO PANDIT JAWAHAR LAL NEHRU

19-A, Ballygunje, Circular Road,
Calcutta,
August, 5th 1940

My dear Jawaharlal,

I reached here yesterday from Wardha, and hope you have also reached Allahabad by now.

I am writing this letter for two things:

You might remember that we had decided at Poona that Babu Rajendra Prasad should report to the next Working Committee after consultation and due deliberation about the critical situation of the Sugar Factories. But it has become rather difficult owing to the illness of Rajendra Babu. Not only his old ailment has recurred, but along with it he is suffering from fever. It had not left him up to the time of my departure from Wardha, and the doctor feared an attack of Pneumonia. I hope he will recover soon, but I do not think he would be able to undertake this work so soon. He is advised to take at least one month's complete rest, which is indeed very necessary. Under the circumstances we should think out some other method for the above-mentioned work.

It there be no hindrance to do so, I would request you to give some time for this work. Both groups of the Sugar Factory Syndicate are to be consulted. After which, some solution may be evolved on behalf of the Congress. Dr. Katju[1] and Mahmood[2] can supply necessary information to you. Moreover you are already in possession of facts beforehand. If you would not give time, there is none amongst the members of the Working Committee who would do the needful in this matter. I would, then, be forced to undertake this work, and you know that I do not have appropriate temperament for such business.

The second thing is that I wish to go to Allahabad for a few days, and spend some time for the office directly.

Please let me know where you are staying in Allahabad or going to Cawanpore. I would not like to disturb your engagement. However, if you are staying on in Allahabad these days, I may go there presently; otherwise I may do so after a few days.

I had finished the letter when I came to know that the Governments of Bihar and U.P. have again recognised the Sugar Syndicate. The Government control of the prices has also been decided.

I think that perhaps it is not much necessary for us to consider the matter, after this action of the Governments.

Yours sincerely,
A.K. Azad

---

1. Dr. Kailashnath Katju.
2. Mr. Syed Mahmood.

Document 77

LETTER FROM JAWAHAR LAL NEHRU TO MAULANA AZAD

Allahabad,
August 7, 1940

My dear Maulana,

I have just received your letter of the 5th.

About the sugar industry, I wrote to Rajendra Babu fully on the subject giving my views only a few days ago. But, as you say, after the action the government has taken, we need not take any further steps just now.

I wrote to you yesterday about the new government order regarding volunteering. It was not my desire to issue a statement on the subject but there is so much confusion and so many people come to me about it that I am issuing the enclosed statement.

You will be welcome in Allahabad whenever you come. My programme is: 11th Cawnpore, 14th Lucknow, and possibly the 15th, 16th Benares. I hope to be back in Allahabad on the 17th and to stay on here till the Working Committee.

Yours sincerely,
Jawahar Lal Nehru

Document 78

TELEGRAM OF MAULANA AZAD TO LORD LINLITHGOW

CALCUTTA,

AUGUST 8, 1940

HIS EXCELLENCY VICEROY
VICEROY'S CAMP

THANKS FOR YOUR EXCELLENCY'S LETTER OF AUGUST FOURTH AND ADVANCE COPY OF DECLARATION RECEIVED LAST EVENING STOP I AM THANKFUL FOR INVITATION TO SEE YOU STOP I WOULD HAVE READILY AVAILED OF PLEASURE OF MEETING YOUR EXCELLENCY BUT WHEN HIS MAJESTY'S GOVERNMENT HAVE ALREADY THOUGHT FIT TO ANNOUNCE A DEFINITE LINE OF ACTION MAY I ASK HOW FAR THERE STILL REMAINS A CHANCE OF USEFULNESS OF FURTHER DISCUSSION.

ABUL KALAM AZAD

Document 79

LETTER FROM THE ASSISTANT SECRETARY TO THE GOVERNOR OF BENGAL, GOVERNMENT HOUSE, CALCUTTA TO THE CONGRESS PRESIDENT CONVEYING H.E. THE VICEROY'S TELEGRAM

August 10, 1940

Dear Maulana Sahib,

I have been asked to send you the following telegram which we have received for you from His Excellency the Viceroy, to whom your Calcutta address is not known:

> Your telegram of 8th August STOP Policy of His Majesty's Government is set out in my statement and it is my hope that within its terms Indian National Congress will as indicated in my letter to you of 4th August feel able to join with me in the Central Government and in the War Advisory Council STOP. As my letter makes clear I should be very glad to see you with any friend whom you may care to bring with you should you desire to pursue the matter in conversation before sending me a more formal reply to my invitation and if you see advantage in this I would be grateful if you would telegraph to let me know as soon as possible date and place which you suggest STOP. My own movements remain as described in my letter to you of 4th August.

Yours sincerely,

Asstt. Secretary
to the Governor

Document 80

TELEGRAM FROM MAULANA AZAD TO THE VICEROY

CALCUTTA,

AUGUST 10, 1940

HIS EXCELLENCY VICEROY
CAMP POONA

THANKS FOR YOUR EXCELLENCY'S TELEGRAM RECEIVED THROUGH GOVERNMENT HOUSE STOP I DO NOT FIND ANY MEETING GROUND FOR CONGRESS IN THE TERMS OF THE DECLARATION OF AUGUST EIGHT STOP. APART FROM OTHER FUNDAMENTAL QUESTIONS THERE IS NOT EVEN ANY SUGGESTION FOR NATIONAL GOVERNMENT STOP UNDER THE CIRCUMSTANCES I AM UNABLE TO FIND ANY SCOPE FOR FURTHER DISCUSSION STOP CALLING WORKING COMMITTEE EIGHTEENTH TO CONSIDER AND DECIDE.

ABUL KALAM AZAD

Document 81

'LETTER FROM THE CONGRESS PRESIDENT TO H.E. THE VICEROY'

Calcutta,
August 11, 1940

Dear Lord Linlithgow,

I had received your Excellency's letter of August 4 on the evening of August 7. As it was necessary to call the Congress Working Committee as soon as possible, and to consider any other thing which might be necessary before calling it, I thought it advisable to reply your Excellency's letter telegraphically. Accordingly I sent the following telegram:

"I received your Excellency second telegram through the Government House Calcutta on August 10, in reply to which I sent the following telegram on the same day.

"I would assure you that it would always be a pleasure to me to pay a visit to your Excellency. When I found that our discussion could not go beyond the terms laid down by the declaration of August 8, I felt that I could not find my way for further discussion."

Yours sincerely,
A.K. Azad

Document 82

LETTER FROM THE CONGRESS PRESIDENT TO H.E. THE VICEROY

Camp : Wardha,
August 19, 1940

Dear Lord Linlithgow,

As I informed your Excellency in my telegram from Calcutta of the 10th August, I convened a meeting of the Congress Working Committee for the 18th August to consider the statement made on behalf of the British Government. The Committee gave their careful consideration to this statement as well as to the amplification of it in the British Parliament.

The Working Committee will express their views in the course of the next few days dealing with this matter more fully, but meanwhile, I may inform you that the Committee have read the statements embodying the British Government's decisions and attitude in regard to India, with deep regret. These are totally at variance with the proposals last put forward by the Congress at Poona and with the objective of the Congress. The Working Committee are of opinion that they cannot associate themselves in anyway with these proposals.

As I ventured to say in my telegram to you, I would have gladly availed myself of the opportunity to meet you and discuss the whole question. But your letter and your wire made it clear that the discussion as to take place within the rigid framework of your announcement which was wholly inadequate for the Congress purpose. Moreover, your letter had left it to me to decide whether I should see you before coming at a final decision. As I did not consider it necessary to trouble you about minor matters, I decided to forego the pleasures of meeting you.

I shall be grateful if you will kindly let me know if you have any objection to my releasing our correspondence to the press.

Yours sincerely,
A.K. Azad

Document 83

TELEGRAM FROM MAULANA AZAD TO C. RAJGOPALACHARIER

BAJAJWADI, WARDHA,

23-8-40

PLEASE REFER WORKING COMMITTEE RESOLUTION SUGGESTING MEETING MEMBERS PROVINCIAL ASSEMBLY EARLY ACTION THROUGH SPEAKER WRITING.

ABUL KALAM AZAD

Document 84

LETTER FROM MAULANA AZAD TO EX-PRIME MINISTERS

Camp : Wardha,
August 23, 1940

Dear friend,

I should like to draw your attention to the Working Committee's two resolutions in regard to the British Government's recent proposals. The Committee have rejected these proposals and a very grave situation has arisen. The Committee have suggested, among other things, that the members of the Provincial Assemblies should meet to consider these proposals and the situation that has arisen. I would request you therefore, to take early steps to have such a meeting, which should be convened by the speaker. At this meeting all the members, including non-Congress members should be invited. The resolution or resolutions to be considered should be on the lines of the Working Committee's resolution. In addition, it is important that the constitutional aspect of the suppression of the Provincial Legislatures preventing them from functioning and the carrying on of autocratic government without consulting them should be emphasised. It may be stated that any decisions or action taken by an autocratic government are not binding on the Legislatures or the people.

We shall endeavour to send you a draft resolution for your considerations.

Please note that the A.I.C.C. is meeting in Bombay on September 15 and the meeting of the members of the Assembly should not conflict with this.

Yours sincerely,
A.K. Azad
President

Document 85

LETTER FROM MAULANA AZAD TO EX-PRIME MINISTERS

Calcutta,

27-8-40

To,

The Ex-Prime Ministers,
and Members of Assemblies,

Dear friends,

I have already drawn your attention to the recent resolutions passed by the Working Committee and suggested to you that a meeting of all members of the Assembly might be summoned at an early, through the Speaker. I now enclose two draft resolutions for your consideration. These drafts indicate generally the type of resolutions that might be put before the meeting. You are at perfect liberty to make any changes in them which you may consider necessary.

Yours sincerely,
A.K. Azad

Document 86

LETTER FROM DR. RAJENDRA PRASAD TO MAULANA AZAD

Camp Wardha,
13th October '40

My dear Maulana Sahib,

You have seen the statement of Sir Sikandar Hayat published in the papers which we got this morning. There is a direct suggestion that the Congress should have consultation with the Muslim League regarding the Communal question and come to an agreement with it. It is a public invitation. You also know that our suggestion for an enquiry by an impartial judge into the allegations against Congress Ministries has been rejected by Mr. Jinnah who has practically barred the door for the present at any rate. I should like to have your views in the matter. I had a talk with Mahatmaji. He is of opinion that I should write to Sir Sikandar Hayat asking him for definite suggestions and pointing out to him that Mr. Jinnah has practically, barred the door at present. But Mahatmaji has said that I should first consult you and get your advice in the matter.

I am leaving this evening and shall be staying at Benaras on the 15th, 16th October with Babu Shivaprasad Gupta, Sevauptan, Benaras Hindu University, Benares and reaching Patna on the 19th. I shall be obliged for an early reply.

Yours sincerely,
Rajendra Prasad

Document 87

A.I.C.C. STATEMENT WITH MAULANA AZAD AS PRESIDENT

The Working Committee issued the following statement at Wardha on the 13th of October 1940.

The Working Committee met at the instance of Mahatma Gandhi and listened to the account of his talks with the Viceroy and the plan of campaign insofar as he has been able to envisage it. The Working Committee approve of what he has done, and repeat the instructions given to Congressmen and Congress Committees by the A.I.C.C. at its last meeting in Bombay that they should give him the fullest possible co-operation in all that he may require or expect them to do.

Document 88

A.I.C.C. RESOLUTION WITH MAULANA AZAD AS PRESIDENT

The following resolution was passed by the A.I.C.C. at Bombay on the 16th of October 1940.

The All India Congress Committee has given its careful attention to the events that have taken place since its last meeting held in Poona on July 27, 1940, and to the resolutions passed by the Working Committee at Wardha in August last. The Committee approves of and endorses these resolutions.

In order to end the deadlock in India and to promote the national cause, in co-operation with the British people, the Working Committee, even at the sacrifice of Mahatma Gandhi's co-operation, made a proposal to the British Government in their Delhi Resolution of July 7th which was subsequently approved by the A.I.C.C. at Poona. This proposal was rejected by the British Government in a manner which left no doubt that they had no intention to recognise India's independence, and would if they could continue to hold this country indefinitely in bondage for British exploitation. This decision of the British Government shows that they will impose their will upon India, and their recent policy has further shown that they will not even tolerate free expression of public opinion in condemnation of their associating India in the War against Germany, against the will of a vast body of the people of India, and of exploiting her national resources and man-power for this purpose.

The All India Congress Committee cannot submit to a policy which is a denial of India's natural right to freedom, which suppresses the free expression of public opinion, and which would lead to the degradation of her people and their continued enslavement. By following this policy the British Government have created an intolerable situation, and are imposing upon the Congress a struggle for the preservation of the honour and the elementary rights of the people. The Congress is pledged under Gandhiji's leadership to non-violence for the vindication of India's freedom. At this grave crisis in the movement for national freedom, the All India Congress Committee therefore, requests him to guide the Congress in the action that should be taken. The Delhi resolution, confirmed by the A.I.C.C. at Poona which prevented him from so doing, no longer applies. It has lapsed.

The A.I.C.C. sympathise with the British people as well as the peoples of all other countries involved in the War. Congressmen cannot withhold their admiration for the bravery and endurance shown by the British nation in the face of danger and peril. They can have no ill-will against them, and the spirit of Satyagraha forbids the Congress from doing anything with a view to embarrass them. But this self-imposed restraint cannot be taken to the extent of self-extinction. The Congress must insist on the fullest freedom to pursue its policy, based on non-violence. The Congress has however no desire at the present moment to extend non-resistance, should this become necessary, beyond what is required for the preservation of the liberties of the people.

In view of certain misapprehensions that have arisen in regard to the Congress policy of non-violence, the A.I.C.C. desire to state this afresh, and to make it clear that this policy continues, notwithstanding anything contained in previous resolutions which may have led to these misapprehensions. This Committee firmly believes in the policy and practice of non-violence not only in the struggle for Swaraj, but also, insofar as this may be possible of application, in free India. The Committee is convinced, and recent world events have demonstrated, that complete world disarmament is necessary, and the establishment of a new and juster political and economic order, if the world is not to destroy itself and revert to barbarism. A free India will, therefore, throw all her weight in favour of world disarmament and should herself be prepared to give a lead in this to the world. Such lead will inevitably depend on external factors and internal conditions, but the state would do its utmost to give effect to this policy of disarmament. Effective disarmament and the establishment of world peace by the ending of national wars, depend ultimately on the removal of the causes of wars and national conflicts. These causes must be rooted out by the ending of the domination of one country over another and the exploitation of one people or group by another. To that end India will peacefully labour, and it is with this objective in view that the people of India desire to attain the status of a free and independent nation. Such freedom will be the prelude to the close association with other countries within a comity of free nations for the peace and progress of the world.

Document 89

LETTER FROM PANDIT JAWAHAR LAL NEHRU TO MAULANA AZAD

October 18, 1940

My dear Maulana,

You may have noticed a message that appeared in the *Hindusthan Standard* from Wardha in which it was stated that you had offered to resign. In the *Leader* today there is another message which I am sending you. This is patently false. I wanted to tell you that no word of mine here or in Wardha to anyone could possibly lead him to come to any such conclusion. In fact I have said nothing at all about this matter to anyone. I did not mention it to the members of the Emergency Committee who were present at Wardha, and in fact met no pressman except Shiva Rao with whom I did not discuss any internal politics.

I issued a brief message yesterday which I enclose. It is just possible that I may issue something more in view of the misstatements in the press.

I am leaving tomorrow morning for a five or six days tour. My programme is: October 18th Pratapgarh, 19th Rae Bareli, 29th Sultanpur, 21st Fyzabad, 22nd Barabanki, 23rd Lucknow, 24th back in Allahabad.

Probably I shall leave Allahabad again on the 25th night. 26th Farrukhabad, 27th Mainpuri, 28th Etah, 29th back in Allahabad.

During these tours I shall be going to rural areas and returning in the evening to the headquarters of the districts where I spend the night. I intend spending a few days in Allahabad during Diwali and Id and then to go out again, probably to Meerut and other places in the north.

All this is of course subject to developments. I am inclined to thinking that these developments will be quicker than I imagine.

Yours sincerely,
Jawahar Lal Nehru

Document 90

LETTER FROM PANDIT JAWAHAR LAL NEHRU TO MAULANA AZAD

October 24, 1940

My dear Maulana

At my suggestion, Kripalani[1] has sent you a telegram requesting you to agree to an extension of the period of making Congress members this year. I hope you will agree to this for many reasons. Just after Ramzan and Diwali, will be the best time for making Congress members. But the chief reason is that people should have some definite work like this to do during the next few weeks.

You will remember that I told you that I had written to Mahmud from Wardha. On my return here today I found that Mahmud had been here for the last four days. He had not received my letter yet or any other during the last 12 days as he had been living in a remote village.

I had a talk with him about many matters. He denied vehemently having made any suggestion, direct or indirect, to the Muslim League people. The very idea seemed to shock him. He said that he had casually met Khaliquazzaman and Jinnah at Brelvi's place just before he left Bombay. Khaliq[2] suggested to him that the Congress should agree to accept the Viceroy's proposals. Mahmood[3] in reply said that this was impossible. This was all the talk he had with him, and he met nobody else and did not write to anybody in regard to the communal or political question. He mentioned to me that both Khaliq and Nawab Ismail[4] had met Bhulabhai[5] twice at the latter's house. What talk they had, he did not know.

I asked Mahmood also if he had in any way mentioned that Gandhiji at one time intended having a fast. I asked this question as Bapu suggested that Mahmood had told some people about this. Mahmood expressed the greatest astonishment and definitely and categorically denied having said anything even casually, or whispered anything on this subject to anyone. The very idea of his doing so painted him.

I mention these two definite facts to you as I think you ought to know them. I think that in these two matters Mahmud must be believed. About other matters he told me that it was true that he had been feeling completely unnerved largely owing to physically ill health, I shall probably have further talks with him.

You need not worry about my accident. It was a very minor one and I am quite well.

I am sending a copy of this letter to Gandhiji.

Yours affectionately,
Jawaharlal Nehru

---

1. Aharya Jivatram Bhagwan Das Kripalani.
2. Chowdhary Khaliquzzaman.
3. Mr. Syed Mahmood.
4. Nawab Ismail Khan.

Document 91

LETTER FROM PANDIT JAWAHAR LAL NEHRU TO MAULANA AZAD

October 24, 1940

My dear Maulana,

I enclose a telegram[1] which I received from Shaukat Ullah Ansari yesterday, at Lucknow. The telegram reached me late as I was touring. It is too late to take any effective action and in any event I do not know what effective action we can take. Still it might be worthwhile for you to send a letter to the Swiss Consul. You could say that you had received a cable from Iqbal Schedai in Switzerland to the effect that he had been ordered to go out of Switzerland. His going out meant necessarily his going to either Italian or German occupied territory and this was bound to lead him to a great deal of trouble. You hoped that the Swiss Government would be good enough to consider the case and not to take this unfortunate step against an Indian.

You need not say anything about the date mentioned or anything else about the man in question.

Iqbal Schedai as a boy took part in the Hajrat from India about 1920. Since then he has been living in Europe, in Italy, France and Switzerland. I believe has also got married there. I met him for the first time in 1926 and since then I have seen him occasionally during my visits to Europe. I cannot say much about him or hold myself responsible for him. But a non-committal letter from you to the Swiss Consul, as suggested above, would do no harm and might possibly do some good.

Yours affectionately,
Jawaharlal Nehru

---

1. Not included.

Document 92

LETTER FROM PANDIT JAWAHAR LAL NEHRU TO MAULANA AZAD

October 25, 1940

My dear Maulana,

I am glad to learn that you are getting over your indisposition. So far as I am concerned, I am quite well.

Yesterday, on arrival here, I received a letter from Bapu asking me if I was in general agreement with what he was doing. If so, to write to him, presumably so that he might instruct me accordingly. It was a difficult matter for me to deal with in a telegram. Ultimately, however, I wired to him briefly 'Agree generally'. I wrote to him somewhat more fully.

I do not think there is any purpose in my staying back. And so I have informed Bapu.

About the Working Committee meeting, I do not think that any useful purpose will be served by all of us going there. Perhaps if you went and conferred with Gandhiji it would be enough. But this is for you to decide.

If you intend holding a Committee meeting in Wardha early in November, this might suit the Ceylon people who could like to get there on the 10th or thereabouts. I suppose the meeting would be after Id. We have a function in Allahabad on the 5th November which I should not like to miss.

Personally I think it would be a good thing if you and I met the Ceylon delegation in Allahabad at some leisure. In Wardha everything is so rushed. Later they could go to Wardha and meet Gandhiji and the others. Even if a Working Committee meeting is held in Wardha it would be desirable for us to meet the Ceylon people in Allahabad. I have had a very long memorandum prepared on India and Ceylon by our Foreign Office and overseas Department. This deals with the question, historically, culturally, economically, *etc.*

So far as the China Mission is concerned, there is no point in its going to Wardha to meet the Working Committee. In fact this will be undesirable and they will not like it. They have come here to meet individuals and not organisations. I am helping them in drawing up their programme and I proposed to the Consul-General in Calcutta that I am prepared to send Dr. B.V. Keskar of our Foreign Department to help in making up the programme. This programme appears to be a lengthy one and includes a visit to Kashmir, Ajanta and Ellora. I have written to Sir Akbar Hydari and am writing to some people in the Kashmir Government. In other places we shall get into touch with our friends. It may be worthwhile for Keskar to accompany the Chinese Mission.

I have today received a cheque for Rs. 500 from the Scindia Steam Navigation Company for the *Hindustan*. I do not know however how long these papers will continue. I agree with you that so far as we can, we should keep the *National Herald* going. I have just heard that Gandhiji has stopped *Harijan* because of restrictions placed upon it.

Yours affectionately,
Jawahar Lal Nehru

Document 93

TELEGRAM OF THE PRESIDENT OF THE C.G.M.A. BOMBAY TO MAULANA AZAD REQUESTING HIM TO STOP THE FAST OF MAHATMA GANDHI IMMEDIATELY

6.11.40

COMMITTEE GRAIN MERCHANTS ASSOCIATION BOMBAY HAVE BEEN EXTREMELY PAINED TO RECEIVE REPORTS ABOUT FAST CONTEMPLATED BY MAHATMAJI STOP IN VIEW OF PRESENT STATE OF HIS HEALTH WHICH WILL NOT PERMIT EXERTION OF FAST AND OF DELICATE POLITICAL SITUATION WITHIN COUNTRY REQUIRING HIS ACTIVE ATTENTION AND GUIDANCE AT ANY MOMENT COMMITTEE BELIEVE SUCH STEP WILL GREATLY SHOCK PEOPLE OF THE COUNTRY WHOSE EYES ARE ALWAYS TURNED TO HIS LEADERSHIP ALONE IN CRITICAL TIMES STOP COMMITTEE EARNESTLY WISH THAT THE IDEA OF FAST SHALL BE DROPPED AT THE PRESENT MOMENTOUS JUNCTURE AND APPEALINGLY REQUEST HIM NOT TO UNDERTAKE PROPOSED FAST.

PRESIDENT

Document 94

LETTER FROM ACHARYA KRIPALANI TO MAULANA AZAD

Wardha,
18.12.1940

My Dear Maulana Saheb,

I was on tour in the province during the last fortnight. The tour had good effect on the masses.

I have decided to offer Satyagraha on the 21st December at Seva Gram Village. You will please let me know your programme as to when you are offering Satyagraha.

Smt. V.M. Jakatdar, M.L.A. from Bhandara (C.P.) had been here yesterday and saw Bapu. Disciplinary action was taken against him in Mishra affairs. He had been here to get permission from Bapu to offer Satyagraha, as is evident from his letter. He fulfils all other conditions of a Satyagrahi. Bapu informed him that unless the ban is lifted it was not possible for Bapu to permit Mr. Jakatdar to offer Satyagraha. At Bapu's instance Mr. Jakatdar had written a letter expressing his regret for the past indiscipline and requesting you to lift the ban. I am herewith enclosing a copy of the said letter. The original is with me. You will receive a letter from Mr. Jakatdar also. I have, therefore, to request you to please lift the ban on him so that he may offer Satyagraha. He is very keen in doing so and wants it to be done as early as possible. You will please inform me your decision by telegram. You will get my letter on the 20th and if you wire me immediately I may get it same evening, so that I may be able to inform Mr. Jakatdar before I go to Jail.

With kind regards,

Yours sincerely,
J.B. Kripalani

Maulana Abul Kalam Azad,
Calcutta

Document 95

LETTER FROM MAULANA AZAD TO DR. RAJENDRA PRASAD

Swaraj Bhawan,
Allahabad,

December 25, 1940

My Dear Rajendra Babu,

I have received today your letter of 21st December and I have received another letter also before it. The matters referred to in your last letter are themselves under my consideration for some time past, specially the matter of local bodies. The Secretary of Purulia Congress Committee had also come here with these questions, a few days ago. Undoubtedly it is necessary to have it clearly decided, having all the *pros* and *cons* of the problem in view. So far as other Provinces are concerned, they are including all such Congressmen in the lists sent to Mahatmaji,[1] who are in the local bodies. And they see the problem in the light of the fact that when we are in the thick of the struggle all other things are of secondary importance, and we should leave them to look after themselves.

However, the decision of all such matters lies with Mahatmaji. You did well in referring the matter to him.

I am leaving for Lahore today, from where I shall go to Wardha. I shall fully discuss the matter with Mahatmaji, and let you know the result.

The matter mentioned in your previous letter needs a detailed discussion. I shall try to write to you in detail during my journey as soon as I get leisure to do so.

You have written nothing about your health. I hope you are quite well by now.

Yours sincerely,
A.K. Azad

---

1. Mahatma Gandhi.

Document 96

LETTER FROM PARSHURAM SHARMA TO MAULANA AZAD

Shri Sanatan Dharam Pratinidhi Sabha, Punjab
Lahore,

December 13, 1941

Respected Maulana Sahib,

This Sabha is very much grateful to yourself and the Congress members of the Punjab Assembly to attend the session on the 11th instant when the Hindu Charitable and Religious Endowments Bill came up before the Assembly. The mover, however, on account of peculiar circumstances on the occasion was forced to get it postponed to the next session of the Assembly. I am confident that the said sub-committee will kindly allow the members to attend the Assembly at that time and to take part in the discussions. At this time the notice to the members to attend was very short. Hence the attendance could not be expected to be as full as possible. My request is that sufficient time be kindly given so that the members could attend conveniently. The Sabha will let you know beforehand of the date when the said Bill come up in the next session.

Once again I express my gratitude to you and other members of the Congress Parliamentary Sub-committee.

With regards.

Yours sincerely,
Parashuram Sharma
Secretary,
Mandir Sudhar Sub-committee

Maulana Abul Kalam Azad,
President, Indian National Congress,
Swaraj Bhawan,
Allahabad

Document 97

C.W.C. RESOLUTION, PASSED AT BARDOLI ON 23-12-1941 WITH MAULANA AZAD AS PRESIDENT

The Congress Working Committee passed the following resolutions:

> "The Working Committee have received a letter from Gandhiji and recognise the validity of the point he has raised and therefore relieve him or the responsibility laid upon him by the Bombay Resolution referred to by Gandhiji, but the Committee assure him that the policy of non-violence adopted under his guidance for the attainment of Swaraj and which has proved so successful in leading to mass awakening and otherwise will be adhered to by the Congress.
>
> "The Working Committee further assures him that it would like to extend its scope as far as possible even in a free India. The Committee hopes that Congressmen will tender him full assistance in the prosecution of his mission including the offering of Civil Disobedience.

The following instructions were issued by the Working Committee to Congressmen:

> "Recent developments in the world situation have brought war near to India's frontiers. This may lead to internal dislocation in certain parts of the country. There is a possibility of some cities being subjected to aerial attack."
>
> "Whatever dangers and difficulties might arise, real antidote to them is to remain cool and collected and on no account to give way to nervousness and excitement. Congressmen must remain at their posts and continue their service of the people wherever necessity arises. They should yield places of safety to those in greater need and be ready to render aid to those who may require it."
>
> "Congress can help and serve people in the difficult times ahead only if its organization is strong and disciplined and Congressmen individually and Congress Committees are able to common confidence in their respective localities."

"Congress Committees and Congressmen should, therefore, address themselves immediately to the task of strengthening organization and reviving and maintaining contacts with people in villages and towns. Every village should as far as possible, receive the message of Congress and be prepared to face such difficulties as might arise."

A statement was immediately issued by Rajendra Babu the Sardar, Kripalaniji and Dr. Ghosh pleading for the exercise of independent judgement at the ensuring meeting of the A.I.C.C.

Further light on the Bardoli Resolution was thrown by the summary of Gandhiji's speech published in the *Harijan*.

"The resolution," he revealed, is a mirror in which all groups can see themselves. The original was Jawaharlalji's draft, but it was referred to a sub-committee at whose hands it has undergone material changes.

"The Original had left no room for Rajaji to work. The sub-committee opened a tiny window for him to squeeze in. Jawaharlalji's opposition to participation in the war effort is almost as strong as mine, though his reasons are different. Rajaji would participate, if certain conditions acceptable to the Congress were fulfilled. The non-violent non-co-operators like Rajendra Babu have certainly a place, for, until the remote event takes place, non-violence rules supreme."

Document 98

LETTER FROM MAHATMA GANDHI TO MAULANA AZAD

Bardoli,
30.12.1941

Dear Maulana Sahib,

In the course of discussion in the Working Committee, I discovered that I had committed a grave error in the interpretation of the Bombay resolution. I had interpreted it to mean that the Congress was to refuse participation in the present or all war on the ground principally of non-violence. I found to my astonishment that most members differed from my interpretation and held that the opposition need not be on the ground of non-violence. On re-reading the Bombay resolution I found that the differing members were right and that I had read into it a meaning which its letter could not bear. The discovery of the error makes it impossible for me to lead the Congress in the struggle for resistance to war effort on grounds in which non-violence was not indispensable. I could not, for instance, identify myself with opposition to war effort on the ground of ill-will against Great Britain. The resolution contemplated material association with Britain in the war effort as a price for guaranteed independence of India. If such was view and I believed in the use of violence for gaining independence and yet refused participation in the effort as the price of that independence I would consider myself guilty of unpatriotic conduct. It is my certain belief that only non-violence can save India and the world from self-extinction. Such being the case, I must continue my mission whether I am alone or assisted by an organisation or individuals. You will, therefore, please relieve me of the responsibility laid upon me by the Bombay resolution. I must continue civil disobedience for free speech against all war with such Congressmen and others whom I select and who believe in the non-violence I have contemplated and are willing to conform to prescribed conditions.

I will not, at this critical period, select for civil disobedience those whose services are required to steady and help the people in their respective localities.

Yours sincerely,
M.K. Gandhi

Document 99

LETTER FROM PARASHURAM SHARMA TO MAULANA AZAD

Sanatan Dharam Pratinidhi Sabha, Punjab
Lahore,
Jan. 1, 1942

Respected Maulana Sahib,

In continuation of this Office Letter No. 8649 of 13th December last I beg to say that the Hindu Charitable and Religious Endowment Bill is expected to come before the Assembly by the end of this month or in the beginning of February next.

You and the Congress Parliamentary Sub-committee was good enough to allow the Congress members to attend the session of the Assembly on the 11th December 1941 when the said Bill came up for discussion. But the time for the Congress members to attend was very short. They could not come in full force to meet the Opposing Party who were in larger numbers and for this reason the mover had to get it postponed.

Now when the Bill is expected to come up in this month I shall feel highly obliged if you and the Sub-committee (be) good enough to give permission beforehand to the Congress members to attend the Assembly on the day when the said Bill comes up for discussion.

This will avoid the adverse situation which appeared last time. I am confident that you will kindly issue instructions to the leader of the Congress Party just now so that we could request them to attend the particular session in time.

Thanking you in anticipation.

Yours very sincerely,
Parashuram Sharma
Secretary
Mandir Sudhar Sub-committee

Maulana Abul Kalam Azad Sahib,
President, Indian National Congress,
Bardoli

Document 100

CONGRESSMEN WILL RENDER FULL ASSISTANCE TO GANDHIJI IN THE PROSECUTION OF HIS MISSION INCLUDING THE OFFERING OF CIVIL DISOBEDIENCE: A STATEMENT OF MAULANA AZAD

3.1.42

The Working Committee have received the letter from Gandhiji and recognise the validity of the point he has raised and therefore relieve him of the responsibility laid upon him by the Bombay resolution referred to by Gandhiji. But the Committee assure him that the policy of non-violence adopted under his guidance for the attainment of Swaraj and which has proved so successful in leading to mass awakening and otherwise will be adhered to by the Congress. The Working Committee further assure him that it would like to extend its scope as far as possible even in free India. The Committee hope that Congressmen will render him full assistance in the prosecution of his mission, including the offering of civil disobedience.

A.K. Azad
President
Indian National Congress

Document 101

THE WORKING COMMITTEE'S DECISION AT BARDOLI ON 14-1-1942 WITH MAULANA AS PRESIDENT

A Report by M. Desai

The Working Committee of the Congress met for days-unconscionably long as the carping critic said but not too long for those who wanted to put themselves right with one another and with the world. From that point of view not a day was wasted, and Gandhiji had enough time to commune with himself and with his colleagues. I shall say nothing about the deliberations in the Working Committee – I have in fact neither the competence nor the right to do so. But I shall make an attempt to indicate broadly a few things that emerged from the discussions inside as well as outside and the talks that followed the decision of the Working Committee. Though the actual decision came to be made on the basis of the interpretation of the Bombay Resolution, what was of vital importance was the actual feeling in the minds of men. No matter how the Bombay Resolution was interpreted were we clear about certain fundamentals? Were we clear that the policy of non-violence that we had followed to the best of our ability for twenty years was no religious creed or for no religious purpose, but a wholly political method for the achievement of the political independence of India? Gandhiji had no doubt on the question. The next question was – could we at this critical hour in our nation's history give up that policy even for the sake of proffered freedom? "So far as I am concerned," says Gandhiji "even if I was given the utmost power conceivable, even if I was made the Viceroy of India today, would I ask the people of India to take up the sword to keep the Empire alive? I for one should feel that I was committing moral suicide in that I would be abandoning the faith of a lifetime, the faith which I had persuaded the Congress to accept for twenty years as a policy. The steady unflinching pursuit of that policy has brought us quite close to the achievement of the objective. Am I to abandon the very boat which has brough me quite close to the shore? Yudhishthira would not forsake his faithful dog and enter the gates of Heaven without him. For he knew that the Kingdom of heaven would be as naught to him without the dog, *i.e.*, his faith. Would the Arab (*i.e.* the Congress) given up towards the end of the journey the faithful steed (*i.e.* non-violence) that had made it possible for it to make that journey? It would be an act of betrayal of faithlessness on my part."

There is another question also. In his open letter to every Briton Gandhiji had advised him not to fight the enemy with the weapons of the enemy but to set an example to the world by abandoning violence and adopting intensive non-cooperation. He had advised the same course to the Abyssineans and the Czechs and the Poles. "Could I, when the war is at my door and when I am in the same predicament as they, forget the sovereign remedy I suggested to them and clutch at the method I have denounced and discarded? No matter what the country would say, what say, what should be the attitude of individual Congressmen who had sworn by the method of non-violence?"

He was clear that, if it was felt that we had committed a mistake, that it was worthwhile bargaining a principle for what seemed to be a richer gain, they should declare their conviction, and if and when the objective was gained, they should convert the whole of India into a recruiting ground, ask every man and woman to contribute his or her share in the war effort, and even extinguish themselves in so doing. What was needed was downright honesty. He at any rate had never conceived this possibility. If he knew that some day India would have to engage in a violent war in order to win Independence, he would long ago have addressed every youth to go in for military discipline, and he would not have placed tireless emphasis, day in and day out, on the various items of the constructive programme.

Document 102

LETTER FROM MAULANA AZAD TO PANDIT JAWAHAR LAL NEHRU

Calcutta,
January 22nd, 1942

My dear Jawaharlal,

I have now decided that I will reach Patna on the 30th January, and shall stay there up to the 1st or the 2nd February. Thus I can reach Allahabad on the morning of the 2nd or 3rd February. If you think it to be advisible, you may call a meeting of those members and workers of the Provincial Committee whose presence you deem necessary on the 3rd or the 4th February, in Allahabad.

Yours sincerely,
A.K. Azad

Pandit Jawaharlal Nehru,
Anand Bhawan
Allahabad

Document 103

LETTER FROM PANDIT JAWAHAR LAL NEHRU TO MAULANA AZAD

Allahabad,
January 24, 1942

My dear Maulana,

I returned from Benares today and received your letter. I note that you intend coming here on the 2nd or 3rd February. It is not clear how long you intend staying here. I should like you of course to meet as many of our provincial workers as possible. There is however one difficulty. A large number of them were made to come to Benares two days ago to meet Gandhiji. Some of them will be coming in the second week of February. In between they have been asked to start work immediately in their districts. It will thus be a little difficult for most of them to undertake a long journey again. Many cannot afford this, especially those living in the Northern and Western parts of the province who have to come a very long way. Meeting of District Congress Committees are being held in various districts and an attempt is being made to give a new impetus to our work.

I am therefore not very sanguine of many people being able to come here at short notice. Perhaps some people from the nearby towns like Lucknow, Cawnpore and Benares might be able to come. I am informing them and suggesting that they might come on the 3rd afternoon.

For my part I had intended remaining here for the next ten days or so. But I may have to go to an important gathering in Gorakhpur district of peasant cane-growers on the 31st of this month. On the 7th I shall go to Cawnpore for two or three days. Meanwhile I shall probably visit certain rural areas in the Allahabad District.

I should particularly like to know if you would be agreeable to addressing a public meeting in Allahabad during your visit here. We would greatly appreciate this and I am sure it would do a lot of good. Please send me a telegram to say if you are willing.

Kripalani[1] is not here. He has gone to Fyzabad district but he will come back within a few days.

Khan Bahadur Allahbux, the Sind Premier, arrived here today and is returning to Karachi tomorrow morning. We had a talk about his constitutional difficulties with the Governor and it seems to me that from every point of view he ought to take up a strong line. Even from a narrow constitutional interpretation he appears to be completely justified. The larger viewpoint, points to the same conclusion. He consulted Kailash Nath Katju and Dr. Tej Bahadur Sapru also. Both agreed that he was completely right and should not yield to the Governor. He hopes to meet you when you go north.

Yours faithfully,
Jawahar Lal Nehru

1. Acharya J.B. Kripalani.

Document 104

ALL INDIA CONGRESS WORKING COMMITTEE'S INSTRUCTIONS WITH MAULANA AZAD AS PRESIDENT

January 25, 1942

This meeting of the A.I.C.C. endorses the following instructions issued by the Working Committee and calls upon all Provincial and other Subordinate Congress Committees to give effect to them within their respective areas. The Provincial Congress Committees are authorised to supplement them wherever necessary. The Committee expects every member of an elective Congress Committee to devote him selectively to the execution of some item of this programme, and to send periodical reports of the work done by him to his Committee.

Recent developments in the world situation have brought war near to India's frontiers. This may lead to internal dislocation in certain parts of the country and there is a possibility of some cities being subjected to aerial attack. Whatever, dangers and difficulties might arise, the real antidote to them is to remain cool and collected and on no account to give way to nervousness and excitement, Congressmen must remain at their posts and continue their service of the people, wherever, necessity arises they should yield places of safety to those in greater need and be ready to render and to those who may require it.

The Congress can help and serve the people in the difficult times ahead only if its organisation is strong and disciplined and Congressmen individually and Congress Committees are able to command confidence in their respective localities. Congress Committees and Congressmen should therefore address themselves immediately to the task of strengthening the organisation and reviving and maintaining contacts with the people in the villages and towns. Every village should as far as possible, receive the message of the Congress and be prepared to face such difficulties as might arise.

The constructive programme adopted by the Congress, and explained from time to time by Gandhiji, is of particular importance at this juncture. It is meant act only to bring about unity among various groups, to remove disabilities which keep sections of the community backward and depressed, to promote self-reliance and the co-operative spirit among the people to increase production and have fairer distributions. The Working Committee therefore call upon Congress Committees and workers to further this programme intensively, and thus exercise a steadying and strengthening influence in times of dislocation and uneasiness.

During such times there is always a possibility of trouble being created by unsocial elements in the country. Two avoid the emergence of such a situation and to meet it when it arises, volunteers should be organised in both the urban and rural areas. Such organisations should be formed on the basis of strict non-violence, and it should always be remembered that the Congress adheres to this principle. These volunteers may co-operate with other organisations working for similar ends. This volunteer organisation is meant for rendering service to the couple both normally and in the event of possible internal commotion. It should therefore avoid conflict with the authorities.

Prices of commodities have already risen and are causing distress among the people and no adequate steps have so far been taken by the authorities to meet this situation. These tendencies are likely to be accentuated in the future, and dislocation of trade and transport, due to stress of war, may lead to scarcity of the necessaries of life as well as of many other things which are of everyday use. Big scale industries in other countries have suffered heavily on account of the war, and transport of goods has become difficult on account of military requirements. China has largely overcome these difficulties by a widespread development of village industries. India may have to face similar problems, and village and cottage industries afford a solution, desirable in itself, and more particularly, suited to the needs of the moment, such Industries can escape to a large extent the effects of dislocation of trade and transport. It is therefore necessary that this item of the constructive programme should be widely taken up and worked up with vigour and earnestness so that the countryside may be rendered, as far as possible, self-sufficient in regard to the necessaries of life. The Committee would especially recommend to the villagers the growing of food crops at least to cover the needs of the village and appeal to the grain dealers not to hold up stores for profit but to release them for consumption at fair prices.

In cases of emergency, when instructions are issued to the public by the authorities for the preservation of life and property and the

maintenance of public order, Congressmen should avoid conflict with the authorities. They should carry out such instructions, unless they are contrary to Congress directions.

Document 105

ALL INDIA CONGRESS WORKING COMMITTEE'S RESOLUTION WITH MAULANA AZAD AS PRESIDENT

(The Working Committee passed the following resolutions at its recent sittings at Bardoli. on 1.2.1942)

Present Situation

Fourteen months have elapsed since the Working Committee held their last meeting and during this period the world has fallen ever deeper into the abyss of war and rushed headlong towards self-destruction. The members of the committee have met again on their release from prison and given earnest though to all the national and international developments during fateful period of human history. The burden of guiding the Congress and the nation at this critical stage when old problems assume a new significance and war approaches the frontiers of India bringing new problems in its train, is a heavy one which the Committee can only shoulder worthily with the full co-operation of the people of India. The Committee have endeavoured to keep in view the principles and objectives for which the Congress has stood during these past many years and considered them in the larger context of world conditions and world freedom. The Committee are convinced that full freedom for the people of India is essential even, and more especially, in the present state of world turmoil, not only for India's sake but for the sake of the world. The Committee also hold that real peace and freedom can only be established and endure on the basis of world co-operation between free nations.

The Committee gave full expression to their attitude towards the War in their statement issued on September 14, 1939, wherein they condemned Nazi and Fascist aggressions and expressed their willingness to help the cause of freedom and democracy, provided the objectives of the war were clearly stated and acted upon in so far as was possible in the present. If freedom and democracy were these objectives, them they must necessarily include the ending of imperialism and the recognition of the independence of India. Subsequent pronouncements made on behalf of the British Government and their reactionary and oppressive policy made it clear that this

Government was determined to maintain and intensify its imperialist hold and exploitation of the Indian people. British policy was one of deliberate insult to Indian nationalism, of a perpetuation of unrestrained authoritarianism, and the encouragement of disruptive and reactionary elements. Not only has every offer made by the Congress for an honourable compromise been rejected, but public opinion voiced by organisation regarded as moderate has also been flouted.

The Congress was, therefore, compelled, in order to defend the honour and the elementary rights of the Indian people and the integrity of the nationalist movement, to request Gandhiji to guide the Congress in the action that should be taken. Mahatma Gandhi desires of avoiding embarrassment to his opponent as far as possible, especially during the perils and dangers of war, limited the Satyagraha movement which he started to selected individuals who conformed to certain tests he had laid down. That Satyagraha has now proceeded for over fourteen months and about twenty-five thousand Congressmen have suffered imprisonment while many thousands of other who offered Satyagraha in the Frontier Province and elsewhere were not arrested. The Committee desire to express their respectful appreciation of Gandhiji's leadership and of the response of the nation to it, and are of opinion that this has strengthened the people.

Throughout this period the attitude of the British Government has been hostile to Indian freedom and it has functioned in India as a completely authoritarian government, insulting the deeply cherished convictions and feelings of the people. Neither the professions of freedom and democracy, nor the perils and catastrophes that have come in the wake of war, have affected this attitude and policy, and such changes as have taken place have been for the worse.

The recent release of a number of political prisoners has no significance or importance, and the circumstances attending it, and official pronouncements made, make it clear that it is not connected with any change of policy. Large numbers of detenus, who are kept in prison under the Defence of India Act without trial and whose only offence seems to be that they are ardent patriots, impatient of foreign rule and determined to achieve the independence of the country, still remain in prison. Recent arrests of prominent persons and their treatment in prison also indicate that the old policy is being pursued as before.

While there has been no change in Britain's policy towards India, the Working Committee must nevertheless take into full consideration the new world situation that has arisen by the development of the war into a world conflict and its approach to India. The sympathies of the Congress must inevitably lie with the people who are the subject of aggression and who are fighting for their freedom. But only a free and independent India can be in a position to undertake the defence of the country on a national basis and be of help in the furtherance of the larger causes that are emerging from the storm of war. The whole background in India is one of hostility and of distrust of the British Government and not even the most far reaching promises can after this background nor can a subject India offer voluntary or willing help to an arrogant imperialism which is indistinguishable from fascist authoritarianism.

The Committee is therefore, of opinion that the resolution of the A.I.C.C. passed in Bombay on September 16, 1940, holds today and defines Congress policy still.

Document 106

LETTER FROM MAULANA AZAD TO PANDIT JAWAHAR LAL NEHRU

19-A, Bally Gunj,
Circular Road,
Calcutta,
February 27, 1942

My dear Jawahar Lal,

The Viceroy has announced to celebrate China day on the 7th of March. The Calcutta Radio informed me that you have given a message in this connection. They had come to record my message for broadcasting on the day. Our sympathy with China needs no further elucidation but would it be a proper way of expression to participate in the function fixed by the Viceroy for their own purpose? I do not think it to be so. I, therefore, could not give a message.

I thought of staying in Allahabad for a day for some office work, as well as to meet you. But you were detained in Calcutta, and then you had to go direct to Lucknow.

I may probably leave for Wardha on Monday. I could not attend the funeral of Jamuna Lalji[1], as the letter sent by Mahatmaji could not be delivered to me in time and I did not know it. Now I think that I should go to Wardha for condolence as soon as possible. And there I have to meet Gandhiji also.

There seems to be no immediate need of calling the working committee. It may be considered later on.

Rajendra Babu had come here yesterday. We had a detailed talk about the Bihar Congress Committee. I wish he could proceed with it with a firm hand. He has, however, agreed to accept my suggestions.

Yours sincerely,
A.K. Azad

Pandit Jawahar Lal Nehru,
Anand Bhawan,
Allahabad

---

1. Seth Jamuna Lal Bajaj.

Document 107

MAULANA AZAD'S APPEAL TO THE MEMBERS OF C.W.C.

19, Ballygunge, Circular Road,
Calcutta,
March 3, 1942

My dear friend,

Reuter's Agency says that the British Premier is going to make a statement about India shortly. We do not know what would be the nature of the statement. Whatever it may be, you would agree with me that considering the delicacy of the situation it is advisable to avoid expressing any opinion individually, and to wait for the meeting of the Congress Working Committee. The proper place to express our views would be the Committee itself.

Yours sincerely,
A.K. Azad
President I.N. Congress

Document 108

LETTER FROM PANDIT JAWAHAR LAL NEHRU TO MAULANA AZAD

Allahabad,

March 4, 1942

My dear Maulana,

Two or three days ago I sent you a letter. This was sent to Wardha, copy to Calcutta. I do not know if it has reached you, nor do I know where you are.

The more I think of it the more worried I am at our not having a meeting of the Working Committee for such a long time. All manner of new and complex problems are arising and we remain passive and do not give much corporate thought to them. We await something affecting us to happen. This seems a weak attitude. It is true that nothing has happened to affect our fundamental position or to make us think of varying it in any way. But quite apart from this, we should give thought to the ever-changing scene and think also of the future as it seems to unfold itself.

If I had known in time that you were going to Wardha, I would have attempted to go there myself. Not being sure I could not do this. Also because I thought that in any event we would have to go there soon. It seems to me very important that we should have full discussions with Gandhiji and our other colleagues at frequent intervals, or else there will be a tendency to interpret events in different ways and to pull in separate directions.

Yours very sincerely,
Jawaharlal Nehru

Document 109

LETTER FROM PANDIT JAWAHAR LAL NEHRU TO MAULANA AZAD

Allahabad,
March 5, 1942

My dear Maulana,

I am not sending you a telegram as it is difficult to say much in a few words.

Your idea of having an advisory committee is good, but a committee spread out all over India can seldom meet. Still it may occasionally meet to consider the problem as a whole. As for the appointment of such a committee, much depends on one's approach to the problem. That is, should there be more or less provincial representation or at any rate representatives from the principal parts of India? Though theoretically this will look well, again it will be difficult for them to meet.

One possible way of dealing with this matter is to zonal representatives who taken together form an advisory committee. In appointing zonal representatives, to some extent local or provincial people will have to be consulted, though this need not be always necessary.

Anyway a committee such as you suggest might be an improvement and would be helpful to Mrs. Kripalani. The names you have suggested are good. It is possible to suggest a few more names but it is difficult to pick and choose. Would not the presence of Sarojini Naidu on such a committee be desirable? Of course as a member of the Working Committee she need not join any such advisory committee and whenever necessary she can always be invited to the advisory committee and meetings.

My own conception of the women's branch of the A.I.C.C. is that it should collect all material relating to women's activities in India, it should keep in touch with all women's organisations in India, it should particularly keep in touch with such women's work as is being done by Congresswomen and through Congress organisations, it should send such suggestions as may be desirable for the coordination of these various activities, and it should issue special directions to provincial Congress committees in this behalf. It cannot undertake direct work of organisation, *etc.*

Again in the present crisis attention should not be given to long distant programmes but rather to the immediate need. Women should address themselves to the local programmes of self-defence and self-sufficiency as outlined by the Congress. Their work will be chiefly confined to women. It is very important that this approach be made to women as public morale depends greatly on how women feel and act. If they are given some work in their own local, they are less likely to give way to a feeling of helplessness and they will feel that they are parts of a larger cooperative enterprise. Immediate problems are arising in some places of molestation of women. This kind of thing is likely to increase as conditions deteriorate. To face this problem women can be of great help, for it is essentially a psychological problem. My own little experience has been that women are anxious to know what they can do at present and any lead given to them will yield results. I am all against treating women as helpless human beings who cannot look after themselves and who must run away from the danger zone. At any time this is bad policy and makes them even more helpless than they are. In present circumstances it is completely pointless as you cannot limit the danger zone. Any and every place may become the danger zone and even the privacy of a house will not be outside this zone. So the only way to tackle the problem is to make women realise that they have to and can face it and to prepare them mentally and otherwise for this.

My sister, Vijayalakshmi, is going to Delhi this evening and she will discuss this matter with Aruna Asaf Ali. I am also sending a copy of this letter to Mrs. Kripalani.[1]

As you know, my sister[2] is the President for this year of the All India Women's Conference and thus she as well as many other Congresswomen are functioning also through the Women's Conference. In some provinces, notably Gujarat, Congresswomen are controlling the women's Conference. It is desirable that every cooperation should be given, whenever possible, to the Women's Conference in doing the work which we think should be done. This may not be possible in all parts of India. Generally speaking a duplication of organisations will lead to waste of efforts and energy.

Yours sincerely,
Jawaharlal Nehru

1. Mrs. Sucheta Kripalani.
2. Mrs. Vijya Lakshmi Pandit.

Document 110

LETTER FROM MAULANA AZAD TO PANDIT JAWAHAR LAL NEHRU

Calcutta,
March 8, 1942

My dear Jawaharlal,

I had already replied your letter when I got your second letter. Previously I had thought that I might go to Wardha for two or three days, but the delicate situation of Bengal kept me back; and some intricate questions in connection with the Civil Protection could not be left behind unsolved. Now the C.W.C. is taking place on the 17th, and I am intending to leave for Wardha on the 11th or 12th instant. It would be useful if you could also reach Wardha two days before the 17th. I will let you know of my departure telegraphically.

Badsha Khan sent me several letters to issue a statement as promised at Wardha. After going into all the aspects of the matter, I had to admit that there is no other way but to fulfil his desire. Accordingly a statement has been given to the Press, which you might have seen. I do not know whether you had correspondence with him in the meantime.

Four or five days ago, a statement of Subhash Babu was broadcast from Berlin, and the next day it was announced that it might be heard in his own voice which had been recorded. I heard it. It was the voice of Subhas Babu. I think that probably it was not a record, he himself was speaking. But the broadcast from Tokyo was certainly a record. The sound of the movement of the record by means of electricity was clearly audible.

The Forward Bloc Ministers Santosh and Bannerji are much distressed here; they say that they have not the nearest connection with the Forward Bloc.

Yours sincerely,
A.K. Azad

Pandit Jawahar Lal Nehru,
Anand Bhawan,
Allahabad

Document 111

TELEGRAM FROM PSV. TO MAULANA AZAD

IMPORTANT

MAULANA ABUL KALAM AZAD
SEVAGRAM WARDHA

IN ACCORDING WITH PROCEDURE DESIRED BY SIR STAFFORD CRIPPS FOR OPENING CONVERSATIONS IT WOULD BE APPRECIATED IF YOU COULD ARRANGE FOR REPRESENTATIVES OF THE CONGRESS WHO IT IS HOPED WILL NOT EXCEED FOUR AND SHOULD PLEASE NOT EXCEED SIX IN NUMBER TO COME TO DELHI TO SEE SIR STAFFORD CRIPPS ON A NEAR DATE AFTER MARCH 25TH MUCH REGRETTED THAT NO MORE PRECISE DATE CAN BE SETTLED AT PRESENT MOMENT BUT THE EARLIEST POSSIBLE NOTICE WILL BE GIVEN TO YOU WHEN EXACT ARRANGEMENTS ARE KNOWN MEANWHILE WOULD YOU KINDLY LET ME KNOW NAMES OF PROPOSED REPRESENTATIVES AND WHERE YOU WILL BE STAYING MEANTIME.

PSV
NEW DELHI
18-03-1942

Document 112

TELEGRAM FROM MAULANA AZAD TO PSV

EXPRESS

PSV.

NEW DELHI 19.3.42

THANKS YOUR TELEGRAM IF SIR STAFFORD CRIPPS DESIRES PRELIMINARY INTERCHANGE VIEWS I SHALL GLADLY MEET HIM STOP MY COMMITTEE DO NOT CONSIDER IT NECESSARY TO SUGGEST ADDITIONAL NAMES STOP AM PROCEEDING LAHORE WHERE MY ADDRESS 21 A I KHAN ROAD TILL TWENTY-FOURTH STOP FROM TWENTY-FIFTH TO TWENTY-EIGHTH MARCH EXPECT TO BE AT ANAND BHAWAN ALLAHABAD LATER CALCUTTA

ABUL KALAM AZAD

Document 113

LETTER FROM MAULANA AZAD TO PANDIT JAWAHAR LAL NEHRU

Calcutta

23-03-42

My dear Jawaharlal,

We have created a Woman's Branch in the A.I.C.C. Office, but it is not enough. We have to do something more to create practical enthusiasm in the work. I wish to appoint an Advisory Committee, the members of which may devote their time in this work.

I have the following names in view:

Mrs. Pandit,[1] Miss Mirdulla,[2] Mrs. Asafali,[3] and Mrs. Iftikharuddin.[4]

Including Mrs. Kripalani[5] as the Secretary incharge, this committee would comprise of five members. Please wire your opinion, and if you have to suggest any more name, you should certainly do so.

Yours sincerely,
A.K. Azad

Pandit Jawaharlal Nehru,
Allahabad

---

1. Mrs. Vijaya Lakshmi Pandit.
2. Miss Mridulla Sarabhai.
3. Mrs. Aruna Asaf Ali.
4. Wife of Mr. Iftikharuddin, a Leading Congressman of Punjab and nearest friend of Pt. Nehru.
5. Mrs. Sucheta Kripalani.

Document 114

WORKING COMMITTEE'S RESOLUTION WITH MAULANA AZAD AS PRESIDENT

Allahabad
27.3.1942

Whereas, the British War Cabinet's proposals sponsored by Sir Stafford Cripps have shown up British imperialism in its nakedness as never before, the A.I.C.C. has come to the following conclusions:

There is an eternal conflict between Indian and British interests. It is natural that whatever Britain does is for her own defence. It follows that their notions of defence would also differ. The British Government has no trust in India's political parties. The Indian army has been maintained up till now mainly to hold India in subjugation. It has been completely segregated from the general population who can in no sense regard it as their own. This policy of distract still continues and is the reason why national defence is not entrusted to India's elected representatives, and India rendered incapable of defending herself.

India's participation in the war has not been with the consent of the representatives of the Indian people. It was purely a British act. If India were free she would wish to keep out of the war, her sympathies with victims of aggression notwithstanding. India would know also how to defend herself in the event of Japanese or any aggressor attacking India.

The plea that the British should remain in India for protecting the Indian Princes is wholly untenable. It is additional proof of their determination to maintain their hold over India. The Princes need have no fear from unarmed India.

The question of majority and minority is a creation of the British Government and would solve itself on their withdrawal.

For all these reasons the Committee appeals to Britain, for the sake of her own safety, for the sake of India's safety and for the cause of world peace to let go her hold on India even if she does not give up all Asiatic and African possessions.

India bears no enmity towards any foreign nation. India only desired freedom from all alien domination. In her fight for freedom the Committee is of opinion that India while welcoming universal sympathy does not stand in need of foreign military aid. Her past experience teaches her that it is harmful to India's interests and dangerous to the cause of India's freedom to introduce foreign soldiers in India. She therefore hopes that the British Government as also other foreign nations will remove their legions and henceforth stop their further introduction. They know full well that there is inexhaustible man-power in India which remains untapped on account of the policy of distrust of the Indian people by the British Government.

India will attain her freedom through her own strength and will retain it likewise. India having no quarrel with Japan or any other nation, the Committee hopes that Japan will not have any designs on India. But no response to her appeal the Committee would expect all those who look to Congress guidance to offer complete non-violent non-cooperation to the Japanese forces and not render any assistance to them.

We may not bend the knee to the aggressor nor obey any of his orders. We may not look to him for any favours nor fall to his bribes. But we may not bear him any malice nor wish him ill. If he wishes to take possession of our homes and our fields we will refuse to give them up even if we have to die in the effort to resist him. If he is attacked by disease or is dying of thirst and seeks our aid we may not refuse it.

In places where the British and Japanese forces are fighting our non-cooperation will be fruitless and unnecessary. Not to put any obstacle in the way of the British forces will often be the only way of demonstrating our non-cooperation with the Japanese. Neither may we assist the British in any active manner. Judging from their attitude, the British Government do not need any help from us beyond our non-interference. They desire our help only as slaves – a position we can never accept.

If, in spite of our non-violent resistance, any part of the country falls into Japanese hands we may not destroy our crops, water supply, *etc.*, if only because it will be our endeavour to regain them. The destruction of war material is another matter and may under certain circumstances be a military necessity. But it can never be the Congress policy to destroy what belongs to or is of use to the masses.

Direct non-cooperation against the Japanese forces will necessarily be limited. Its complete and lasting success as also the true building up of Swaraj depend on the millions of India wholeheartedly working the constructive programme. Without it the whole nation cannot rise from its age long torpor. Whether the British remain or not it is our duty always to wipe out unemployment to bridge the gulf between rich and poor, to banish communal strife, to exercise the demon of untouchability, to reform dacoits and save the people from them. If crores of people do not take a living interest in this nation building work, freedom in terms of the masses must remain a dream and unattainable by either non-violence or violence.

Document 115

AZAD'S TELEGRAMS TO FOUR DIFFERENT ADDRESSES

(EXPRESS)

(1) B.G. KHER
KHAR (BOMBAY SUB)

(2) RAVISHANKAR SHUKLA
RAIPUR

(3) BISWANATH DAS
CARE PROVINCIAL CONGRESS, CUTTACK

(4) SRIKRISHNA SINHA
PATNA

UNDERSTAND CRIPPS INVITED YOU STOP MAY INFORM HIM PRESIDENT CONDUCTING TALKS ON BEHALF OF CONGRESS AS DESIRED BY WORKING COMMITTEE STOP IF HE STILL WISH SEE YOU MAY MEET HIM AFTER MAKING POSITION CLEAR STOP ASCERTAIN HIS WISHES BEFORE STARTING.

ABUL KALAM AZAD

Swaraj Bhawan, Allahabad, March 27, 1942.

Document 116

LETTER FROM STAFFORD CRIPPS TO MAULANA AZAD

3, Queen Victoria Road,
New Delhi, 30.3.42

My dear Maulana Sahib,

I had the opportunity of a short talk with H.E. the Viceroy last night, during which he discussed with me his views as to the implementation of clause (e) of the draft declaration.[1]

It must be clearly understood that the final definition of the division of responsibilities between His Majesty's Government and the Government of India is as stated in paragraph (e) of the document. I propose to make the position as to this as clear as I can in my broadcast tonight.

The Viceroy would be prepared to consult with Indian leaders on this basis to see whether it were possible to designate an Indian to some office connected with the Government of India's defence responsibilities without in any way impinging upon the functions and duties of the Commander-in-Chief either in his capacity as supreme commander of the armed forces in India or as the member of the Executive Council incharge of Defence.

I give you this information as you put the question to me when last I had the pleasure of seeing you.

Yours sincerely,
Stafford Cripps

---

1. See Appendix.

Document 117

LETTER FROM CRIPPS TO MAULANA AZAD

3, Queen Victoria Road
New Delhi, 1.4.42

My dear Maulana Saheb,

I understand from the Hindu press that difficulties are still in the mind of Congress as to the question of the responsibility for the Defence of India.

I have done what I could to clarify this point but as I think it would be a tragedy if negotiations were to break down upon any misunderstanding of the position I should like to suggest that I should ask the Commander-in-Chief to meet yourself and Pandit Jawaharlal Nehru with myself in order that he may explain fully to you the technical difficulties of the situation and in order that you may make to him any suggestions you wish as to the division of responsibilities in this sphere of government. Unfortunately he is at the moment away at Calcutta but he is expected back on Saturday next at the latest (and possibly earlier). If you consider this a helpful suggestion – as I hope you will – I will ask him the moment he returns whether he will be prepared to attend such a meeting and I do not anticipate that there will be any difficulty about it.

I am sure you will realise that I do not want to be met with an impasse if there is any reasonable way out.

Yours sincerely,
Stafford Cripps

Maulana Abdul Kalam Azad,
Kucha Chelan
Delhi

Document 118

LETTER FROM MAULANA AZAD TO CRIPPS

New Delhi, Apr. 1, 1942

Dear Sir Stafford

I have your letter of today's date, for which I thank you.

If you so desire it, I shall gladly meet the Commander-in-Chief and Pandit Jawaharlal Nehru will, I hope, be able to accompany me.

My Committee have already arrived at a decision in regard to the proposals communicated by you to us. It was my intention to send this to you this evening, or possibly to take it over in person, in case you wished to discuss any point contained in it. This decision naturally covers other points also apart from Defence. I hope to send it to you some time today. If you wish to meet me again in regard to this I shall gladly meet you.

In your letter you refer to the "Hindu Press". I do not know what exactly you mean by this.

Yours sincerely,
A.K. Azad

The Rt. Hon. Sir Stafford Cripps, K.C., M.P.

Document 119

LETTER FROM CRIPPS TO MAULANA AZAD

3, Queen Victoria Road, N. Delhi,
The 1st April, 1942

My dear Maulana Sahib,

Thank you very much for your letter.

I will make the arrangement for the meeting with the Commander-in-Chief the moment he returns.

As to the document you are sending over, I understand this expresses the views of the Congress Working Committee upon the proposals, but that it is not intended to be a definite and final statement as to the Congress attitude, in view of our meeting again.

I should be most grateful if you could come over and see me with regard to it tomorrow morning at 10 A.M.

I apologise for the reference to the "Hindu Press" I was referring to the *Hindustan Times* amongst other papers.

Yours sincerely,
Stafford Cripps

Document 120

LETTER FROM CRIPPS TO MAULANA AZAD

3, Queen Victoria road,
New Delhi.

2nd April, 1942

Dear Maulana Sahib,

Mr. Jinnah[1] has asked me to give him a clear picture of the method by which I have proposed that a Province should decide whether it will or will not join an Indian Union set up in accordance with the procedure laid down in His Majesty's Government draft declaration. I have told him in reply that the proposition which I have put orally to him and to the other leaders is that a Province should reach its decision by a vote in the Legislative Assembly on a resolution that the Province should join the Indian Union, and that if the majority for accession is less than 60%, the minority would have the right to demand a plebiscite of the adult male population.

I explained this to you at our first meeting, but as I have written to Mr. Jinnah in this sense, I thought it desirable to give you a similar letter.

Yours sincerely,
Stafford Cripps

Maulana Abul Kalam Azad,
Kucha Chelan

---

1. Mr. M.A. Jinnah.

Document 121

LETTER FROM CRIPPS TO MAULANA AZAD

3rd April, 1942

Dear Maulana Sahib,

I have now been able to see His Excellency the Commender-in-Chief and he will be very glad to meet you and Pandit Jawaharlal Nehru to discuss the position regarding Defence. Subject to your convenience, 6 o'clock tomorrow evening would suit General Wavell and if you can manage this, I suggest that you should come here at 10 minutes to 6 p.m. and I will go up with you to the Commander-in-Chief's Office.

If there are any specific points of detail about organisation which you wish to raise, I should be very much obliged if you could let me have a note of them tonight or first thing tomorrow morning so that the Commander-in-Chief can consider them before the meeting.

Yours very sincerely,
Stafford Cripps

Document 122

LETTER FROM MAULANA AZAD TO CRIPPS

New Delhi,
4 April, 1942

Dear Sir Stafford,

Thanks for your letter of today's date. From our talk yesterday I had gathered the impression that we were likely to meet the Commander-in-Chief some time today and we had arranged our programme accordingly, but as this is not convenient to him we shall meet him tomorrow at 6 p.m. as suggested and reach your house at 5.50 p.m. I do not think it is necessary for me to send a note about organisational details. We are interested as you know in the political aspect of the problem, the full popular control of defence as well as all other departments of administration. We consider such control essential before responsibility can be undertaken. Our views on this subject and others are embodied in the resolution I gave you yesterday and it is with that background that we should like to consider the subject of defence. Problems of higher strategy may well be controlled by inter-Allied Cabinet Councils, but the effectual control of the defence of India should rest with the Indian National Government.

Yours sincerely,
A.K. Azad

Document 123

LETTER FROM CRIPPS TO MAULANA AZAD

New Delhi,
7 April, 1942

Dear Maulana Saheb,

I have as I promised when I last saw you consulted His Majesty's Government as to what further step could be taken in order to meet the criticism of your Working Committee, that under clause (e) of the draft declaration the defence of India would not fall to be administered by a representative Indian. Although, as the Working Committee have fully understood, it is impossible to make any change in the existing constitution during the period of hostilities, His Majesty's Government are anxious to give representative Indians the maximum possible participation in the Government during that period. In accordance with the principle laid down in clause (e) of the draft declaration I have explained to you the technical difficulties with regard to the position of the Commander-in-Chief and will not here reiterate them. I have also pointed out that all those main aspects of the defence of India which at present fall under the care of other members of the Executive (*e.g.*, civil defence, supply, home affairs, communications, *etc., etc.*) will, if the scheme is accepted, be administered by representative members in the New National Government. His Majesty's Government are however anxious to do their utmost to meet the wishes of the Indian people and to demonstrate their complete trust in the co-operative effort of the two peoples, British and Indian, which they hope may reinforce the defence of India. They also appreciate the force of the arguments that have been put forward as to the necessities of an effective appeal to the Indian peoples for their own defence.

I am therefore authorised to propose to you as a way out of the present difficulties that (a) the Commander-in-Chief should retain a seat on the Viceroy's Executive Council as War Member and should retain his full control over all the war activities of the armed forces in India subject to the control of His Majesty's Government and the War Cabinet, upon which body a representative Indian should sit with equal powers in all matters relating to the defence of India. Membership of the Pacific Council would likewise be offered to a representative Indian. (b) An Indian representative member would be added to the Viceroy's Executive who would take over those sections of the Department of Defence which can organisationally be separated immediately from the Commander-in-Chief's War Department and which are specified under head (I) of the annexure. In addition this member would take over the Defence Co-ordination Department which is at present directly under the Viceroy and certain other important functions of the Government of India which are directly related to defence and which do not fall under any of the other existing departments, and which are specified under head (II) of the annexure.

His Majesty's Government very much hope, as I personally hope, that this arrangement will enable the Congress to come into the scheme, so that if other important bodies of Indian opinion are also willing it will be possible for His Excellency the Viceroy to embark forthwith upon the task of framing the New National Government in consultation with the leaders of Indian opinion.

Yours sincerely,
Stafford Cripps

ANNEX I

Matters now dealt with in the Defence Department which would be transferred to a Defence Co-ordination Department:

(a) Public relations
(b) Demobilisation and post-war reconstruction.
(c) Petroleum officer whose functions are to calculate the requirements of and make provision for all petroleum products required for the Army, Navy and Air Force, and for the civil departments, including storage and distribution.
(d) Indian representation on the Eastern Group Supply Council.
(e) Amenities for the welfare of troops and their dependants including Indian soldiers' boards.
(f) All canteen organisations.
(g) Certain non-technical educational institutions, *e.g.*, Lawrence Schools, K.G.R.I.M. School, and the Prince of Wales' Royal Indian Military College,

(h) Stationery, printing, and forms for the Army.
(i) Reception, accommodation, and social arrangements for all foreign missions, representatives, and offices.

ANNEX II

In addition the Defence Co-ordination Department would take over many major questions bearing directly on defence but difficult to locate in any particular existing departments; examples are denial policy, evacuation from threatened areas, signals co-ordination, economic warfare.

Document 124

LETTER FROM MAULANA AZAD TO SIR STAFFORD CRIPPS

New Delhi,
April 10, 1942

Dear Sir Stafford,

On the 2nd April I sent you the Resolution of the Working Committee of the Congress containing their views on the tentative proposals put forward by you on behalf of the British Government. In this resolution we expressed our dissent from several important and far-reaching proposals for the future. Further consideration of those proposals has only strengthened us in our conviction in regard to them, and we should like to repeat that we cannot accept them as suggested. The Working Committee's Resolution gives expression to our conclusions relating to them which we reached after the most earnest consideration.

That resolution, however, emphasized the gravity of the present situation and stated that the ultimate decision that we might take would be governed by the changes made in the present. The overriding problems before all of us, and more especially before all Indians, is the defence of the country from aggression and invasion. The future, important as it is, will depend on what happens in the next few months and years. We were therefore prepared to do without any assurances for this uncertain future, hoping that through our sacrifices in the defence of our country we would lay the solid and enduring foundations for a free and independent India. We concentrated, therefore, on the present.

Your original proposals in regard to the present, as contained in clause (e) of the proposed declaration, were vague and incomplete, except in so far as it was made clear that "His Majesty's Government must inevitably bear the full responsibility for the defence of India." These proposals, in effect, asked for participation in the tasks of today with a view to ensure "the future freedom of India." Freedom was for an uncertain future, not for the present; and no indication was given in clause (e) of what arrangements or governmental and other changes would be made in the present. When this vagueness was pointed out, you said that this was deliberate, so as to give you freedom to determine these changes in consultation with others. In our talks you gave us to understand that you envisaged a National Government which would deal with all matters except Defence.

Defence at any time, and more particularly in war time, is of essential importance and without it a National Government functions in a very limited field. Apart from this consideration, it was obvious that the whole purpose of your proposals and our talks centred round the urgency of the problems created by the threat of the invasion of India. The chief functions of a National Government must necessarily be to organize Defence both intensively and on the widest popular basis and to create a mass psychology of resistance to an invader. Only a National Government could do that, and only a government on whom this responsibility was laid. Popular resistance must have a national background, and with this soldier and the citizen must feel that they are fighting for their country's freedom under national leadership.

We pointed this out to you. The question became one not of just satisfying our national aspirations but of effective prosecution of the war and fighting to the last any invader who set foot on the soil of India. On general principles a National Government would control defence through a Defence Minister, and the Commander-in-Chief would control the armed forces and would have full latitude in the carrying out of operations connected with the war. An Indian National Government should have normally functioned in this way. We made it clear that the Commander-in-Chief in India would have control of the armed forces and the conduct of operations and other matters connected therewith. With a view to arriving at a settlement, we were prepared to accept certain limitations on the normal powers of the Defence Minister. We had no desire to upset in the middle of the war the present military organization or arrangements. We accepted also that the higher strategy of the war should be controlled by the War Cabinet in London which would have an Indian member. The immediate object before us was to make the defence of India more effective, to strengthen it, to broad base it on the popular will, and to reduce all red tape, delay and inefficiency from it. There was no question of our interfering with the technical and operational sides. One thing, of course, was of paramount importance to us: India's safety and defence. Subject to this primary consideration, there was no reason why there should be any difficulty in finding a way out of the present impasse in accordance with the unanimous desire of the Indian people, for in this matter there are no differences amongst us.

The emphasis on Defence led you to reconsider the matter and you wrote to me on the 7th April suggesting a formula for Defence.

In this letter you said: "As the Working Committee have fully understood, it is impossible to make any change in the existing constitution during the period of hostilities." The Working Committee's attitude in the matter has been completely misunderstood and I should like to clear this up, although we are not immediately concerned with it. The Committee do not think that there is any inherent difficulty in the way of constitutional changes during the war. Everything that helps in the war not only can be but must be done, and done with speed. That is the only way to carry on and win a war. No complicated enactments are necessary. A recognition of India's freedom and right to self-determination could easily be made, if it was so wished, together with certain other consequential but important changes. The rest can be left to future arrangements and adjustments. I might remind you that the British Prime Minister actually proposed a union of France and England on the eve of the fall of France. No greater or more fundamental change could be imagined, and this was suggested at a period of grave crisis and peril. War accelerates changes; it does not fit in with static conceptions.

The formula for Defence that you sent us was considered by us together with its annexure which gave a list of subjects or departments which were to be transferred to the Defence Department. This list was a revealing one as it proved that the Defence Minister would deal with relatively unimportant matters. We were unable to accept this and we informed you accordingly.

Subsequently, a new formula for Defence was suggested to us, but without any list of subjects. This formula seemed to us to be based on more healthy approach and we suggested certain changes pointing out that our ultimate decision would necessarily depend on the allocation of subjects. A revised formula was then sent back to us together with an indication of the functions of the War Department. This was so widely and comprehensively framed that it was difficult for us to know what the actual allocation of subjects and departments, as between the Defence Department and the War Department, would be. A request was made on our behalf that illustrative lists of these subjects might be supplied to enable us to consider the matter. No such lists were supplied to us.

In the interview we had with you yesterday we discussed the new formula and expressed our viewpoint in regard to it. I need not repeat what I said then. The wording of the formula is after all a minor matter and we would not allow that to come in our way, unless some important principle is at stake. But behind that wording lay certain ideas and we were surprised to find that during the past few days we have been proceeding on wrong assumptions.

When we asked you for illustrative lists of subjects for the two Departments, you referred us to the old list for the Defence Department which you had previously sent us and which had been unable to accept. You added that certain residuary subjects might be added to this but, in effect, there was not likely to be any such subject as the allocation was complete. Thus, you said, that substantially there was no change between the old list and any new one that might be prepared. If this was so, and we were to go back ultimately to the place we started from, then what was the purpose of our searching for new formulae? A new set of words meaning the same thing made no difference.

In the course of our talks many other matters were also cleared up, unfortunately to our disadvantage. You had referred both privately and in the course of public statements to a National Government and a 'cabinet' consisting of 'ministers'. These words has a certain significance and we had imagined that the new Government would function with full powers as a Cabinet, with the Viceroy acting as a constitutional head. But the new picture that you placed before us was really not very different from the old, the difference being one of degree and not of kind. The new Government could neither be called, except vaguely and inaccurately, nor could it function as a National Government. It would just be the Viceroy and his Executive Council with the Viceroy having all his old powers. We did not ask for any legal changes but we did ask for definite assurances and conventions which would indicate that the new Government would function as a free government the members of which act as members of a cabinet in a constitutional government. In regard to the conduct of the war and connected activities the Commander-in-Chief would have freedom, and he would also act as War Minister.

We were informed that nothing can be said at this stage, even vaguely and generally, about the conventions that should govern the new Government and the Viceroy. This was a matter in the Viceroy's sole discretion and, at a later stage, it could be discussed directly with the Viceroy. Ultimately there was always the possibility of the members of the Executive Council, resigning or threatening to resign if they disagreed with the Viceroy. That sanction or remedy is of course always open, but it is curious that we should base our approach to a new government on the probability of conflict and resignation at the very outset.

The Picture therefore placed before us is not essentially different from the old one. The whole object which we and I believe you, have in view – that is, to create a new psychological approach to the people, to make them feel that their own National Government had come, that they were defending their newly-won freedom – would be completely frustrated when they saw this old picture again, with even the old labels on. The continuation of the India office, which has been a symbol of evil to us, would confirm this picture. It has almost been taken for granted for some time past that the India Office would soon disappear as it was an anachronism. But now we are told that even this undesirable relic of a past age is going to continue.

The picture of the government, which was so like the old in all essential features, is such that we cannot fit into it. Normally we would have had little difficulty in disposing of this matter for it is so far removed from all that we have striven for, but in the circumstances of today we were prepared to give full consideration to every proposal which might lead to an effective organization of the defence of India. The peril that faces India affects us more than it can possibly affect any foreigner, and we are anxious and eager to do our utmost to face it and overcome it. But we cannot undertake responsibilities when we are not given the freedom and power to shoulder them effectively and when an old environment continues which hampers the national effort.

While we cannot accept the proposals you have made, we want to inform you that we are yet prepared to assume responsibility, provided a truly national Government is formed. We are prepared to put aside for the present all questions about the future, though, as we have indicated, we hold definite views about it. But in the present, the National Government must be a cabinet government with full power and must not merely be a continuation of the Viceroy's Executive Council. In regard to defence we have already stated what, in our opinion, the position should be at present. We feel that such an arrangement is the very minimum that is essential for the functioning of a National Government and for making the popular appeal which is urgently needed.

We would point out to you that the suggestions we have put forward are not ours only but may be considered to be the unanimous demand of the Indian people. On these matters there is no difference of opinion among various groups and parties, and the difference is as between the Indian people as a whole and the British Government. Such differences as exist in India relate to constitutional changes in the future. We are agreeable to the postponement of this issue so that the largest possible measure of unity might be achieved in the present crisis for the defence of India. It would be a tragedy that even when there is this unanimity of opinion in India, the British Government should prevent a free National Government from functioning, and from serving the cause of India as well as the larger causes for which millions are suffering and dying today.

Yours sincerely,
A.K. Azad

Document 125

MAULANA AZAD'S EXPLANATION OF THE CONGRESS POSITION ON DELHI TALKS

April 10, 1942

Maulana Azad, Congress President, at a Press Conference today, referred to his first interview at which, he said he had laid emphasis on three issues.

Firstly, Maulana Azad had told Sir Stafford that the approach to the Indian problem made in the Draft Declaration was not only not correct but was likely to lead to greater complications. If the British Government desire to infuse a new spirit in India even at this eleventh hour, and send out a person like Sir Stafford for the task, the simple method would have been to send out through Sir Stafford the announcement that Britain was prepared to party with power. Sir Stafford could then have asked Indians to draw up a scheme. If we failed to draw one up, the entire responsibility would have been ours. Sir Stafford, in reply, had referred to the first part of the Draft Declaration and asserted that it was a considered decision of the War Cabinet and it constituted a fundamental principle. He added that provision had already been made in it for different political organisations and it was open to them to come to an agreement at any time.

'I pointed out' said the Maulana, that after concrete proposals had been introduced by him, the task of independent agreement among the parties in India had been made difficult.

'Secondly,' proceeded the Maulana, 'I told Sir Stafford that the Draft Declaration laid much greater emphasis on the future than on the immediate present, while India demanded changes in the present system. The proposals relating to the present were not positive, they were negative. I said to him that as far as the Congress was concerned, I do not see how it could accept the proposals. War, I said, was threatening India, but the light had gone out of the hearts of the millions, who might have sacrificed themselves for their country. Our common task now demanded that we should find a psychological approach in order to rekindle the spark of patriotic fervour in those hearts. This could not be achieved merely by holding out promises for the future but people must be made to feel that they were free in their own country today and made to defend their own freedom and their own country.'

'Sir Stafford speaking with great confidence, assured me that Clause(e) of the Draft Declaration provided for complete freedom and transfer of power with only one reservation about Defence.

'I then pointed out that defence of the country was the demand of the moment as far as the country was concerned, and during the war, civil administration had disappeared, because problems of defence permeated every civil department and if you reserve Defence, you practically reserve all the powers whieh you say, are being transferred to India.

'Sir Stafford said by way of reassurance that the reservations related only to the functions of the Commander-in-Chief. The rest of the discussion proceeded in respect of the particular question.

'The third point emphasised by me was that in tackling the political question in India communal questions were bound to arise at some stage or other and would have to be solved. I assured him that as soon as the main political problem was settled, the responsibility of ending a satisfactory solution of the communal and other problems would be ours, and I could confidently assert that we would find a satisfactory solution.

'Sir Stafford entirely agreed with me and said this was exact in what he has said before the War Cabinet before he came out to India.

'This naturally conjured up in my mind a picture of the present not found in the cold words of the Draft Declaration, and I therefore, naturally decided to call a meeting of the Working Committee to examine it. I however, regret to say that the first impression of the picture created as a result of my earlier interviews with Sir Stafford gradually became blurred as the discussions on material points proceeded from stage to stage. And when I last met him on the night of April 9 the whole picture had completely faded out.'

Interview with General Wavell

Referring to his interview with General Wavell, the Maulana said, 'In the course of our talks Sir Stafford Cripps had repeatedly emphasised the technical difficulties in the way of transferring Defence to an Indian Member. He had suggested that we should meet General

Wavell, because he could explain that technical side of the question much better. But curiously enough, throughout our interview with the Commander-in-Chief, at which other military officers were present, not a word was spoken about any technical difficulty, the entire discussion proceeded on political lines. It did not strike me for a moment that we were interviewing military experts, but expert politicians.

'I think' the Maulana went on 'I must clarify the position created by certain speculations in a section of the Press as regards Mahatma Gandhi's part in the discussions. The Mahatma's views as regards participation in any war are well-known and it would be entirely untrue to suggest that the Working Committee's decisions have in any way, been influenced by those views. In fact, Mahatma Gandhi made it clear to the Working Committee that they were perfectly free to come to their own decisions on the merits of the proposals. He did not really want to participate even in the sittings of the Working Committee, but he was persuaded by me to stay on from day to day as long as he could afford to do so. Eventually, my persuasion proved powerless to make his stay longer.

'I want to repeat what I said yesterday that the Working Committee's decision has at every stage, been unanimous'. Maulana Azad said, 'It is deeply to be regretted that the aim which all of us had passionately desired has not been reached, but I must acknowledge that all these discussions were carried on in a friendly atmosphere and in spite of profound differences which at times led to heated controversy. We and Sir Stafford have parted as friends. The cordiality of the talks was maintained to the last.'

Document 126

LETTER FROM CRIPPS TO MAULANA AZAD

3, Queen Victoria Road,
New Delhi, the 10th April 1942

My Dear Maulana Sahib,

I was extremely sorry to receive from you your letter of April 10th expressing the rejection by the Congress Working Committee of His Majesty's Government's draft declaration.

I will not deal with those points which are covered by the original resolution of your Committee which you sent me, as they were clearly not the reason for your decision.

Nor need I go into the question of the division of duties between the Defence Minister and the Commander-in-Chief as War Member with which you deal at length. This division allotted to the Defence Minister all functions outside those actually connected with the General Headquarters, Navy Headquarters and Air Headquarters which are under the Commander-in-Chief as head of the fighting force in India.

In addition to these functions in the narrow field of "Defence" it was suggested that all other portfolios relating to that subject such as:

Home Department – Internal order, police, refugees, *etc.*

Finance Department – All war finance in India.

Communications Department – Railways, Roads, Transport, *etc.*

Supply Department – Supplies for all forces and munitions

Information and Broadcasting Department – Propaganda, publicity, *etc.*

Civil Defence Department – A.R.P. and all forms of civilian defence.

Legislative Department – Regulations and orders

Labour Department – Man-power

Defence Department – Administration of Indian personnel, *etc.*

should be put in the hands of representative Indians as members of the Executive Council.

Nothing further could have been done by way of giving responsibility for Defence services to representative Indian members without jeopardising the immediate defence of India under the Commander-in-Chief. This defence is, as you know, a paramount duty and responsibility of His Majesty's Government, while unity of Command is essential in the interests of the Allied help to India.

The real substance of your refusal to take part in a National Government is that the form of Government suggested is not such as would enable you to rally the Indian people as you desire.

You make two suggestions. First that the constitution might now be changed. In this respect I would point out that you made this suggestion for the first time last night, nearly three weeks after you had received the proposals, and I would further remark that every other representative with whom I have discussed this view has accepted the practical impossibility of any such legislative change in the middle of a war and at such a moment as the present.

Second you suggest "a truly National Government" be formed, which must be a "Cabinet Government with full power."

Without constitutional changes of a most complicated character and on a very large scale this would not be possible, as you realise.

Were such a system to be introduced by convention under the existing circumstances, the nominated cabinet (nominated presumably by the major political organisations) would be responsible to no one but itself, could not be removed and would in fact constitute an absolute dictatorship of the majority.

This suggestion would be rejected by all minorities in India, since it would subject all of them to a permanent and autocratic majority in the Cabinet. Nor would it be consistent with the pledges already given by His Majesty's Government to protect the rights of these minorities.

In a country such as India where communal divisions are still so deep an irresponsible majority Government of this kind is not possible.

Apart from this, however, until such time as the Indian peoples frame their new constitution, His Majesty's Government must continue to carry out its duties to those large sections of the Indian people to whom it has given its pledges.

The proposals of His Majesty's Government went as far as possible short of a complete change in the constitution which is generally acknowledged as impracticable in the circumstances of today.

While therefore both I and His Majesty's Government recognise the keen desire of your Working Committee to carry on the war against the enemy by every means in their power, they regret that your Working Committee has not seen its way to join in the war effort upon the conditions sincerely offered, the only conditions which could have brought together all the different communities and sections of the Indian people.

Yours sincerely,
Stafford Cripps

I propose to publish this answer.

Maulana Abul Kalam Azad,
Birla House,
New Delhi.

Document 127

CONGRESS COMMITTEE'S RESOLUTION ON DELHI TALK WITH MAULANA AZAD AS PRESIDENT

April 11, 1942

'The Working Committee have given their full and earnest consideration to the proposals made by the British War Cabinet in regard to India and the elucidation thereof by Sir Stafford Cripps. These proposals, which have been made at the very last hour because of the compulsion of events, have to be considered not only in relation to India's demand for independence, but more especially in the present grave war crisis, with a view to meeting effectively the perils and dangers that confront India and involve the world.

'The Congress has repeatedly stated, ever since the commencement of the War in September 1939, the people of India would line themselves with the progressive forces of the world and assume full responsibility to face the new problems and shoulder the new burdens that had arisen, and it asked for the necessary conditions to enable them to do so to be created. An essential conditions was the freedom of India, for only the realisation of present freedom could light the flame which would illumine millions of hearts and move them to action. At the last meeting of the All India Congress Committee, after the commencement of the War in the Pacific, it was stated that: Only a free and independent India can be in a position to undertake the defence of the country on a national basis and be of help in the furtherance of the larger causes that are emerging from the storm of war.

Objections to Cabinet's Proposals

'The British War Cabinet's new proposals relate principally to the future upon the causation of hostilities. The Committee, while recognising that self-determination for the people of India is accepted in principle in that uncertain future, regret that is fettered and circumscribed and certain provisions have been introduced which gravely imperil the development of a free and united nation and the establishment of a democratic state. Even the constitution-making body is so constituted that the people's right to self-determination is vitiated by the introduction of non-representative elements. The people of India have as a whole, clearly demand full independence and the Congress has repeatedly declared that no other status except that of independence for the whole of India could be agreed to or could meet the essential requirements of the present situation.

States People's Interests

'The Committee recognise that future independence may be implicit in the proposals, but the accompanying provisions and restrictions are such that, real freedom may well become an illusion. The complete ignoring of the ninety millions of the people of the Indian States and their treatment as commodities at the disposal of their Rulers is a negation of both democracy and self-determination. While the representation of an Indian State in the constitution-making body is fixed on a population basis, the people of the State have no voice in choosing those representatives, nor are they to be consulted at any stage, while decisions vitally affecting them are to be taken. Such State may, in many ways, become barriers to the growth of Indian freedom, enclaves where foreign authority still prevails and where the possibility of maintaining foreign armed forces has been stated to be a likely contingency, and a perpetual menace into the freedom of the people of the States as well or the rest of India.

Non-Accession Clause – An Apple of Discord

'The acceptance before hand of the novel principle of non-accession for a Province is also a severe below to the conception of Indian unity and an apple of discord likely to generate growing trouble in the Provinces, and which may well lead to further difficulties in the way of the Indian States merging themselves in the Indian Union. The Congress has been wedded to Indian freedom and any break in that unity, especially in the modern world when people's minds inevitably think in terms of ever larger federations would be injurious to all concerned and exceedingly painful to contemplate. Nevertheless, the Committee cannot think in terms of compelling the people in any territorial unit to remain in an Indian Union against their declared and established will. While recognising this principle the Committee feel that every effort should be made to create conditions which would help the different units in developing a common and co-operative national life. The acceptance of the principle inevitably involves that no changes should be made, which result in fresh problems being created and compulsion being exercised on other substantial groups within that area. Each territorial unit should have the fullest possible autonomy within the Union consistently with a strong National State. The proposal now made on the part of the British War Cabinet encourages and will lead to attempts at separation at the very inception of the Union and thus create friction just when the utmost co-operation and goodwill are most needed. This proposal has been presumably made to meet a communal demand, but it will have other consequences also and lead politically reactionary and obscurantist groups among different communities to create trouble and divert public attention from the vital issue before the country.

Transfer of Defence Essential

'Any proposal concerning the future of India must demand attention and scrutiny. But in today's grave crisis, it is the present that counts and even proposals for the future are important insofar as they affect the present. The Committee have necessarily attached the greatest importance to this aspect of the question and on this ultimately depends what advice they should give to those who look to them for guidance. For the present, the British War Cabinet's proposals are vague and altogether incomplete, and it would appear that no vital changes in the present structure are contemplated. It has been made clear that the defence of India will, in any event, remain under British control. At any time Defence is a vital subject: during war time it is all important and covers almost every sphere of life and administration. To take away defence from the sphere of responsibility at this stage is to reduce that responsibility to a farce and a nullity, and to make it perfectly clear that India is not going to be free in any way and her Government is not going to function as a free and independent Government during the pendency of the war.

'The Committee would repeat that an essential and fundamental prerequisite for the assumption of responsibility by the Indian people in the present is their realisation as a fact that they are free and are incharge of maintaining and defending their freedom. What is most wanted is the enthusiastic response of the people which cannot be evoked without the fullest trust in them and the devolution of responsibility on them in the matter of defence. It is only thus that even at this grave eleventh hour, it may be possible to galvanise the people of India to rise to the height of the occasion. It is manifest that the present Government of India, as well as its provincial agencies, are lacking in competence, and are incapable of shouldering the burden of India's defence. It is only the people of India through their popular representatives who may shoulder this burden worthily. But that can only be done by present freedom and full responsibility being cast upon them.

'The Committee, therefore, is unable to accept the proposals put forward on behalf of the British War Cabinet.'

Document 128

LETTER FROM MAULANA AZAD TO STAFFORD CRIPPS

Birla House, Albuquerque Road,
New Delhi,

April 11, 1949

Dear Sir Stafford,

I have just received your letter of April 10th and I must confess that my colleagues and I were considerably surprised to read it. I am sending you this reply immediately and can only deal briefly here with some of the points you have raised.

The points covered by our original resolution are important and represent my Committee's well-considered views on the British proposals as a whole. But we pointed out to you that so far as the proposals relate to the future they might be set aside, as we were anxious to assume responsibility for India's government and defence in this hour of danger. This responsibility could only be undertaken, however, if it was real responsibility and power.

As regards the division of functions between the Defence Minister and the War Minister you did not give illustrative lists, as requested by us, and referred us to the previous list of the Defence Minister's functions, which, as you know, we have been wholly unable to accept. In your letter under reply you mention certain subjects, directly or indirectly related to the war, which will be administered by other departments. So far as the Defence Minister is concerned, it is clear that his functions will be limited by the first list that you sent.

No one has suggested any restrictions on the normal powers of the Commander-in-Chief. Indeed we went beyond this and were prepared to agree to further powers being given to him as War Minister. But it is clear that the British Government's conception and ours in regard to defence differ greatly. For us it means giving it a national character and calling upon every man and woman in India to participate in it. It means trusting our own people and seeking their full cooperation in this great effort. The British

Government's view seems to be based on an batter lack of confidence in the Indian people and in withholding real power from them. You refer to the paramount duty and responsibility of His Majesty's Government in regard to defence. That duty and responsibility cannot be discharged effectively unless the Indian people are made to have and feel their responsibility, and the recent past stands witness to this. The Government of India do not seem to realise that the war can only be fought on a popular basis.

Your statement that we have for the first time after three weeks suggested a change in the constitution is hardly correct. In the course of our talks reference was made to it, but it is true that we did not lay stress on it as we did not want to introduce new issues. But when you stated explicitly in your letter that we had agreed that no constitutional changes could be made during the war, we had to deny this and correct your impression.

It is the last part of your letter that has especially surprised and pained us. It seems that there has been a progressive deterioration in the British Government's attitude as our negotiations proceeded. What we were told in our very first talk with you is now denied or explained away. You told me then that there would be a National Government which would function as a Cabinet and that the position of the Viceroy would be analogous to that of the King in England *vis-a-vis* his Cabinet. In regard to the India Office, you told me, that you were surprised that no one had so far mentioned this important matter, and that the practical course was to havc this attached or incorporated with the Dominions' office.

The whole of this picture which you sketched before us, now been completely shattered by what you told us during our last interview.

You have put forward an argument in your letter which at no time during our talks was mentioned by you. You refer to the 'absolute dictatorship of the majority.' It is astonishing that such a statement should be made in this connection and at this stage. This difficulty is inherent in any scheme of a mixed cabinet formed to meet an emergency, but there are many ways in which it can be provided for. Had you raised this question we would have discussed it and found a satisfactory solution. The whole approach to this question has been that a mixed cabinet should be formed and should cooperate together. We accepted this. We are not interested in the Congress as such gaining power, but we are interested in the Indian people as a whole having freedom and power. How the Cabinet should be formed and should function was a question which might have been considered after the main question was decided; that is, the extent of power which the British Government, would give up to the Indian people. Because of this we never discussed it with you or even referred to it. Nevertheless you have raised this matter for the first time, in what is presumably your last letter to us, and tried most unjustifiably to side-track the real issue between us.

You will remember that in my very first talk with you, I pointed out that the communal or like questions did not arise at this stage. As soon as the Britain Government made up its mind to transfer real power and responsibility, the other questions could be tackled successfully by those concerned. You gave me the impression that you agreed with this approach.

We are convinced that if the British Government did not pursue a policy of encouraging disruption, all of us, to whatever party or group we belonged, would be able to come together and find a common line of action. But, unhappily, even in this grave hour of peril, the British Government is unable to give up its wreeking policy. We are driven to the conclusion that it attached more importance to holding on to its rule in India, as long as it can, and promoting discord and disruption here with that end in view, than to an effective defence of India against the aggression and invasion that overhang us. To us, and to all Indians, the dominant consideration is the defence and safety of India, and it is by that test that we judge.

You mention that you propose to publish your letter too. I presume that you have no objection now to our publishing our original resolution, your letters to us, and our letters to you.

Yours sincerely,
A.K. Azad

The Right Hon'ble Sir Stafford Cripps
Queen Victoria Road, New Delhi

Document 129

MAULANA AZAD'S INSTRUCTIONS TO THE ALL LEADERS OF P.C.C.

Letters have been received from some provinces asking whether in view of the fact that most of the members of the provincial and other Congress committees are out of Jail, it is desirable for the Committee to function.

It seems that these Committees have not grasped the real position in this respect. The constitution was never suspended during the last 15 months. The committees formed after the last election did not cease to function, and there is no reason why their normal activities should not continue. The situation in the beginning of the present struggle was that the Congress had asked the members of Committee to offer Satyagraha. And when all or most of the members were arrested Gandhiji instructed them not to fill the vacancies thus caused, and the offices were put incharge of an organiser during the state of emergency. It did not, however, mean the suspension of the Committees. Now, when all the members of the committees have come out of the jails there is no reason why the committees should not function as before.

Abul Kalam Azad
15-4-42

Document 130

MAULANA'S REACTION THROUGH AN OPEN LETTER ON THE RESOLUTION PASSED BY THE MADRAS CONGRESS LEGISLATIVE PARTY

IT GREATLY ASTONISHED AND PAINED ME THAT A MAN LIKE MR. RAJAGOPALACHARI IN SPITE OF HIS BEING A MEMBER OF THE CONGRESS WORKING COMMITTEE SHOULD HAVE ADOPTED SUCH AN ATTITUDE. ...I AM IN COMMUNICATION WITH HIM. I WOULD ASSURE YOU THAT ANY PERSONAL RELATIONSHIP HOWEVER DEAR TO. CANNOT DETER ME FOR A MOMENT FOR....FROM DISCHARGING MY DUTY AS A PRESIDENT OF THE CONGRESS.

I MAY POINT OUT IN THIS CONNECTION THAT IN THE CONGRESS ORGANISATION ONLY THE PROVINCIAL CONGRESS COMMITTEE IS THE COMPETENT BODY TO REPRESENT PROVINCIAL VIEWS...NOT THE CONGRESS LEGISLATURES....PARTY DESPITE THIS FACT THE PARTY ITSELF WAS NOT FULLY REPRESENTED IN THE MEETING. THE INFORMATION ABOUT THE MEETING INDICATES THAT OUT OF 191 CONGRESS MEMBERS OF BOTH THE HOUSES ONLY 52 ATTENDED THE MEETING. AND WHEN VOTES CAME.....WERE TAKEN ONLY 36 PARTICIPATED IN THE VOTING. IT CLEARLY SHOWS THAT IT WOULD BE WRONG TO ATTRIBUTE THE DECISION TO THE MAJORITY OF THE CONGRESSMEN OF THE PROVINCE.

25-4-42

Document 131

ABDULLAH BUT'S ANALYSIS OF THE PERSONALITY OF MAULANA AZAD

It is always difficult to write about a person one has come to know well. It is still more difficult when that person is a political colleague with whom one has shared the burdens and responsibilities of public work. And so I do not find it easy to write anything about Maulana Abul Kalam Azad.

It was about 22 years ago when I first met the Maulana. Of course I had heard about him previously, of his great learning of his integrity in the national cause, and of his internment during the last World War. So I was eager to see him. He was fairly young in years. And yet he had somehow the impress of maturity about him. Inevitably he took his place among the elders of the Congress, though he was much younger in years. I had occasion to see him and watch him from some distance, for at that time I was not intimately associated with the inner Council of the Congress. In later years, I saw a great deal of him at work in the Working Committee of the Congress, and especially during the last dozen years I have been closely associated with him. Except for our long periods in prison and except for my absence from India, I have been in continuous touch with him in our day-to-day work in the Congress, as well in the taking of weighty decisions. In Congress history, and therefore in recent Indian history, few people perhaps know what a great part he has played in shaping decisions. Whether as the President or as a member of the Working Committee, his opinion has carried very great weight with all the other members. This was so because more and more we came to recognise the ripe wisdom which lay behind those opinions.

The Maulana is an unusual type of politician. He lacks the usual temperament of a successful politician who becomes tough and insensitive and capable of giving and receiving hard blows. He is the very opposite of this. He is exceedingly sensitive and retiring. A fine and moving orator, he yet dislikes the rough and tumble of the crowd and it is no easy matter to get him to address public meetings. He is essentially the scholar whom circumstances have forced into a life of action.

He reminds me often of the French encyclopaedists who preceded the great French Revolution. His knowledge of past history is vast and all this is arranged in a well ordered way in his mind. One is continually astonished at odd bits of knowledge that come out of him most unawares. His mind is logical and precise and one would think that it had been trained in the old schools of formal logic and philosophy. His general outlook is rational. And yet with all this there is a human background which softens the weight of learning and shows itself in a rich, though sometimes dry, humour.

Probably if he had not been so retiring by nature he would have played an even greater part in the public life of our country, because he has it in him to move millions by his voice and his pen. We have heard that voice much too seldom in public, and unfortunately for many years his pen has not functioned as of old.

I have always regretted this neglect of the pen on his part. For the language he writes is full of winged words. Indeed it was through the pen that he became known, while he was yet in his teens, not only in India but in the Arabic countries of Western Asia and Egypt. Even now a traveller in those Arabic-speaking lands is asked about Abul Kalam Azad. If he had carried on his crusade of the pen, what tremendous service he could have rendered to the cause of clear thinking and, therefore, right action, amongst our people.

Circumstances, however, forced him to shoulder other burdens and responsibilities. History will tell of how he did so. But we, who have had the privilege of close comradeship with him, need not await the verdict of history. He has been a tower of strength to us and to the country and whether one agreed with him or not, we always knew that his opinion mattered and could never be lightly brushed aside. Far behind that opinion lay a keen and well trained mind, knowledge of the past and of the present, and a ripe wisdom which is given to few.

The Younger generation can learn much from this great Indian. He has found no difficulty in being a most learned of Muslim divines and at the same time an exponent and an emblem of India's unity. Lesser men have sometimes found conflict in the rich variety of Indian life. But he has been big enough not only to see the essential unity behind all that diversity but also to realise that only in this unity can there be hope for India as a whole and for those great and varied currents of national life which course through her veins.

Lahore
24-6-1942

Document 132

LETTER FROM C. RAJGOPALACHARIER TO MAULANA AZAD

30-4-1942

Dear Maulana Sahib,

With reference to your observation on the resolutions passed on my motion by the Madras Congress Legislative Party, I admit that I should have talked the matter over with you and other colleagues of the Working Committee before the resolution, knowing as I find their disagreement on the subject. I write this to express in regard.

I have explained to you already how strongly I feel. I believe that I should be talking in my duty if I do not endeavour to get people to think and act in the direction. I feel that in the future interest I should move the resolution as already notified by me. I desire therefore to request you to permit me to resign my place in the working committee.

Let me tender my grateful thanks for the unqualified thereof and affection bestowned on me by you and the other colleagues during all these many years that I have served in the Committee.

Yours Sincerely,
C. Rajagopalacharier

Document 133

LETTER FROM JAWAHAR LAL NEHRU TO MAULANA AZAD

New Delhi,
May 8, 1942

My dear Maulana,

I had no time then to consult many of my colleagues, I had a talk, however, with Rafi Ahmad Kidwai and one or two others. En route to Deoli I met Paliwal, our provincial President.

We are all agreeable to help you as far as we can in the matter of making arrangements for evacuee children from Calcutta. It was not possible to form a committee immediately for the purpose because our members had dispersed. But this can be done a little later. Meanwhile I have asked Rafi Ahmed to deal with this matter in cooperating with our provincial office and with Sucheta Kripalani and others.

This work will largely be women's work. We have just appointed a women's sub-committee of the P.C.C. and we can ask them to help fully in the matter. I am writing to Sucheta about it. In order, however, to avoid duplication, I would suggest your sending directions to Rafi Ahmed directly for the present.

Many questions arise and before any arrangement are made definite particulars should be obtained about the children concerned their numbers, their ages, sex, kind of living they have been accustomed to, *etc. etc.* It is possible to spread out a number of them in existing families, chiefly Bengali, or we can keep most of them in large hostels or both these methods can be adopted. Perhaps it will be better if you send for Rafi Ahmed and Sucheta to Calcutta so that they can discuss the matter with you and at the same time see for themselves what has to be done.

As arranged, I am leaving tomorrow night for Lahore.

Yours affectionately,
Jawaharlal Nehru

Document 134

LETTER FROM MAULANA AZAD TO JAWAHAR LAL NEHRU

Allahabad,
Dated 9th May 42

My dear Jawaharlal,

I do not know whether you received my letter sent to you care of the U.P.P.C.C. Lucknow. An important matter was mentioned in the letter. You might have received the reply to your Lucknow letter on reaching Lahore.

I have received a letter from Bapu,[1] through Profulla Babu.[2] He wants me to see. The papers say that he is leaving for Bombay for a week. I am, therefore, intending to leave for Bombay on Monday or Tuesday. The selfish feeling of taking rest is to a certain extent working behind this intention. The weather of Bombay would after all be less oppressive to me than that of Wardha.

Bapu also mentioned in his letter that you may also meet him if possible, but I do not think that there is any need for it at present. If this need will be felt after the Bombay meeting, then an occasion may arise by the end of this month, after your return from Kulu.

I shall stay at Bhulabhai's House in Bombay, and if possible I might go for a day or two to Juhu.

Please convey my salams to Mrs. and Mr. Iftikhar. I have received letters of Rajendra Babu and Patel also.

Yours Sincerely,
A.K. Azad

---

1. Mahatma Gandhi.
2. Mr. Profulla Chandra Ghosh.

Document 135

LETTER FROM MAULANA AZAD TO J.B. KRIPALANI

Calcutta,
May 13, 1942

My dear Kripalani,

I forgot to consult you about a matter in Allahabad.

You know Anis-ur-Rahman full well. I think it would be good to keep him in the office permanently. The work of Hindustani will increase in the office, for which we have none there. Anis-Ur-Rahman knows Hindi also, and has sufficient experience of our office routine. You may call him if you agree with it. He lives in Allahabad. For the present he may be given Rs. 75 per month; later on you do whatever may be suitable.

Poor Mahesh Prasad is also desirous of getting a chance of work in the office. Previously he was a despatch clerk there. He was discharged in the beginning of the movement, and he went to the office of the National Herald. Please consider his case also. He seems to be an energetic man. He can be engaged in the office as a Hindi clerk or as a Despatch clerk, as he previously was.

I somehow pulled on in Allahabad, but not I feel much tired and over-worked.

Yours Sincerely,
A.K. Azad

PS: Please Direct the office to send some office pads, as they are out of stock.

Document 136

LETTER FROM MAULANA AZAD TO JAWAHAR LAL NEHRU

19-A, Bally Gunj,
Circular Road,
Calcutta,

Dated, the 13th May '42

My dear Jawahar Lal,

I thank you for the telegram and the letter, you have sent to me from Delhi. Please note that I have said, "I thank you. I have issued only an appeal." Thus I have fully kept up the distinction between the two modes of discussion which you had indicated to me in Delhi.

I have received a letter from Kidwai, and Paliwal has also wired to me his readiness in connection with the evacuation of children. I am settling the details with the Bengal Government. As soon as they reach a definite point, I shall inform the U.P. friends.

But I came to know today that Kidwai has yesterday been arrested suddenly, under the Defence of India Act. I am at a loss to understand what has he done within the last few days that he has became a dangerous man now for the U.P. Government.

I had written to you in my last letter that I was leaving for Bombay. But the affairs of Bengal have stuck to me in such a way that I had to postpone my visit. The Chittagong air attack has created a feeling here that Calcutta will also be attacked within a few days. Moreover, now and difficult problems have suddenly arisen in connection with the coastal population of Bengal. Under the circumstances I could not propose myself to go out.

It pained me to find that Iftikhar is going out of the right way. I do not know whether you tried to bring him round and with what result.

I was much concerned to what you had asked in Ahmedabad. Now you should admit that you are going to leave the wrong side. You should be little more careful about your health.

Yours sincerely,
A.K. Azad

Document 137

LETTER FROM SUCHETA TO MAULANA AZAD

Swaraj Bhawan
Allahabad,

May 14, 1942

My dear Maulana Sahib,

Rafi Sahib[1] told me that he had written to you to give some details about the plan of evacuated children from Calcutta for which the Bengal Government was prepared to bear the expenses. Jawaharlalji[2] wrote to Rafi Sahib and me that we might go to Calcutta and consult you and other concerned and see things for ourselves. We had called a joint meeting of the Women's Sub-committee and the current programme Sub-committee of the P.C.C. at Lucknow on the 18th to consider ways and means for the arrangement of the evacuee children.

I do not know whether you conveyed any detailed information to Rafi Sahib. I heard nothing from him till he was arrested. If you have sent anything I would request you to send me a copy of your communication. If you have not written anything then you will please let me have such details as I would be able to place before this joint meeting on the 18th and which will be helpful in its deliberation. I am here till the 17th evening. If I cannot get your letter by that time you will please address it to Lucknow care the P.C.C. Office, 61 Abott Road to reach me there on the 18th at the latest. If no details are available, I am afraid, the joint meeting will not be able to devise any concrete plan.

You will also please inform me that with whom future correspondence in this matter may be carried on. Will there be any need for some of us to go there and see things for ourselves and talk over matters with these concerned?

Yours sincerely,
Sucheta Devi

---

1. Mr. Rafi Ahmed Kidwai.
2. Pt. Jawaharlal Nehru.

Document 138

TELEGRAM FROM MAULNA AZAD TO M.S. ANNEY

NEW DELHI,
18-5-42

M.S. ANNEY,

THANKS FOR YOUR TELEGRAM ACCEPTING OUR OFFER TO SEND MEDICAL UNIT ALONG MANIPUR-BURMA ROAD STOP.

WE ARE TAKING IMMEDIATE STEPS TO ORGANIZE UNIT AND HAVE REQUESTED DR. BIDHANCHANDRA ROY TO DO SO STOP SHALL INFORM.

ABUL KALAM AZAD

Document 139

LETTER FROM MAULANA AZAD TO JAWAHARLAL NEHRU

Calcutta,
18th May 1942

My dear Jawaharlal,

It seems that my letters to you on the Kulu address did not reach you, otherwise you would have known that I had cancelled my journey to Bombay, and you would not have wired to me there. I am sorry that you had to wire to Bombay owing to have missed my letters.

I want to meet Bapu alone first, and then we may meet him together. I shall leave for Wardha as soon as the urgent affairs allow me to do so. In the meantime, I request you to spare some time for Madras, if there be no other pressing engagement. You had told me in Allahabad that you would do so. It is necessary from every point of view. I would be thankful to you, if you could leave for Madras after staying in Allahabad for a few days. Thus on your return from Madras you can break journey at Wardha.

It is also possible, that if you could leave sooner for Madras, I may reach Wardha a few days before the probable date of your return from Madras, and then we may meet there.

Yours sincerely,
A.K. Azad

Document 140

LETTER FROM MAULANA AZAD TO J.B. KRIPALANI

Calcutta,

Dated, the 20th May '42

My Dear Kripalani,

I had written to you to send me without delay all the donations received directly in the office about the Congress Medical Mission, and to write to Messrs. Bachhraj Co., to send me all the amount received in this connection. In reply Mr. Sadiq Ali wrote that arrangements had been made about it. But more than a week has elasped and I have received neither the amount sent by the office, nor from Bombay.

I do not understand the cause of delay. Kindly send me all the amount received under this head.

My travelling and office bills have already been sent. I am waiting for their clearance also.

Hope you are doing well.

Yours sincerely,
A.K. Azad

Acharia J.B. Kripalani
A.I.C.C. Office
Allahabad.

Document 141

LETTER FROM MAULANA AZAD TO J.B. KRIPALANI

Calcutta,
23rd May
1942

My dear Kripalani,

Sometime in the year before last the attention of the office was drawn to the fact that the title head of office letter papers should be uniform in both Hindustani and English. The All India Congress Committee is not only known to the remotest villager but it has become an international term, moreover it is wrong on principle to translate proper nouns in other languages. Since the very time, the Congress came into existence, its name is Indian National Congress; we cannot adopt another name for it, unless the Congress itself does not change it. But in Nagri Script it has been translated into Akhil Bharatiya Congress Committee. Please get it changed into All India Congress Committee in Nagri Character also. If we change the name in Nagri characters, it becomes necessary to do the same in Urdu characters. If this is done, the same organisation will be called by three different names. This would be not only wrong but ridiculous. Names are never translated.

Only two writing pads were sent by the office last month. Please instruct them to send a few more. The paper used is rather thick, and carbon copies become faint. If possible, thinner paper might be used for some pads. But the first thing to be done is to have one name only in all the three characters. I hope you will pay immediate attention to this matter.

Yours sincerely,
A.K. Azad

Document 142

LETTER FROM J.B. KRIPALANI TO MAULANA AZAD

May 25, 1942

My dear Maulana Sahib,

Your letter of the 20th instt. received yesterday. Thanks. It would appear that you are not getting your post regularly or in due time. As soon as your wire about the money was received the office wired to the treasurer to send you the whole amount of the receipt up-to-date. The office had also informed you that we have taken this step. As soon as monies are received in the office they are transferred to Bombay. Therefore, money can be sent to you only from there.

The office has also sent you a cheque in payment of your travelling and office bills.

Yours sincerely,
J.B. Kripalani

Document 143

LETTER FROM JAWAHAR LAL NEHRU TO MAULANA AZAD

Station Road,
Lucknow, May 30, 1942

My dear Maulana,

I arrived here last night. I ought to have reached in the morning but, as usual, the Grand Trunk Express was five hours late and missed my connection at Jhansi, where I had to spend another eight or nine hours. Thus I missed an important day's sitting of our Provincial Council. Railway travelling is becoming increasingly difficult, especially when there is a change. Almost invariably one misses the connection. From Allahabad to Wardha is now a much more difficult journey than it was. There is only one partly suitable train and this lands one in Nagpur where one must stop for some hours.

Apart from other problems, I have to face the question of forfeiture of the security from the *National Herald*. We have filed another declaration today but no order has been passed upon it. This will probably be done on Monday. I am, therefore, staying on here till the night of Monday June 1st, and shall reach Allahabad on June 2nd morning.

I shall then be away from Allahabad for nearly a month. I have much to do there and many matters to attend to, but I shall keep myself ready to go to Wardha whenever you want me to do so. I should, however, like to have at least two clear days in Allahabad and, if possible, three. I hope you will send me directions as to when I should reach Wardha. My journey there will be a longer one than yours.

I spent just one day with Gandhiji. I am glad I went because I got to know a little of what he was thinking. During my stay at Kulu I was almost out off from newspapers and outside news. On coming back I was confronted by many new developments and I found myself rather at sea. The visit to Gandhiji and now the meeting of our Provincial Congress Committee, have helped me to understand the present situation. I told Gandhiji that I had come to listen to him and not to talk much, as I wanted to have time to think over what he said.

I understand here that the scheme for making provision for evacuee children from calcutta has fallen through or at any rate has made no progress. So we are not taking any further steps in the matter.

Yours
Jawahar Lal Nehru

Maulana Abul Kalam Azad

Document 144

LETTER FROM MAULANA AZAD TO JAWAHAR LAL NEHRU

Calcutta,

31st May 1942

My dear Jawaharlal,

Your letter of 27th May from Wardha had reached me day before yesterday. I am sending this letter to Allahabad, so that you may get it as soon as you reach there.

When you were staying in Calcutta en route to Assam, you might remember that one day I had a sudden attack of giddiness while talking to you. At Allahabad too, this complaint had happened once, but I did not take any notice of it. Recently it has recurred many a time, specially when I work long. The remedy seems to be, that I should give up the work for a few days and take rest; but you know the circumstances cannot permit me to do so. Even if I am allowed to do so, how would it be possible to take rest after leaving work?

I am much disturbed over certain matters. I do not know what are your feelings now. My mind seems to be much oppressed, which burden I cannot remove in any way.

You write that you will be ready after the 3rd June, owing to my present state of health, I think I shall not be able to leave on the 4th. I might be delayed for a few days. However, it is certain that we have to go to Wardha next week. If my complaint does not increase I may probably be able to leave on the 5th or 6th instant. In any case I shall let you know by telegram beforehand, so that you may also be able to leave Allahabad the same day.

The Medical Mission is working in Silchar satisfactorily. The local responsible men are praising its work. A number of refugees is coming to Goalundo. A Unit has, therefore, been sent there also. Kiran Sankar Roy is going there for its opening ceremony.

The refugees from Burma are also pouring in Sylhet and Karimganj. Most of them succumb to epidemic diseases. The local Congress Committee had made arrangements for doctors. They were in need of medicines, clothes and male-nurses, which we have supplied them.

Owing to the air raid by Japan on the borders of Assam, a new situation has arisen in the whole province. People leave the cities for villages, where owing to rains a great danger of seasonal diseases is imminent. Moreover, the Marwari grain dealers have totally vacated the province, which has caused great dislocation of grain business. There is no purchaser of the Assam paddy, and no one is there to supply them with other kinds of grains which are needed by Assam. The military is purchasing away all the local stock of medicines, and there is a great dearth of necessary medicines.

These conditions required our utmost vigilance to relieve the distress of Assam. I have done whatever I possibly could immediately, and I hope I shall be able to help them sufficiently from Calcutta.

Yours sincerely,

A.K. Azad

Pandit Jawahar Lal Nehru
Ananad Bhavan,
Allahabad

Document 145

LETTER FROM MAULANA AZAD TO JAWAHR LAL NEHRU

My Dear Jawahar Lal,

I am in receipt of your letter of 2nd June, and I got your telegram also. I wonder why my letters do not reach you. As you were reaching Allahabad on the Ist June I had despatched a letter on 31st May to your Allahabad address, so that you may get as soon as you reach there, later on I sent another letter on 3rd June in which I have informed you that I am leaving for Wardha on the 8th June, and hope that you would also be able to proceed the same day.

You have been writting to me from every place you visited in your tour. I am thankful to you for the same. I had similarly tried to keep you informed of my activities constantly, but it seems that you got my letters up to Lahore, after which you somehow missed them. I had written two letters to your Kulu address.

Probably the letters are now-a-days delayed owing to censorship, and perhaps they are lost also. Please ask the servants of Anand Bhavan about my letter of May 31, which might have been misplaced.

Owing to the matters connected with the Medical Mission, my departure to Wardha was delayed for three or four days. The Government of Assam had put certain obstacles in the smooth working of the Mission in Silchar. I was, therefore, prepared to withdraw it. But they are after all, now being removed by the intervention of General Wood. He has further requested the Congress to send a complete Unit with fifty volunteers to Dimapur also. I am, therefore, arranging to send it. Dr. Roy[1] is taking rest in Shillong.

However, I am leaving for Wardha on the 8th June, and I hope that you would also be able to proceed on the 8th.

I am sorry that you were troubled by not receiving my letters; but you may realise that it is not my fault.

Yours sincerely,
A.K. Azad

Pt. Jawahar Lal Nehru
Anand Bhawan
Allahabad

---

1. Dr. Bidhan Chandra Roy.

Document 146

LETTER FROM JAWAHAR LAL NEHRU TO MAULANA AZAD

Anand Bhawan
Allahabad,
June 5, 1942

My dear Maulana,

Ever since my return to Allahabad I have been anxiously waiting for news from you. I have sent you three telegrams but so far there has been no reply. I do hope you are well.

Ordinarily it would not have mattered much if I stayed here a few days more or not. I have plenty of work to do here. But I feel a little oppressed at the fact that big things are happening and we are passively looking on. I know that we cannot do much but even so this inactive condition is bound to injure the Congress. What we should do is another matter.

Invevitably this depends on full and frank talks with Gandhiji. He has taken up a certain attitude, with part of which I agree and part of which I do not. Or rather it would be more correct to say that I do not agree with his approach though generally speaking I agree with the actual work to be done. That of course is an old argument between us. But in the present circumstances it has ceased to be academic and is likely to affect all our work. Therefore, it is essential, as you yourself suggested, to have these talks with Gandhiji and not allow matters to drift any further. My brief talk with him last week, short as it was, had I think some good effect.

When I came away from Wardha, it was understood that I should be back by about the 4th June. It was presumed then that you would be going there about that time or earlier. Accordingly I promised to return by that date and I made an engagement with an American friend to meet me there. This American is already there waiting for me.

I feel that I should now go to Wardha as soon as possible in order not to upset arrangements any more. Even if I get there a day or two before you, I shall of course wait for you and remain there as long as you wish.

Last evening I sent you another express telegram. I am waiting for your reply. Unless I hear to the contrary from you, I should like to go to Wardha tomorrow morning reaching there on the 7th afternoon.

I am anxious about your health. I hope you have got over the feeling of giddiness that you simetimes had. Travelling in this weather is a trail but there is no help for it. Your journey to Wardha direct from Calcutta will at least be no-change one and more comfortable that mine is likely to be *via* Itarsi where I shall have to spend many hours.

Yours,
Jawahar Lal Nehru

Document 147

ALL INDIA CONGRESS WORKING COMMITTEE'S RESOLUTION WITH MAULANA AZAD AS PRESIDENT

Resolution passed by the Working Committee at Wardha on July 14, 1942.

Events happening from day to day, and the experience that the people of India are passing through, confirm the opinion of Congressmen that British rule in India must end immediately, not merely because foreign domination, even at its best, is an evil in itself and a continuing injury to the subject people, but because India in bondage can play no effective part in defending herself and in affecting the fortunes of the war that is desolating humanity. The freedom of India is thus necessary not only in the interest of India but also for the safety of the world and for the ending of Nazism, militarism and other forms of imperialism, and the aggression of one nation over an other.

Ever since the outbreak of the World War, the Congress has studiedly pursued a policy of non-embarrassment. Even at the risk of making its Satyagraha ineffective, it deliberately gave it a symbolic character, in the hope that this policy of non-embarrassment, carried to its logical extreme would be duly appreciated and that real power would be duly transferred to popular representatives, so as to enable the nation to make its fullest contribution towards the realisation of human freedom throughout the world, which is in danger of being crushed. It had also hoped that negatively nothing would be done which was calculated to tighten Britain's stranglehold on India.

These hopes have, however, been dashed to pieces. The abortive Cripps proposals showed in the clearest possible manner that there was no change in the British Government's attitude towards India and that the British hold on India was on no way to be relaxed. In the negotiations with Sir Stafford Cripps, Congress representatives tried their utmost to achieve a minimum consistent with the national demand, but to no avail. This frustration has resulted in a rapid and widespread increase of ill-will against Britain and a growing satisfaction at the success of Japanese arms. The Working Committee views this developments with grave apprehension as this, unless checked, will inevitably lead to a passive acceptance of aggression. The Committee hold that all aggression must be resisted, for any submission to it must mean the degradation of the Indian people and the continuation of their subjection. The Congress is anxious to avoid the experience of Malaya, Singapore, and Burma and desires to build up resistance to any aggression on or invasion of India by the Japanese or any foreign power.

The Congress would change the present ill-will against Britain into good-will and make India a willing partner in a joint enterprise of securing freedom for the nations and peoples of the world and in the trials and tribulations which accompany it. This is only possible if India feels the glow of freedom.

The Congress representatives have tried their utmost to bring about a solution of the communal tangle. But this has been made impossible by the presence of the foreign power whose long record has been to pursue relentlessly the policy of divide and rule. Only after the ending of foreign domination and intervention, can the present unreality give place to reality, and the people of India, belonging to all groups and parties, face India's problems and solve them on a mutually agreed basis. The present political parties, formed chiefly with a view to attract the attention of and influence the British Power, will then probably cease to function. For the first time in India's history, realisation will come home that princes, jagirdars, zamindars, and propertied and monied classes, derive their wealth and property from the workers in the fields and factories and elsewhere, to whom essentially power and authority must belong. On the withdrawal of British Rule in India, responsible men and women of the country will come together to form a Provisional Government, representatives of all important sections of the people of India, which will later evolve a scheme whereby a Constituent Assembly can be convened in order to prepare a constitution for the government of India acceptable to all sections of the people. Representatives of Free India and representatives of Great Britain will confer together for the adjustment of future relations and for the cooperation of the two countries as allies in the common task of meeting aggression. It is the earnest desire of the Congress to enable India to resist aggression effectively with the people's united will and strength behind it.

In making the proposal for the withdrawal of British Rule from India, the Congress has no desire whatsoever to embarrass Great Britain or the Allied Powers in their prosecution of the war, or in any way to encourage aggression on India or increased pressure on

China by the Japanese or any other Power associated with the Axis group. Nor does the Congress intend to jeopardise the defensive capacity of the Allied Powers. The Congress is therefore agreeable to the stationing of the armed forces of the Allies in India, should they so desire, in order to ward off and resist Japanese or other aggression, and to protect and help China.

The proposal of withdrawal of the British Power from India was never intended to mean the physical withdrawal of all Britishers from India, and certainly not of those who would make India their home and live there as citizens and as equals with the others. If such withdrawal takes place with goodwill, it would result in establishing a stable Provisional Government in India and co-operation between this Government and the United Nations in resisting aggession and helping China.

The Congress realises that there may be risks involved in such a course. Such risks, however, have to be faced by any country in order to achieve freedom and more especially at the present critical juncture, in order to save the country and the larger cause of freedom the world over from far greater risks and perils.

While, therefore, the Congress is impatient to achieve the national purpose, it wishes to take no hasty step and would like to avoid, insofar as is possible, any cause of action that might embarrass the United Nations. The Congress would plead with the British Power to accept the very reasonable and just proposal herein made, not only in the interest of India but also that of Britain and of the cause of freedom to which the United Nations proclaim their adherence.

Should however this appeal fail, the Congress cannot view without the gravest apprehension the continuation of the present state of affairs, involving a progressive deterioration in the situation and weakening of India's will and power to resist aggression. The Congress will then be reluctantly compelled to utilise all the non-violent strength it might have gathered since 1920, when it adopted non-violence as part of its policy for the vindication of political rights and liberty. Such a widespread struggle would inevitably be under the leadership of Gandhiji. As the issues raised are of the most vital and far reaching importance to the people of India as well as to the peoples of the United Nations, the Working Committee refer them to the All India Congress Committee for final decision. For this purpose the A.I.C.C. will meet in Bombay on the seventh of August, 1942.

2

Re: Evacuation and other Orders

Whereas, complaints have been received from various places regarding Government orders for evacuation of villages, lands and building without due notice and proper compensation, seizure and destruction of country boats, even where life is impossible without them, requisition of cycles, motor vehicles and carts without proper compensation and without regard for the needs of the civil population.

The Working Committee deem it necessary to issue the following instructions for the guidance of the people concerned and hope that the Government will take immediate and necessary steps to remove the grievances and that the people will carry out their instructions as circumstances demand, provided that in all cases before the final decision to disobey an order or resist any measure is taken, all possible avenues of negotiations and relief through negotiation shall be thoroughly explored.

With regard to evacuation and other orders involving loss, either temporary or permanent, of landed property of any kind full compensation should be demanded. In fixing the compensation the factors to be taken into consideration are the value of the land and the crops, the inconvenience and expenses likely to be caused to the holder of the land by having to move to another place and the difficulty and delay likely to be involved in obtaining other land where the dispossessed land holder could settle.

Wherever possible arrangement should be made for providing other land to agriculturists where their agricultural land is acquired. Where this is impossible compensation in money should be paid.

Value of trees, water-channels, and wells etc. taken over or destroyed should be included in the compensation.

In case of temporary acquisition of agricultural land the full value of the crop plus 15% of it should be paid for each crop lost and when the occupation by Government terminates compensation should be paid for restoring the land to its previous conditions for agricultural purposes.

Where the bulk of the land of an agricuturist is acquired and the balance left over is so small that it may not be worth cultivating, the balance too should be acquired.

Houses where acquired should be fully paid for where the whole or bulk of the agricultural land of an agriculturist is acquired and only his house is left over, the house should also be acquired by paying full compensation if the agriculturist so desires.

Where a house is to be occupied temporarily for Government purposes fair rent should be paid and the owner compensated for the inconvenience and discomfort caused.

No one should be required to vacate his house without arrangement being made elsewhere for his residence, and full compensation should be paid for transport of the evacuee's belongings and for his maintenance for a reasonable period to enable him to find suitable occupation in his new suroundings.

Compensation should in all cases be paid promptly and on the spot by a responsible officer and not at the headquarters of a District. In case no agreement is reached between the authorities and the evacuee regarding the amount of compensation and the matter has to be referred to a tribunal for decision, the amount of compensation proposed by the authorities should be paid forthwith and should not be withheld pending the adjudication of the claim.

There should be no interference with the use or disposal of private property except with the consent of the owner or on payment of adequate compensation.

In case of requisition of boats full compensation should be demanded and no boats should be surrendered till the question of compensation is settled. In areas surrounded by water boats are indispensable for normal everyday life they should not be surrendered at all.

Fishermen who depend upon their boats for earning their livelihood should be compensated for loss of their employment in addition to the price of their boat.

In case of requisition of cycles, motor vehicles, cars etc. full compensation should be demanded and until the question of compensation is settled they should not be parted with.

In view of scarcity of salt and apprehended famine of it due to war conditions, facilities should be provided for collection, preparation and transport of salt on the sea-coast and in inland areas, free of duty, by individuals. People may manufacture salt for their own consumption and that of their cattle.

With regard to restrictions on organisations for self-protection, the Committee is of opinion that it is the inherent right of all to protect their own life and property and those of their neighbours and therefore all restrictions on them should be disregarded.

Document 148

LETTER FROM C. RAJGOPALACHARIER TO MAULANA AZAD

48, Bazlullah Road,
Thyagarajyanagar, Madras,
August 4, 1942

Dear Maulana Sahib,

I have no right to advise you. Still I crave your leave to send these few words on this critical occasion for the consideration of colleagues with whom I have worked so long.

Whoever, may be in the wrong and whoever, may be to blame for it, so long as we cannot form a strong Provisional Government commanding the willing and immediate allegiance of the people of this vast country we have no rational basis for non-violent mass action of the kind now contemplated. We have no right at this juncture to plunge the country into disorder when we are so near to if not actually in the zone of war. A definite understanding and support from the enemy may justify revolutionary action on the part of a suffering and himiliated people, but that principle has no application in the present case.

I beg that you at once offer to Mr. Jinnah[1] – the clearest assurance that the people of every territorial area will have the right of political self-determination and ask him to co-operate with you now in the nomination of twelve trusted men to take over the entire Government of India from Britain pending the settlement of the constitution.

You say that the present proposal for direct action against British authority is the only way to achieve a rational basis for the proper defence of the country and that the British attitude has left no other alternative. I respectfully urge that this is far too artificial an argument and that in view of the anormous peril involved it should be given up.

I beg that Gandhiji may be given fullest authority to come to terms with the Muslim League and then lead the country either in negotiations with Britain or otherwise.

Yours sincerely,
C. Rajagopalacharier

---

1. Mr. M.A. Jinnah.

Document 149

ALL INDIA CONGRESS COMMITTEE'S RESOLUTION WITH MAULANA AZAD AS PRESIDENT

(The Congress Working Committee has passed the following Resolution at Bombay on August 7, 1942)

The All India Congress Committee has given the most careful consideration to the reference made to it by the Working Committee in their resolution dated July 14, 1942, and to subsequent events, including the development of the war situation, the utterances of responsible spokesman of the British Government, and the comments and criticisms made in India and abroad. The Committee approves of and endorse that resolution and is of opinion that events subsequent to it have given it further justification and have made it clear that the immediate ending of British rule in India is an urgent necessity, both for the sake of India and for the success of the cause of the United Nations. The continuation of that rule is degrading and enfeebling India and making her progressively less capable of defending herself and of contributing to the cause of world freedom.

The Committee has viewed with dismay the deterioration of the situation on the Russian and Chinese fronts and conveys to the Russian and Chinese peoples its high appreciation of their heroism in defence of their freedom. This increasing peril makes it incumbent on all those who strive for freedom, and who sympathise with the victims of aggression, to examine the foundations of the policy so far pursued by the Allied Nations, which have led to repeated and disastrous failure. It is not by adhering to such aims and policies and methods that failure can be converted into success, for past experience has shown that failure is inherent in them. These policies have been based not on freedom so much as on domination of subject and colonial countries and the continuation of the imperialist tradition and method.

The possession of empire, instead of adding to the strength of the ruling power, has become a burden and a cursed India, the classic land of modern imperialism, has become the crux of the question, for by the freedom of India will Britain and the United

Nations be judged, and the people of Asia and Africa be filled with hope and enthusiasm. The ending of British rule in this country is thus a vital and immediate issue on which depend the future of the war and the success of freedom and democracy.

A free India will assure the success by throwing all her great resources in the struggle for freedom and against the aggression of nazism, fascism and imperialism, This will not only affect materially the fortunes of the war, but will bring all subjected and oppressed humanity on the side of the United Nations, and give these Nations, whose ally India would be, the moral and spiritual leadership of the world. India in bondage will continue to be the symbol of British imperialism and the taint of the imperialism will affect the fortunes of all the United Nations.

The peril of today, therefore, necessitates the independence of India and the ending of British domination. No future promises or guarantees can effect the present situation or meet the peril. They cannot produce the needed psychological effect on the mind of the masses. Only the glow of freedom now can release that energy and enthusiasm of millions of people which will immediately transform the nature of the war.

The AICC therefore repeats with all emphasis the demand for the withdrawal of the British power from India. On the declaration of India's independence, a Provisional Government will be formed and Free India will become an ally of the United Nations, sharing with them in the trials and tribulations of the joint enterprise of the struggle for freedom. The Provisional Government can only be formed by the cooperation of the principal parties and groups in the country. It will thus be a composite government, representative of all important sections of the people of India. Its primary functions must be to defend India and resist aggression with all the armed as well as the non-violent forces at its command, together with its allied powers, to promote the well-being and progress of the workers in the fields and factories and elsewhere to whom essentially all power and authority must belong.

The Provisional Government will evolve a scheme for a Constituent Assembly which will prepare a constitution for the Government of India acceptable to all sections of the people. This Constitution according to the Congress view should be a federal one, with the largest measure of autonomy for the federating units, and with the residuary powers vesting in these units. The future relations between India and the Allied Nationas will be adjusted by representatives of all these free countires conferring together for their mutual advantage and for their cooperation in the common task of resisting aggression. Freedom will enable India to resist aggression effectively with the people's united will and strength behind it.

The freedom of India must be symbol of and prelude to the freedom of all other Asiatic nations under foreign dominations. Burma, Malaya, Indo-China, the Dutch Indies, Iran, Iraq must also attain their complete freedom. It must be clearly understood that such of these countries as are under Japanese control now must not subsequently be placed under the rule or control of any other colonial power.

While the AICC must primarily be concerned with the independence and defence of India in this hour of danger, the Committee is of opinion that the future peace, security and ordered progress of the world demand a World Federation of free nations, and on no other basis can the problems of the modern would be solved. Such a World federation would ensure the freedom of its constituent nations, the prevention of aggression and exploitation by one nation over another, the protection of national minorities, the advancement of all backward areas and peoples, and the pooling of the world's resources for common good of all. On the establishment of such a World Federation, disarmament would be practicable in all countries, national armies, navies and air forces no longer be necessary, and a World Federal Defence Force would keep the world peace and prevent aggression.

An independent India would gladly join such a World Federation and cooperate on an equal basis with other nations in the solution of international problems.

Such a federation should be open to all nations who agree with its fundamental principles. In view of the war, however, the Federation must inevitably, to begin with, be confined to the United Nations. Such a step taken now will have a most powerful effect on the war, on the peoples of the Axis countries, and on the peace to come.

The Committee regretfully realises, however, that despite the tragic and overwhelming lessons of the war and perils that overhang the world, the governments of few countries are yet prepared to take this inevitable step towards World Federation. The reaction of the British Government and the misguided criticisms of the foreign press also make it clear that even the obvious demand for India's independence is resisted though this has been made essentially to meet the present peril and to enable India to defend herself and help

China and Russia in their hour of need. The Committee is anxious not to embarrass in any way the defence of China or Russia, whose freedom is precious and must be preserved, or to jeopardise the defensive capacity of the United Nations. But the peril grows both to India and these nations, and inaction and submission to a foreign administration at this stage is not only degrading India and reducing her capacity to defend herself and resist aggression, but is no answer to that growing peril and is no service to the peoples of the United Nations. The earnest appeals of the Working Committee to Great Britain and the United Nations have so far met with no response, and the criticisms made in many foreign quarters have shown an ignorance of India's and the world's stand, and sometimes even hostility to India's freedom, which is significant of a mentality of domination and racial superiority which cannot be tolerated by a proud people conscious of their strength and of the justice of their cause.

The AICC would yet again, at this last moment, in the interest of world freedom, renew this appeal to Britain and the United Nations. But the Committee feels that it is no longer justified in holding the nation back from endeavouring to assert its will against an imperialist and authoritarian government which dominates over it and prevents it from functioning in its own interest and in the interest of humanity. The Committee resolves, therefore, to sanction for the vindication of India's inalienable right to freedom and independence, the starting of a mass struggle on non-violent lines on the widest possible scale, so that the country might utilise all the non-violent strength it has gathered during the last 22 years of peaceful struggle. Such a struggle must inevitably be under the leadership of Gandhiji and the Committee requests him to take the lead and guide the nation in the steps to be taken.

The Committee appeals to the people of India to face the dangers and hardships that will fall to their lot with courage and endurance, and to hold together under the leadership of Gandhiji, and carry out his instructions as disciplined soldiers of Indian freedom. They must remember that non-violence is the basis of this movement. A time may come when it may not be possible to issue instructions or for instructions to reach our people, and when no Congress Committee can function. When this happens, every man and women, who is participating in this movement must function for himself or herself within the four corners of the general instructions issued. Every Indian who desires freedom and strives for it must be his own guide urging him on along the hard road where there is no resting place

and which leads ultimately to the independence and deliverance of India.

Lastly, whilst the AICC has stated its own view of the future government under freed India, the AICC wishes to make it quite clear to all concerned that by embarking on mass struggle it has no intention of gaining power for the Congress. The power when it comes, will belong to the whole people of India.

Document 150

(Appendix-1)

Statement of Sardar Vallbhbhai Patel on C.P. Affair

The offence of rape was committed in 1936, in Wardha, in the house of Sub-Inspector Dawood, and the accused involved in the case were Jaffar, an officer of the Educational Department, the Sub-Inspector Dawood, a pleader named Surfuddin of Amraoti and three others, who were instruments employed by the principal accused. the last three were convicted and sentenced to two years. Jaffar was sentenced to three years and Dawood to four years Rigorous Imprisonment. The pleader Surfuddin was let off for want of identification. All accused happened to be Musalmans and the victim a girl of Mochi class – Hindu Harijan community of thirteen years of age. It was a most heinous offence and naturally it had become a sensational affair in C.P. for a long time till the trial ended some time in 1937, April, when the revision petition was finally rejected by the Chief Justice of the High Court and the sentences were confirmed. The case was tried in the court of an experienced Magistrate and the accused were ably defended by five lawyers. The girl was cross examined for six days and her deposition contained 111 pages. In the Appellate Court the case was referred by an European I.C.S. Officer, in whose court the appeal was transferred at the instance of the accused when the sentences were confirmed. A revision petition was refiled in the High Court where the Chief Justice himself read the petition at greater length than usual on account of the importance of the case. The petition was rejected and the findings and sentences were confirmed in April 1938. Jaffar was all along on bail till the revision petition was rejected in the High Court. No argument was advanced in any of the three Courts that there was any consent on the part of the girl, or that the offence was a technical. No plea for the reduction of sentences was made at all in any court.

Mercy petition was made on behalf of Jaffar during the past regime by his relatives but it was rejected by the then Home Member expressing surprise that the case was recommended in the absence of any petition from the prisoner concerned.

In January 1938, Mr. Sharif, the Minister of Justice passed orders for releasing the three less important prisoners by reducing their sentences for one year and in doing so, he seems to have examined the judgments of the three courts and recorded a finding that the decisions of the Judicial Courts were based either on incorrect appreciation of facts, or on some such other grounds. In his order he has stated that the offence was merely technical and the girl was a willing party to the inter-course and the sentences passed were severe and unjustified. After the release of these prisoners Jaffar's own application appears to have been entertained, evidently the way for exercise of clemency in his case being made clear by the above order in the other case. On this petition Mr. Shareef recorded an order stating that the reasons given by him for clemency in the other case applied in this case also. In addition he noted that Jaffar having lost his wife and having minor children with nobody to look after, he should be released. At this time he had only put in less than one year's period in jail. This petition of Jaffar's was recommended by the legal Secretary, who had suggested that one year's remission of sentence may be given. The D.C. had not recommended the petition. It may be noted that except Mr. Shareef nobody, not even the accused, had ever dared to suggest that the offence was technical or that there was any consent on the part of the girl. It has been argued by him that the girl had previous sexual experience, but there is no such positive proof for such inference. The Medical evidence is quite consistent with the opposite theory.

After the release of Jaffar in the beginning of February, Sub-Inspector Dawood's application was entertained and he would naturally, in view of the orders in the other cases have been released as a matter of course. The order in Dawood's petition is said to be that the papers should be placed before him after the 10th April. The explanation given for such order is that he wanted to allow the Legislative Assembly Sessions to be over before passing orders in this case.

In the meanwhile, an attempt was made by Mr. Shareef to appoint Mr. Surfuddin, the pleader who was involved in this case, but was discharged for want of identification, as Public Prosecutor of Amraoti. This was stoutly opposed by all the other Ministers and the attempt had to be given up. Mr. Shareef then also admitted that there was pressure from his (Shareef's) wife in this affair, because she happens to be the sister of Surfuddin's wife.

About the 9th or the 10th of March, the party meeting was called at the instance of some of the members of the Congress

Assembly party to discuss this question as there was a lot of agitation in the city. In this meeting Mr. Shareef himself was present. Mrs. Kale, the Deputy Speaker bitterly attacked the action of Mr. Shareef and she broke down and wept. Mr. Shareef in that meeting took a defiant attitude and said that the matter as such that it could not be discussed in detail in the presence of ladies and that he had full justification for the release.

In my capacity as the Chairman of the All India Congress Parliamentary Sub-Committee went to Wardha on the 11th March 1938 and called for Dr. Khare, the Prime Minister and Mr. Ravishankar Shukla in order to ascertain the true facts in the case. They pleaded absolute ignorance and said they also learnt about the release of Jaffar from the Press for the first time. The whole thing was kept secret for over two months and both of them were very angry and felt that there was no alternative, but to ask him to resign. I took Dr. Khare with me to Shegaon, there we met Mahatma Gandhi. Dr. Khare narrated the whole story to Mahatmaji. He agreed that there was no alternative and Mr. Shareef must resign. As the matter involved serious consequences which may have repercussions even outside the province, it was decided that the matter should be reported to the Working Committee, who should take the responsibility of the decision.

It is admitted by Mr. Shareef that he had not informed any of his colleagues about these orders.

Mr. Shareef is not an inexperienced man. He was Minister of Education for a fairly long time in the past regime, when he was Education Minister he knew Jaffar because Jaffar was under him and had joined him in his tours in the Amraoti division. It is admitted that Jaffar and Surfuddin were both known to Mr. Shareef. As there were rumours about some other cases in which prisoners convicted of offences involving moral turpitude were released Dr. Khare was asked to submit his report on this case and also a statement of other cases in which sentences were remitted together with Mr. Shareef's explanation in the matter.

Before submitting the report a party meeting of the Assembly members was held which lasted for about eight hours. It was a stormy meeting. Mrs. Kale led the attack again and when she could not bear the agony she wept bitterly. Mr. Shareef left the meeting at this stage. He went home and sent a note saying that "he could not bear the sight of a sister weeping in his presence and therefore he left the meeting. But if his resignation was the only thing that would satisfy her he was prepared to do so. At the end of the meeting a resolution of vote of confidence was passed with a recommendation to the Working Committee for the acceptance. This resolution was passed on the understanding that Mr. Shareef had given an apology or expressed regret for his having committed a grave error of judgment in releasing Jaffar. It is admitted by the Ministers that neither they nor the party would have accepted this apology as sufficient, if it was given for his effort in not consulting his colleagues before passing the order of release in such a sensational case, which he must have known would result in raising the storm in the province. Mr. Shareef contends that he was not given an apology for his action of releasing Jaffar. He contends that his action was justified as he considered the offence to be a technical one. He says his apology was only with regard to his having failed to consult his colleagues in a case of this nature, which he after the agitation realised was an error of judgement.

Vallabhbhai Patel,
Chairman
All India Congress Parliamentary Sub-Committee.

Congress House,
Bombay-4
1-6-1938

Copy to Maulana Abul Kalam Azad

Document 151

(Appendix - 2)

WORKING COMMITTEE'S RESOLUTIONS

(The Congress Working Committee, at its meeting held in Bombay from the 2nd to the 4th inst. has passed the following important Resolutions regarding the Congress Ministries)

1. The Working Committee have considered the motion relating to the release of political prisoners, the repeal of repressive laws and other allied matters, which was referred to them by the A.I.C.C. at Calcutta. The Committee, after full and careful consideration of the situation in the various provinces and the difficulties inherent in the present position record their approval of the work done so far by the Congress Ministries, and appreciate that further efforts are being made to enlarge the bounds of civil liberty and implement the Congress programme. The Committee are confident that such efforts will be continued by the Ministries and will have the full co-operation of all Congressmen. The Committee are of opinion that in order to facilitate and expedite progress in this direction, as well as to strengthen the Congress organization in the struggle for Swaraj, it is necessary to adhere to the Congress policy of non-violence and to discourage, all incitements to violence. The Committee apeal to Congress Committee and individual Congressmen to help create an atmosphere of peaceful disciplined action in the country and to warn any erring Congressman against any tendency which militates against our policy of non-violence. Where necessary, Congress Committees should take disciplinary action against Congressmen who offend against the Congress policy.

Congress Ministries must guide themselves by the principle of civil liberty and the democratic approach by means of persuasion rather than by coercive action. But in spite of every desire to avoid it, coercive action may become necessary, and in such cases Ministries will inevitably have to undertake it. Such coercive action should only be undertaken where there has been violence or incitement to violence or communal strife.

2. The Working Committee considered the resolution of the Executive of the Bihar P.C.C. regarding the activities of some members of the Kisan Sabha in that province, and also considered representation in connection therewith. The Committee desire to make it clear that while the Congress fully recognises the rights of Kisans to organise themselves in Kisan Sabhas, it cannot associate itself with any activities which run counter to the basic principles of the Congress. The Working Committee are in agreement with the Executive of the Bihar P.C.C. in disapproving of the activities of those Congressmen who as members of the Kisan Sabha help in creating an atmosphere of violence. Such conduct renders them liable to disciplinary action, and the Bihar P.C.C. should take such action wherever necessary, after due notice to the parties concerned.

3. The Working Committee has learnt with strong disapproval that in the course of recent Congress delegate elections in some provinces, violence and other objectionable behaviour was resorted to by some candidates or their supporters. Such behaviour on the part of Congressman cannot be tolerated and the Provincial Congress Committees concerned should institute immediate enquiries and take strongest action whenever called for.

Document 152

(Appendix-3)

Text of the judgment delivered by the City Magistrate of Allahabad in the case against Maulana Azad, Congress President, sentencing him to eighteen months' simple imprisonment under the Defence of India Act:[1]

"Maulana Abul Kalam Azad, President of the Indian National Congress, admits having made the speech in the Purushottamdas Park, Allahabad, on December 13, 1940, which as recorded by shorthand report and later read out by him to witnesses who signed the shorthand version. This speech is proved by the shorthand reporter.

"Maulana Azad, in his statement says that the recorded speech is full of mistakes and errors, but inasmuch as it proclaims the declared Policy of the Congress not to assist in the prosecution of the war, it is correct and he assumes full responsibility not only for having proclaimed this in the speech here but also all over India and also for having instructed several other to proclaim this policy all over. The speech abounds in passages which aim at bringing the British Government into hatred and contempt and at prejudicing the efficient prosecution of the war. These are prejudicial acts under Rule 34 and he has accordingly been charged under Rule 38(5) of the Defence of India Rules to which charge he has pleaded guilty.

"It is to be noted that although the Congress has drawn up the well ordered programme of informing the authorities in time of the date, time and place of carrying out anti-war slogan in this instance, the Congress President himself delivered a violent anti-war speech in total disregard of the well-disciplined programme evolved by the Congress in conducting Satyagraha.

1. 'The Hindu', January 10, 1941

Document 153

(Appendix-3)

SIR STAFFORD CRIPPS' DRAFT DECLARATION ON BEHALF OF THE BRITISH GOVERNMENT

His Majesty's Government having considered the anxieties expressed in this country and in India as to the fulfilment of promise made in regard to the future of India, steps which they propose shall be taken for the earliest possible realization of self-government in India. The object is the creation of a new Indian Union which shall constitute a Dominion associated with the United Kingdom and other Dominions by a common allegiance to the Crown but equal to them in every respect, in no way subordinate in any aspect of its domestic and external affairs.

His Majesty's Government therefore make the following declaration:

(a) Immediately upon cessation of hostilities steps shall be taken to set up in India in manner described hereafter an elected body charged with the task of framing a new Constitution for India.

(b) Provision shall be made, as set out below, for participation of Indian States in the constitution-making body.

(c) His Majesty's Government undertake to accept and implement forthwith the Constitution so framed subject only to (i) the right of any province of British India that is not prepared to accept the new Constitution to retain its present constitutional position, provision being made for its subsequent accession if it so decides.

With such non-acceding provinces, should they so desire, His Majesty's Government will be prepared to agree upon a new Constitution giving them the same full status as the Indian Union and arrived at by a procedure analogous to that here laid down.

(ii) The signing of a treaty which shall be negotiated between His Majesty's Government and the constitution making body. This treaty will cover all necessary matters arising out of the complete transfer of responsibility from British to Indian hands; it will make provision, in accordance with undertakings given by His Majesty's Government for the protection of racial and religious minorities; but will not impose any restriction on the power of the Indian Union to decide in future its relationship to other member States of the British Commonwealth.

Whether or not an Indian State elects to adhere to the Constitution it will be necessary to negotiate a revision of its treaty arrangements so far as this may be required in the new situation.

(d) The constitution-making body shall be composed as follows unless the leaders of Indian opinion in the principal communities agree upon some other form before the end of hostilities.

Immediately upon the result being known of provincial elections which will be necessary at the end of hostilities, the entire membership of the Lower Houses of Provincial Legislatures shall as a single electoral college proceed to the election of the constitution-making body by the system of proportional representation. This new body shall be in number about 1/10th of the number of the electoral college.

Indian States shall be invited to appoint representatives in the same proportion as to their total population as in the case of representatives of British India as a whole and with the same powers as British Indian members.

(e) During the critical period which now faces India and until the new constitution can be framed His Majesty's Government must inevitably bear the responsibility for and retain the control and direction of the Defence of India as part of their World War effort but the task of organizing to the full the military, moral and material resources of India must be the responsibility of the Government of India with the co-operation of the peoples of India. His Majesty's Government desire and invite the immediate and effective participation of the leaders of the principal sections of the Indian people in the counsels of their country, of the Commonwealth and of the United Nations. Thus they will be enabled to give their active and constructive help in the discharge of a task which is vital and essential for the future freedom of India.

Document 154

Appendix 5

GANDHIJI'S APPEAL TO MUSLIMS

Sevagram,

20-7-1942

I have read with attention Quaid-e-Azam's reply to my article in *Harijan*. "Pakistan" according to him in a nutshell" "is a demand for carving out of India a portion to be wholly treated as an independent and Sovereign State." This Soverign State can conceivably go to war against the one of which it was but yesterday a part. It can also equally conceivably make treaties with other States. All this can certainly be had, but surely not by the willing consent of the rest.

But it seems he does not want it by consent. For he says, "Pakistan is an article of faith with Muslim India and we depend upon nobody except ourselves for the achievement of our goal." How is one to offer one's service in these circumstances?

But later he gives me hope, for he says: "Show your sincerity and frankness for an honourable settlement." In order to show both, I wrote the article to which the Quaid-e-Azam has objected. How also is one to show sincerity and frankness expect through one's action and speech or pen?

Let me state my limitations. I cannot speak as a mere Hindu, for my Hinduism includes all religions. I can speak only as an Indian. If Pakistan as defined above is an article of faith with him, indivisible India is equally an article of faith with me. Hence, there is a stalemate.

But today there is neither Pakistan nor Hindustan. It is Englistan. So I say to all-India, let us first convert it into the original Hindustan and then adjust all rival claims. This is surely clear. After the restoration of India to the nation, there will be no Central Government. The representatives all have to construct it. It may be one Hindustan many Pakistans.

If the Quaid-e-Azam really wants a settlement, I am more than willing and so is the Congress. He will forgive me for suggesting that his reply leaves on one the impression that he does not want a settlement. If he wants one, why not accept the Congress President offer that Congress and League representatives should put their heads together and never part until they have reached a settlement. Is there any flaw or want of sincerity in this offer?

Who's Who

Abdullah, Sheikh Muhammad	: A Prominent leader of Kashmir Valley; was sent to jail in 1946 by Maharaja, became the head of Government of State of Jammu and Kashmir (1947) and the Premier since 1948.
Alexender, A.V.	: A prominent figure of British Cabinet, headed by Clement Attlee in 1945, a member of Cabinet mission plan sent to India by British Government in 1946.
Amery, L.S.	: Secretary of State for India during the Second World War.
Anney, M.S.	: Reputed national leader, some time member of Viceroy's Council; was the president of first session of All India Hindu League held at Lucknow in 1935.
Anugraha Narayan Singh	: A leading Congressmen of Bihar, Finance Minister in the Cabinet of Shri Krishna Sinha in 1946.
Asaf Ali	: A prominent Congess leader of Delhi, was appointed a Minister in Interim Government in 1946.
Asaf Ali, Aruna	: Wife of Mr. Asaf Ali who actively took part in the Quit India Movement, launched by Mahatma Gandhi in 1942.
Attlee, Clement	: Labour Party Leader and the Prime Minister of Great Britain in 1945. Many important events relating to Indian Independence including Cabinet Mission Plan accrued during his tenure of Prime Ministership.

Bajaj, Jamuna Lal	:	Prominent Congress leader of Central Provinces and businessman, President Charkha Sangh and the trasurer of A.I.C.C., took active part in the Nagpur Flag satyagraha in 1923.
Bardoloi, Gopinath	:	Prominent Congess leader of Assam; became the Premier of the State in 1937 and Chief Minister in 1946.
Bhave, Vinoba	:	Gandhian thinker and Bhoodan leader.
Birla, G.D.	:	Well-known industrialist and a devotee of Mahatma Gandhi, was president of Harijan Sevak Sangh, became member of Central Legislative Assembly.
Bose, Sarat Chandra	:	Prominent Congress leader of Bengal and elder brother of Netaji Subhas Chandra Bose. He was a member of Interim Government, headed by Pandit Nehru in 1946.
Bose, Subhas Chandra	:	Great Patriot and front-ranking Congress leader of Bengal, elected President of Indian National Congress twice in 1938 at Haripura and in 1939 at Tripuri; founder of Forward Bloc (1939), Indian National Army and Indian National Government during the Second World War, imprisoned several times during National Liberation Movement.
Choudhry Khaliquzzaman	:	A prominent leader of United Provinces Muslim League; was elected to U.P. Legislative Assembly in 1937.
Cripps, Sir Stafford	:	A Minister in the Cabinet of C.R. Attlee, was a member of Cabinet Mission Plan, sent to India by British Government in 1946. He is also popular for his proposals of 1942.
Das, Biswanath	:	Leader of Orissa Congress Legislative Party and the Premier of the State in 1937.
Deo, Shankarrao	:	A front ranking Congress leader of Maharashtra, was appointed a member to the Working Committee of Indian National Congress by Maulana Azad in 1940.

Desai, Bhulabhai J.	: A prominent Congress leader and well-known Advocate of Bombay; Leader of Congress Party in Central Legislative Assembly (1946), Marvellously pleaded for I.N.A. Convicts (1946). His parleys with Liyakat Ali Khan when Congress Leaders were in jail regarding the future set-up of National Government had been one of the reasons for Congress, this commands cool attitude towards him. A nearest friend of Maulana Azad.
Deshmukh, R.M.	: Chief Minister of Vindhya Pradesh (1947-50).
Diwakar, R.R.	: Well-known Congress leader of Karnataka; was appointed a Minister of State in Central Government in 1948.
Gadgil, N.V.	: A prominent Congress leader of Maharashtra was appointed a minister in Union Cabinet by Nehruji.
Gandhi, Devadas	: Youngest son of Mahatma Gandhi and son-in-law of C. Rajgopalacharier. A managing editor of the Hindustan Times.
Gandhi, M.K.	: Supreme Leader of National Liberation Movement and Indian National Congress (1920-47), President of I.N.C. (1925), Editor of Young India and Navjeevan (1920-31), Harijan, Harijan Bandhu and Harijan Sewak (1933-42), Participated in the Second Round Table Conference, held in London in 1931.
Ghose, P.C.	: A Congress leader of Bengal; was the Chief Minister of West Bengal before Dr. B.C. Roy.
Hafiz Abrahim	: A Congressman of U.P. and freedom fighter.
Hakim Ajmal Khan	: Front ranking Congress leader of Delhi and a prominent figure of Non-co-operation and Khilafat movement (1920), was a member of Congress Working Committee (1923-26); was elected President to 36th Session of Indian National Congress, held at Ahmedabad in 1921.
Haq, A.K. Fazlul	: Leader of Krishak Praja Party of Bengal and Premier of Bengal.

Hasan, S.M. : A member in the Central Provinces Ministry in 1937 and again in 1946.

Humayun Kabir : A close associate of Maulana Azad, was appointed a State Minister in the Union Government in 1959.

Jairamdas Daulataram : Congress leader of Sind; member Working Committee (1940-46), Minister in the Union Cabinet, headed by Pt. Nehru; Governor of Bihar in 1947.

Jinnah, M.A. : Vice-Chancellor of Osmania University; Supreme leader of Muslim League since 1934; member Indian Legislative Assembly (1924-34); first Governor General of Pakistan.

Khan Abdul Ghaffar Khan : Frontier Gandhi and Organiser of Khudai Khidmatgars in N.W.F.P. Started Red Shirt movement in the province (1930); member Congress Working Committee from 1936 to 1947.

Khan Saheb, Dr. : Elder brother of Frontier Gandhi and a leading Congressman, became the Premier of N.W.F.P. in 1946.

Khare, N.B. : Premier of Central Provinces in 1937.

Kidwai, Rafi Ahmad: Prominent Congress leader of U.P.; a nearest friend of Pandit Nehru; became a member of the Union Cabinet in 1952.

Kripalani, J.B. : A front ranking Congress leader; was appointed the Principal of Gujarat Vidyapith; imprisoned several times during the National Liberation Movement; elected President to the Meerut Session of I.N.C. in 1946.

Liquat Ali Khan : Prominent leader of U.P. Muslim League; leader Muslim League Parliamentry Party (1946); became the first Prime Minister of Pakistan in 1947.

Pathick Lawrance, Sir : A sinior British Statesman; was a member of Cabinet Mission Plan, sent to India by the

British Government in 1946; was appointed Secretary of State for India in 1945 in place of Amery.

Madni, Hussain Ahmed : President Jamiat Ulema-i-Hind and noted scholar of Islamic Philosophy, founder of Darul Ulum, Deoband and a nearest friend of Maulana Azad.

Mahtab, H.K. : Veteran freedom fighter and Congress leader of Orissa; was the Chief Minister of the state from 1946 to 1950.

Misra, Chintamani : Congressman and Journalist of Orissa.

Misra, D.P. : Leading Congressman of Central Province, Minister in the State Government in 1937 and again in 1946.

Mufti, Kifaytullah : Scholar and freedom fighter of U.P.

Munshi, K.M. : A well-known Barrister and Congress leader of Bombay; was appointed Agent General by Government of India in Hyderabad State in 1948.

Naidu, Sarojini : Top ranking Congress Worker of Hyderabad; was elected the President of Indian National Congress (1926); became the first Governor of U.P. after independence.

Narayan, Jaiprakash : Founder Secretary of the Socialist Party of India and a noted freedom fighter.

Ram, Narayan : Famous Congress worker of Bihar; was an associate of Dr. Rajendra Prasad.

Nawab Ismail Khan : Leader of U.P. Muslim League; was elected to the State Assembly in 1937 and again in 1946.

Nehru, Jawahar Lal : A leading figure of National liberation movement, was elected President of Indian National Congress in 1929, 1936, 1937 and 1946; founder, All India Kisan Sabha, Bharat Krishak Samaj and the President of States Peoples Organisation; became the first Prime Minister of India after independence in 1947.

Pandit, Nilakantha Das	: Leading Congressman of Orissa.
Pandit, Ranjit	: A well-known freedom fighter and Congress worker of U.P. Brother-in-law of Pandit Jawahar Lal Nehru.
Pandit, Vijaya Lakshmi	: Younger sister of Pandit Jawahar Lal Nehru; was elected to the Legislative Assembly of U.P. (1937); became the Chair-person of the General Assembly of U.N.O.; appointed Indian Ambassador to Soviet Union.
Paliwal, S. K.D.	: A leading Congress worker of U.P.
Pant, G.B.	: Front ranking Congress leader of U.P.; became the Premier of the state in 1937 and the Chief Minister in 1946; elected to the Working Committee of I.N.C. several times between 1936 and 1950; was appointed Home Minister in the Union Cabinet headed by Pandit Nehru.
Patel, Manibehn	: Famous social worker and freedom fighter; became the member of Congress Working Committee in 1950; was elected to the Indian Parliament several times between 1952 and 1980. She was the daughter of Sardar Vallabhbhai Patel.
Patwardhan, Achyut	: Noted freedom fighter and Socialist Party leader.
Prakasam, T.	: Leading Congressman of Andhra Pradesh; became the Chief Minister in 1946.
Prasad, Rajendra	: Top-ranking Congress leader and constructive worker of Bihar; was a colleague of Maulana Azad, Sardar Patel and Pandit Nehru and associate of Mahatma Gandhi; elected President of Indian National Congress (1935); became a member Congress Parliamentary Board (1937); appointed Food and Civil Supplies Minister in the interim government (1946); elected Chairman Constituent Assembly (1946) and the President of Indian Republic in 1950, 1952 and 1957.
Rajagopalachari, C.	: Gandhian thinker and front ranking Congressman of Madras, became Premier of

Madras in 1937, later on was also its Chief Minister; was the first and last Indian Governor-General (1948-50); appointed Minister for Home Affairs in the Government of India in 1950. Well-known for his suave diplomacy and cruditeness; founder of Swatantra Party of India.

Roy, B.C. : Renowned doctor and Congress leader of Bengal, became the Chief Minister of W.B. in 1939.

Roy, M.N. : Well-known thinker and freedom fighter of Bengal; participated in Communist International, held in Moscow in 1920; was defeated by Maulana Azad in the election of Congress Presidentship at Wardha in 1940.

Sahay, K.B. : A Parliamentary Secretary in Bihar Ministry in 1937.

Sadulla, Muhammad: Leader of Assam Muslim League; became Premier of the State in 1939.

Sanskrityayan, Rahul: A noted freedom fighter and progressive writer.

Shah, Shantilal Harjivanlal : Constructive worker of Gujarat; was a founder member of Indian National Trade Union Congress and Incharge of Congress Election Office in 1945-46.

Singh, Sardar Baldev : Senior Akali leader, was included as Sikh representative in the Interim Government (1946); appointed as a senior member in free India's cabinet of Pandit Jawaharlal Nehru.

Sinha, Sri Krishna : A well known Congress leader of Bihar, became the Chief Minister of the province.

Singh, Tara (Master) : Akali leader of Punjab who started agitation for separate Sikh State.

Sitaramaiyya B., Pattabhi : Leading Congressman of Andhra; was elected President of Indian National Congress in 1948.

Sri Prakasa : Congress leader of U.P.; appointed Indian High Commissioner to Pakistan (1947); became Governor of Assam in 1945.

Glossary

Ahimsa	:	Non-violence
Akali Dal	:	Religious and Political Organization of the Sikhs.
All India Spinners Association	:	An all-India body, formed by Gandhiji in 1925 to provide employment to the starving millions of India.
Bapu	:	Literally father, a generic term to denote respect to elder, a term widely used by Indian people for Gandhiji.
Civil Disobedience Movement	:	Non-violent or Satyagaraha Movement of Mahatma Gandhi to resist British Rule in India.
Charkha	:	Spinning wheel.
Constructive Programme	:	Mahatma Gandhi's eighteen point programme for India's resurgence.
Dharma	:	Religion
Gurudwara	:	Worship place of Sikhs.
Harijan	:	The term used by Mahatma Gandhi for the people belonging to Scheduled Castes of India; weekly started by Gandhiji since 1933.
Individual Satyagraha	:	Mahatma Gandhi's campaign of 1940 through Satyagrahis of his choice of protest against Britain's war-effort in India.
Khadi	:	Hand-Spun and hand-woven cloth.
Lahore Resolution	:	A Resolution passed by All India Muslim League in March, 1940 at Lahore, under the Presidentship of Mr. Mohammed Ali Jinnah, to launch

an agitation to get India divided into two nations.

Mahatma : A title bestowed on Gandhiji by Dr. Rabindra Nath Tagore.

Non-Violence : Ahimsa which along with truth and love formed the *summum bonum* of the Philosophical view of Mahatma Gandhi's positive force to resist tyranny and injustice.

Qaumi Ekta : National Unity. The Rule of God, Mahatma Gandhi's conception on ideal non-exploitation human society wedded to truth, non-violence, brotherhood, love and communal harmony.

Quit India Movement : Started by Mahatma Gandhi on August 9, 1942 to force the Britain to quit India. Gandhiji, by starting the movement, exhorted the people to adopt any means to fight against the civil designs of imperialistic government which were ruthlessly suppressing people.

Quit India Resolution : A resolution adopted by the All India Congress Committee in Bombay on 8 August, 1942, under the presidentship of Maulana Abul Kalam Azad to force the British to withdraw from India.

Rajaji formula : A formula, popularly known as 'Rajaji formula' put forward by Chakraborty Rajgopalacharier in connection with the working arrangement with the Muslim League. Rajaji had developed a conviction that only division of the country was the appropriate political solution for the constitutional problem of India.

Sardar : Leader or captain; a title bestowed on Vallabhbhai Patel by Mahatma Gandhi in 1928 after the victory of Bardoli Kisan Satyagraha.

Satyagraha : Literally insistence on truth, Mahatma Gandhi's weapon of truth and love (with non-violence) for mass action.

Satyagrahi : A believer of Satyagraha.

Swaraj	: Self Rule with complete independence.
Zamindar	: Landlord.
Zamindari	: Landlordism.
Zulum	: Atrocities.

Chronology of Events

1936	: Elected a member to the Parliamentary Board of Indian National Congress. Sardar Vallabhbhai Patel was its Chairman and Dr. Rajendra Prasad another member.
1937	: Took the view that the Congress members of Sind Legislative Assembly should not support the Allah Bux Ministry, under any circumstances.
1938: July 17	: Sent his confidential report on the Political situation of Bihar Province to the All India Congress Parliamentary Board.
1939	: Working Committee of Indian National Congress favoured Maulana Azad for the Presidentship of Tripuri Session but he declined to contest.
Feb. 27	: Presided over the open Session of Indian National Congress in Place of Babu Subhash Chandra Bose.
Sept. 16	: Maulana Azad, along with Sardar Patel and Pandit Nehru, appealed the Congressmen to maintain unity and discipline in the party.
Dec. 21	: Issued a statement against the deliverance day of Muslim League.
1940: March 19	: Presided over the Congress Session at Wardha.
July 31	: Tried to minimise the apprehension of Congressmen on Gandhiji's separation from Congress by issuing a public statement.
Nov. 6	: C.G.M.A. of Bombay requested Maulana Azad to stop the fast of Mahatma Gandhi.
Nov. 19	: Arrested in Caluctta in the Individual Civil Disobedience Movement launched to protest against the war and uphold the freedom of speech.

Index

A

Abdullah Butt of Lahore, 8, 16, 22, 49
Abyssinia, 80
African Countries, 115
Africa, South, 99
Agra, 42
Ahimsa (Non-violence), 296
Ahmedabad, 4, 8
Ahmed Nagar, 153
Akali Dal, 118, 296
Akalis and the Congress, 154
Akbar Hyderi, 188
Albania, 88
Al-Hilal, 18; an Urdu Weekly, 18, 109, 112, 128
Ali Asaf, 155, Aruna, 213, 289
Ali, Hyder Khan, 76
Ali, Sadiq, 259
Ali, Shaukat, 54
Ali, Zaheer, 53
Allahabad, 17, 57, 61, 66, 120, 142, 149, 150, 153, 154, 169, 170, 187, 200, 201, 257, 262, 284, 285,
City Majistrate of, 204,
District, 202
Allahbax Khan Bahadur, 202, 299
All India Congress Committee, 9, 16, 17, 19, 20, 22, 39, 42, 43, 44, 45, 57, 59, 61, 63, 64, 66, 76, 77, 80, 98, 100, 105, 108, 115, 116, 117, 118, 139, 144, 146, 150, 151, 159, 161, 163, 164, 165, 168, 170, 173, 174, 175, 176, 177, 178, 179, 180, 181, 182, 188, 189, 192, 193, 194, 195, 196, 198, 199, 207, 212, 213, 214, 216, 217, 223, 224, 230, 237, 238, 240, 241, 242, 243, 244, 247, 248, 249, 251, 268, 272, 273, 274, 275, 276, 277, 282, 283, 297, 299, 300, Also see Congress, Indian National and Working Committee of the Congress.
All India Hindu League, 289.
All India Radio, 3, 52; Calcutta, 208
All India Muslim League, 9, 13, 39, 53, 90, 91, 133, 161, 296, 297, 299.
All India Spinners' Association, 9
Almora, 146
America, 143, 144, 146,
American, 177
Amraoti, 270
Andhra, 124
Anney, M.S., 17, 289
Angel, 1
Anis-Ur-Rehman, 255
Ansari, M.A.'s Wife, 54
Anti-British, 18.
Anti-German, 89
Anti-Wafdist, 40
Appellate Court, 270
Arabic Scholar, 18
Arrah, 68
Assam, 6, 7, 66, 74, 85, 263
Assam Cabinet, 66
Assembly Party Central, 29
Assembly Party of Congress, 45
Association, British India of Oudh, 42
Atrocities, 298
Attlee, Clement, 289
Auckland Colvin, 109; A former Lt. Governor of N.W.F.P., 109
Australia, 99
Austria, 88
Austrian, 88
A. Wahid, 54
Axis Countries, 276
Azad, Maulana Abul Kalam, 1, 2, 3, 4, 6, 7, 8, 11, 12, 13, 15, 16, 17, 18, 20, 22, 23, 24, 25, 26, 28, 37, 38, 39, 40, 41, 42, 43, 44, 46, 47, 48, 49, 50, 51, 52, 53, 54, 55, 56, 57, 58, 59, 61, 62, 63, 64, 65, 66, 69, 70, 71, 72, 75, 76, 77, 78, 80, 81, 82, 83,

84, 85, 86, 88, 93, 94, 95, 115, 118, 119, 120, 122, 126, 127, 132, 133, 134, 135, 136, 137, 138, 139, 140, 142, 143, 146, 147, 149, 150, 151, 152, 155, 157, 158, 159, 160, 161, 162, 163, 164, 165, 166, 168, 169, 170, 171, 172, 173, 174, 175, 176, 177, 178, 179, 180, 181, 183, 184, 186, 187, 189, 190, 191, 192, 193, 195, 196, 197, 198, 200, 201, 203, 206, 209, 210, 211, 212, 214, 215, 216, 217, 218, 220, 221, 222, 223, 224, 225, 226, 227, 228, 229, 235, 236, 237, 238, 240, 241, 244, 246, 247, 248, 249, 251, 252, 253, 254, 255, 256, 257, 258, 259, 260, 261, 262, 263, 264, 265, 266, 268, 274, 281, 284, 297, 299, 300; As an Excellent Representative, 2, Best Person to Judge 3, Congress President, 4, 6, 7, 95; Elected the President, 7, 8, 12, 13, 18, 56, 95, 96; Elder Brother, 4; Eminent Organiser, 6; Nationalist to the Core, 7; Opposed Muslim League, 7; Perfect Organiser, 5; Responsibility for National Welfare, 4; Sincerity towards Mahatama Gandhi, 6; Statemanship of, 7, On the Question of India's Participation in War, 7; Tenure of Congress Presidentship, 8; Tripuri's Acting President, 12; Withdrawal of the Name, 52, To Contest the Election Against Subhash Chandra Bose, 52.

B

Bachhraj and Co. 149; of Bombay, 149,
Bajaj, Jamuna Lal, 30, 208, 290,
Balwantrai, P., 54
Bardoli, 6, 15, 78, 79, 80, 193, 194,206, 297
Bardoloi, Gopinath, 13, 38, 290.
Basic Education Court, 123, 124.
Begum Ansari, 54.
Benaras, 9, Hindu University of, 9, 76, 178, 201
Bengal, 5, 14, 18.
Bengal Government, 9,
Bengal P.C.C. 64
Berlin, 215
Bettia, 32
Bhagalpore, 41, 68
Bhargava, Gopichand, 13.
Bhatt, K.H. 54.
Bhave, Vinoba, 290.
Bhumihar, 32.
Bihar, 5, 9, 11, 27, 31, 32, 35, 42, 85, 169
Bihar Provincial Congress Committee, 9, 27, 208, 282, 283
Bihar's Situation, 31
Bihar Tenancy Amendment Bill, 26
Birla, G.D. 290
Bombay, 4, 8, 9, 15, 20, 22, 26, 34, 43, 61, 124, 152, 176, 208,
Bombay Provincial Congress Committee, 9
Bombay Resolution, 198
Bose, Netaji Subhash Chandra, 3, 57, 63, 64, 66, 67, 214, 290, 299,
Bose, Sharat Chandra, 80, 290.
British, 4, 6, 7, 9, 18.
Britishers, 4, 6,
British Government, 7, 88, 89, 93, 100, 101, 103, 208.
British Influence, 40
British Imperialism, 90, 91, 98, 100, 105
British Newspapers, 8, 94
British Parliament, 92
British Policy, 40; With Soviet Russia, 89, 90, 115, 207.
British Premier, 208
British War Cabinet, 9
British War Aim, 103
Burma, 276

C

Cabinet, 6, 7,
Calcutta City 3, 8, 18, 23, 26, 46, 47, 48, 51, 57, 60, 64, 72, 149, 209
Cavesheer, S. Mangal Singh, 18.
Central Provinces Affairs, 17
Central Provinces Ministry, 11, 29, 30, 139
Ceylon, 61, 165
Ceylon Delegation, 195,
Champaran, 32, 100
Charkha, 125, 296
Chhapra, 68
Chamerlain, 88, 90, 103
Chhotanagpur, 68
Chief Justice, 278; of High Court, 278.
China, 54, 164, 204

China and Russia, 276
China Mission, 186
China or Russia, 276
Christian Nation of Europe, 103
Christians, 124
City Magistrate of Allahabad, 17
Citizen, 114
Civil Disobedience, 6, 9, 116, 300
Civil Disobedience Movement, 9, 18, 156, 196, 300
Cloth, India Loin, 122
Common Achievements, 113
Common Language, 114
Commander-in-Chief, 7,
Committee, Bihar Hindustani of Patna, 43
Complete, 6,
Communal Harmony, 1, 2, 7; Bickering and Bitterness, 1
Communal Problem, 106
Commission, 31
Communal Question, 106
Concept, 102
Congress and League, 88
Congress City, 121
Congress Election Manifesto, 20
Congress, Indian National, 2, 3, 4, 6, 7, 9, 12, 14, 15, 16, 17, 18, 20, 21, 22, 26, 27, 28, 29, 34, 38, 39, 42, 43, 44, 45, 52, 54, 57, 63, 64, 69, 73, 74, 78, 81, 90, 94, 95, 96, 97, 98, 100, 101, 103, 105, 107, 108, 115, 116, 121, 126, 131, 139, 145, 147, 148, 151, 154, 155, 160, 171, 175, 182, 184, 191, 203, 204, 207, 208, 211, 212, 217, 236, 245, 249, 259, 269, 270, 284, 289, 290-95,
Congress Delagates, 126
Congress Direction, 205
Congress Funds, 21
Congress Leaders, 6, 7
Congress Medical Mission, 6, 149
Congress Member, 78,
Congress Men, 6, 73, 78, 205
Congress Ministries, 17, 81, 282
Congress Organisation, 6, 9, 27
Congress Position on Delhi Talk, 16, 107
Congress Programme 80
Congress Resolution, 118
Congress Session, 3, 13; at Bombay, 19; at Wardha, 13; in Ramgarh, 121
Congrss Socialist Party, 9,
Congress Sub-Committee on Parliamentary Affairs, 9
Congress Traditions, 30
Congress Zamindar Agreement, 36
Constituent Assembly, 92, 108, 115, 116, 131, 153, 156, 269, 275, 296
Consul General in Calcutta, 188
Cripps Draft Declaration, 17,
Cripps Formula, 9
Cripps Plan, 7
Cripps, Stafford, 7, 16, 215, 221, 222, 223, 224, 225, 226, 227, 229, 230, 235, 236, 238, 240, 241, 244, 246, 290.
Culture, 114
Customs, 114
Cuttack, 22, 48, 51
Czechoslovakia, 88

D

Dara Nagar, 121
Darul Irshad College of Calcutta, 18.
Das, B.N., 11, 46, 47, 48, 49, 50, 51, 290.
Das, Chaturanan, 54
Das, Nilakanth, 12, 46, 48, 49, 50, 294
Dawood, 278
Das, Shrinath, 54
Delhi, 1, 9, 18, 38, 49, 61, 158, 164, 165, 182, 213; Session of Congress, 118, Talk, 9, 16, 158,
Deliverence Day of Muslim League, 13, 81.
Demand of Muslim League, 7
D.I.A. 207
Deoband Jehad Conspiracy, 18.
Deo, Shankar Rao, 290.
Desai, Bhulabhai, J., 87, 184, 290
Desai, Mahadeo, 4, 5, 7, 11, 13, 26, 121, 198
Deshmukh, C.D., 290
Devi, Asha, 123, 124
Dharma, 296
District Congress Committees, 27
Diwali, 184
Divide India, 116
Dress, 114

Dufferin, Lord, 109; A Former Viceroy of India, 109
Dutch, 276
Dutta, Girija Bhushan, 54
Dwivedi Pandit Mahaveer, P., 54.

E

Egypt, 18, 54
English, 4, 119, 287
English People, 4; man, 4
English Power, 288
Europe, 2, 18, 88, 102, 103, 125, 186
European, 103, 278
European Element, 37
European Nation, 103
Exploitation of India, 21
Ex-Prime Ministers, 14

F

Faizpur, 121
Fair Deal Politics, 8
Fascism, 97; and Nazism, 97, 98, 100
Fascist, 207
Finland, 89
Flood in Bihar, 33
France, 89
Freedom, 54, 102
Freedom and Democracy, 102
Freedom of India, 21
Frontier, 64
Fundamental Basis, 20
Fyzabad, 202

G

Gandhi Devdas, 212, 290
Gandhi, Mahatma, 1, 2, 3, 4, 5, 6, 13, 15, 54, 57, 74, 76, 102, 105, 114, 121, 125, 127, 133, 134, 136, 137, 152, 153, 165, 179, 180, 181, 183, 185, 187, 189, 191, 194, 195, 197, 198, 201, 207, 212, 214, 237, 247, 253, 262, 266, 273, 280, 287, 291, 296, 297, 299, 300; Appealed Maulana Azad to Relieve, 6; Indifferent Attitude from Congress, 5, 6; To Muslims, 17; Statement of, 102.
Ganga and Jamuna, 113
Gaya, 41, 68, 69
General People of the Country, 8
General Policy of the Congress, 57
Germany, 89, 100
Germany Nazi, 100, 270, 275
Ghosh, P.C. 4, 194, 291.
God, 81
Gopichand, 153
Government, 6, 9, 11, 14, 42, 45, 90
Government Printing Press, 32.
Governor, 31, 34, 80, 202
Great Britain, 99, 102
Gupta, Shiv Prasad, 76, 176,
Gurudwara, 296.

H

Hafiz Ibrahim, 55, 60, 291
Haq, A.J.F., 291
Harijan Colony of Delhi, 38
High Court, 278
High Heavens, 1
Hijarat, 186
Hindi, The National Language, 6
Hinduism, 113
Hindu-Muslim Unity, 1, 128
Hindus Majority, 109
Hindus, 9, 31, 114, 124
Hindustan Standard, 183
His Majesty's Government, 7, 9, 166
Historians, 8
History, 1, 7, 18,
History of India, 7
Hitler, 88, 89, 90, 92
Humanity, 101,
Human Right, 103
Human World, 1
Humayun Kabir, 292
Hussain Ahmed Madni, 55, 293.

I

Iftikhar, 154, 252,
Imperialism, 110
Imperialistic, 107
Imperialists, 89
Independence, 6, 106; Of India, 6
India, 1, 2, 6, 7, 10, 21, 39, 45, 73, 74, 97, 101, 103, 106, 107, 103, 113, 135, 143, 145, 158, 198, 208, 218, 219, 270, 275, 277, 285, 286.
Indian, 1, 4, 78, 113, 129

Indian Christianity, 113
Indian cultural heritage, 1
Indian Dominion, 20
Indian Muslims, 109
Indian National Congress, See Cong.
Indian People, 20, 106
Individual Civil Disobedience Movement, 9, 296, 299
Indo-China, 276
I.N.G., 290
Inhuman Imperialism, 54
Iqbal, Muhammad, 54, 186
Iran, 276
Iraq, 276
Islam, 112, 129; Spirit of, 113
Islamic Religion, 113
Italy, 89

J

Jafar, 278
Jagpat Nathuji, 54
Jakatdar, V.M. 190
Jamia Milia, 123
Jamiat, 39
Jaunpur, 52
Jerabai, 123
Jhansi, 262
Jinnah, M.A., 14, 76, 176, 224, 292

K

Kale, Mrs. 280
Kanpur, 64, 169, 170, 201
Kanungo, N., 12, 47, 49
Kashmir, 154, 188
Khadi Court, 120
Khadi Mandal, 120
Khadi Programme, 9, 296
Khaliquzama, 184, 290
Khan, A. (Hakim), 291
Khan, Abdul Gaffar, 42, 165, 214, 292
Khan, Ali Hyder, 78
Khan, Dr. Saheb, 157, 165, 292.
Khan, Sir Sikander Hyat, 76, 91, 157
Khaparde, G.S., 54
Khare, N.B., 280, 292
Kher, B.G., 220.
Khilafat Non-Cooperation Movement, 18; in Bengal, 18
Khudhai Khidmatgars, 165
Khuddam-e-Kaba Movement, 18
Kingdom, 198
Kisan, 26, 27, 28, 31, 36
Kisans and Zamindars, 27
Kisan Sabha, 27, 283
K.N. Katju, 168, 202
Kripalani, J.B., 5, 6, 13, 14, 15, 16, 86, 118, 122, 149, 184, 190, 194, 202, 212, 259, 260, 261
Kripalani, Sucheta, 17, 213,
Krishna Menon, V.K., 143, 144, 145, 146

L

Lahore, 8, 9, 154, 191, 250, 252, 296
Lahore Resolution, 9, 13, 135, 296
Lal, Chaman, 61
Legislative Party of Madras Congress, 7, 9, 10, 16
Liaquat Ali Khan, 291, 292
Linlithgow, Lord, 6, 7, 14, 133, 134, 135, 167, 170, 174, 175
Local Self Government, 67
Lokamat, 43,
London, 2, 39, 53
Lucknow, 8, 58, 70, 72, 97, 151, 154, 201, 252, 256, 262

M

Madras, 9, 10, 258
Madras Congress Legislative Party, 10
Madhusudan Das, 125
Mahanty, Bachchanidhi, 54
Majlis-e-Khilafat, 1
Manbhum, 68
Maulana Khairuddin, 18
Meerut City, 18, 124
Members of Assemblies, 15
Menon, K. Raman, 54
Messaage of Congress, 21
Minorities, 108, 111
Mishra, B.C., 6, 12
Mishra, Chintamani, 43, 46, 47, 293.
Mishra, G., 12, 47, 51
Mission, Medical of Congress, 54
Moulvi Abdul Shakur, 54

Mufti Kifaytullah, 40, 293.
Mukharji, Upendranath, 54
Municipal Amendment Bill, 32, 66
Muslim Mass Contact, 68
Muslims, 17, 31, 39, 81, 108, 124
Muslims Minority, 67
Muslim Nationalists, 42
Mussolini, 89
Mussorie, 146

N

Nainital, 146, 150, 151
Nazi Power, 88
Nagpur, 64
Nahas Pasha, 2, 39, 40
Naik, Dhundiraj Mahadeo, 54
National Cause, 8
National Herald, 188
Nationalism, 1
National and International, 2
National Liberation Movement, 1, 29.
National Planning Committee 141, 142, 158
National Unity, 5, 7, 8; and Integrity, 8
Nehru, Pt. Jawahar Lal, 2, 3, 4, 5, 11, 12, 13, 14, 15, 16, 17, 20, 21, 39, 52, 53, 56, 57, 59, 60, 61, 62, 63, 66, 75, 76, 77, 88, 93, 119, 120, 140, 142, 143, 145, 146, 150, 151, 152, 154, 155, 157, 158, 162, 163, 164, 165, 166, 168, 170, 183, 184, 185, 186, 187, 188, 200, 201, 202, 209, 211, 212, 213, 217, 222, 226, 252, 253, 255, 256, 258, 262, 263, 264, 265, 266, 267, 293; a Sentimental, 3
Nehru, Pandit Moti Lal, 18,
Nehru Report, 147
New Delhi, 8
Nigam, Maheshwar Prasad, 54
Non-Cooperation and Khilafat Movement, 1; against British Government, 7
Non-Violence, 10, 182, 297
N.W.F.P., 64, 85, 153

O

Officials 31; Non, 31
Official Literature, 101
Orissa, 43, 47, 85, 123, 124
Orissa's Premier, 48
Orissa Tenancy Amendment Bill, 48, 50
Orissa University Committee, 49
Oudh, 42

P

Pachmarhi, 29
Pakistan, 135, 286
Pakistan Scheme, 147
Palestine, 40
Paliwal, Shri Krishna Dutta, 260
Pan-Islamism, 91
Pant, G.B., 55, 57, 58, 60, 146, 294
Pant Resolution, 57
Parliamentary Board of I.N.C., 5, 19, 281
Parliamentary Secretariat of Bihar, 33
Parliamentary work, 7
P.C.C.S., 21, 81, 83, 85, 282, 283
Patel, Manibehn, V. 294
Patel, Rajab Ali, 54
Patel, Sardar Vallabhbhai, 3, 5, 11, 12, 13, 17, 20, 21, 24, 25, 28, 42, 44, 45, 46, 63, 66, 75, 84, 85, 86, 88, 139, 194, 253, 275, 281, 297, 299; Sardar of Bardoli, 297.
Patna, 8, 10, 22, 34, 36, 46, 53, 69, 76, 80, 200
Patwardhan, A., 149, 150, 151, 294
Peace and Freedom, 54
Peasants, 5
Peasants and Landholders of Bihar, 5
People of Bihar, 34
Peshawar, 154
Policies of Congress, 283
Political Arena of India, 7; Aspect of the Problem, 7
Politicians, 8
Poona, 165, 175, 180, 182
Potala, 124
Prakasham, T., 294
Prasad Mahesh, 260
Prasad, Dr. Rajendra, 5, 11, 12, 13, 14, 15, 22, 23, 25, 26, 27, 38, 39, 41, 42, 43, 53, 62, 63, 64, 66, 70, 71, 72, 74, 80, 82, 83, 85, 88, 120, 152, 155, 166, 170, 179, 191, 194, 209, 253, 294, 299; Association with Azad, 5; Congress President, 5
Premiers Conference, 33
Premiers, 47,
Prime-Minister, 43, 45; of Britain, 102
Prohibition, 34, 35

Provisional Government, 275
Punjab, 5, 82, 83, 152, 192
Puri, 46
Puri Express, 46
Punrnea, 68

Q

Quit India Movement, 4, Resolution, 297, 300
Qutub Minar, 1

R

Rafi Ahmed Kidwai, 54, 60, 252, 256, 257, 292
Raja Bahadur, 42, 43
Raja Bahadur of Tiloi, 42
Raja of, 201
Rajagopalacharier, C., 7, 14, 16, 17, 194, 242, 250, 272, 291, 294, 295
Rajaji Formula, 297
Ram Babu Kamakhyadutt, 42
Ramgarh, 7, 70, 72, 121, 126
Ramgarh Congress, 7
Ramzan, 184
Ram Narayan, 23, 283
Ranchi, 34, 71
Rau, B. Raju, 54
Rau, K. Nageshwar, 54
Religion, 296
Religious, 198
Roy, B.C., 61, 119, 256, 265, 295
Roy, M.N., 295
Roy Nickolas, 78; As Lear, 78; of Assam, 78.
Rule of God, 297
Russia, 88, 89, 100, 273, 274; Soviet, 89, 90

S

Sadullah, 80, 295
Sahay, K.B., 34, 295
Sapru, T.B., 202.
Sanskrityayan Rahul, 36
Sarabhai Mridul, 215
Satyagraha, 35, 190, 297
Scindhia, S.N.C., 188
Security of Humanity, 6
Separate Nation for Muslims, 7
Sethi, Mr., 86
Shariff, M., 29, 278, 279
Sharma, Parshuram, 15,
Shia-Sunni Affair, 60
Shilong, 38
Singh, Jwala, 54
Singh, Master Tara, 14, 119, 147, 148, 295
Singh, Pratap, 54
Singh, Thakur Gulzar, 54
Shrinagar, 154
Shukla, Devi Prasad, 54
Shukla, Rajaram, 54
Shukla, Ravishankar, 220
Sinha, A.N., 12, 68, 69, 289
Sinha, S.K., 220
Sitaramaiah, B. Pattabi, 118, 136, 295
Socialist Friends, 150
Solidarity, 54
Spain, 88
Sultan Ahmed, 55, 58, 60
Surfuddin, 278
Surma Valley, 7, 65
Surma Valley Congress, 66
Swaraj, 1, 18, 282, 298; Movement in Bengal, 18
Switzerland, 186
Syed Mahmood, 168, 184
Syndicate, Sugar, 169

T

Tagore, R.N., 297
Taluqdars Association, 42
Taluqdars, 42, 43
Thakur Dutt, 136
The Cumbha Mela, 125
The Daily Telegraph, 126
The Hindustan Standard, 183
The Hindustan Times, 8, 61
The Leader, 183
The League of Nations, 89
The Times, 127
Tiloi, 42
Tribunal, 82
Tripuri, 12, 57, 290, 299
Trojans, 121
Troops of India, 115

U

Ultra vires, 58
Unislamic, 135
United Front, 20, 75
United Nations, 276, 277
United Provinces, 10, 34, 66, 83, 85, 109, 124, 153, 169
United Provinces Ministry, 34
Unity and Discipline in Congress, 12, 73,
Unity in Diversity, 2
University, 29
U.P. Legislative Assembly, 290
Urdu, 119, 155
Utkal, 5, 81

V

Vaid, 138
Vakil, Kuwerbai, 123
Valley, Surma, 6, 7
Venkat, Ghaltu, 54
Verma, Bipin Bihari, 32
Viceregal Declaration, 120
Viceroy, 6, 7, 14, 101, 133, 170, 172, 173, 174, 175, 180, 184, 209, 215, 221, 225, 245,
Viceroy's P.S., 215, 216
Vijayalaxmi, Pandit, 213

W

Wafd, 54; Party of Egypt, 54
Wafdist Congress, 2, 39, 40
Wardha, 13, 54, 96, 102, 115, 180, 209, 214
Welfare of The Country, 8
Westminster, 134
Whole Nation, 116
Working Committee of I.N.C., 3, 4, 6, 15, 19, 39, 42, 58, 64, 66, 80, 81, 100, 102, 117, 126, 138, 151, 194
World, 1
World Federation, 276
World Progress, 98
Wars, 88, 207
World War, Second, 3, 5, 7, 88, 290
War Resolution, 127
Wavell, 237

Y

Yudhishthira, 198

Z

Zaffar-ul-Mulk, 55
Zakir Husain, 124
Zamindar, 26, 27, 28, 36, 298
Zamindari, 298
Ziradei, 42
Zulum, 298.